Ball, Bat and Bitumen

CONTRIBUTIONS TO SOUTHERN APPALACHIAN STUDIES

1. *Memoirs of Grassy Creek: Growing Up in the Mountains on the Virginia–North Carolina Line.* Zetta Barker Hamby. 1998

2. *The Pond Mountain Chronicle: Self-Portrait of a Southern Appalachian Community.* Leland R. Cooper and Mary Lee Cooper. 1998

3. *Traditional Musicians of the Central Blue Ridge: Old Time, Early Country, Folk and Bluegrass Label Recording Artists, with Discographies.* Marty McGee. 2000

4. *W.R. Trivett, Appalachian Pictureman: Photographs of a Bygone Time.* Ralph E. Lentz, II. 2001

5. *The People of the New River: Oral Histories from the Ashe, Alleghany and Watauga Counties of North Carolina.* Leland R. Cooper and Mary Lee Cooper. 2001

6. *John Fox, Jr., Appalachian Author.* Bill York. 2003

7. *The Thistle and the Brier: Historical Links and Cultural Parallels Between Scotland and Appalachia.* Richard Blaustein. 2003

8. *Tales from Sacred Wind: Coming of Age in Appalachia. The Cratis Williams Chronicles.* Cratis D. Williams. Edited by David Cratis Williams and Patricia D. Beaver. 2003

9. *Willard Gayheart, Appalachian Artist.* Willard Gayheart and Donia S. Eley. 2003

10. *The Forest City Lynching of 1900: Populism, Racism, and White Supremacy in Rutherford County, North Carolina.* J. Timothy Cole. 2003

11. *The Brevard Rosenwald School: Black Education and Community Building in a Southern Appalachian Town, 1920–1966.* Betty Jamerson Reed. 2004

12. *The Bristol Sessions: Writings About the Big Bang of Country Music.* Edited by Charles K. Wolfe and Ted Olson. 2005

13. *Community and Change in the North Carolina Mountains: Oral Histories and Profiles of People from Western Watauga County.* Compiled by Nannie Greene and Catherine Stokes Sheppard. 2006

14. *Ashe County: A History.* Arthur Lloyd Fletcher (1963). New edition, 2006

15. *The New River Controversy.* Thomas J. Schoenbaum (1979). New edition, 2007

16. *The Blue Ridge Parkway by Foot: A Park Ranger's Memoir.* Tim Pegram. 2007

17. *James Still: Critical Essays on the Dean of Appalachian Literature.* Edited by Ted Olson and Kathy H. Olson. 2007

18. *Owsley County, Kentucky, and the Perpetuation of Poverty.* John R. Burch, Jr. 2007

19. *Asheville: A History.* Nan K. Chase. 2007

20. *Southern Appalachian Poetry: An Anthology of Works by 37 Poets.* Edited by Marita Garin. 2008

21. *Ball, Bat and Bitumen: A History of Coalfield Baseball in the Appalachian South.* L.M. Sutter. 2008

22. *The Frontier Nursing Service: America's First Rural Nurse-Midwife Service and School.* Marie Bartlett. 2009

23. *James Still in Interviews, Oral Histories and Memoirs.* Edited by Ted Olson. 2009

24. *The Millstone Quarries of Powell County, Kentucky.* Charles D. Hockensmith. 2009

25. *The Bibliography of Appalachia: More Than 4,700 Books, Articles, Monographs and Dissertations, Topically Arranged and Indexed.* John R. Burch, Jr. 2009

Ball, Bat and Bitumen

A History of Coalfield Baseball in the Appalachian South

L. M. SUTTER

Contributions to Southern Appalachian Studies, 21

McFarland & Company, Inc., Publishers
Jefferson, North Carolina, and London

To the ballplayers of the coalfields.
May the stories of your skill, your grace,
and your spirit radiate from the heart
of Appalachia and live forever.

LIBRARY OF CONGRESS CATALOGUING-IN-PUBLICATION DATA

Sutter, L.M., 1959–
Ball, bat and bitumen : a history of coalfield baseball
in the Appalachian south / by L.M. Sutter.
p. cm. — (Contributions to Southern Appalachian Studies ; 21)
Includes bibliographical references and index.

ISBN 978-0-7864-3594-4
softcover : 50# alkaline paper ∞

1. Baseball—Appalachian Region, Southern—History. 2. Appalachian Region, Southern—Social life and customs.   I. Title.
II. Title: History of coalfield baseball in the Appalachian South.
GV863.A53S87   2009   796.3570973—dc22   2008049102

British Library cataloguing data are available

©2009 L.M. Sutter. All rights reserved

*No part of this book may be reproduced or transmitted in any form
or by any means, electronic or mechanical, including photocopying
or recording, or by any information storage and retrieval system,
without permission in writing from the publisher.*

On the cover: The Lonesome Pine League's 1934 champions, the
Lee Smokies (courtesy of Ty Harber, Jr.); inset ©2008 Clipart.com

Manufactured in the United States of America

*McFarland & Company, Inc., Publishers
Box 611, Jefferson, North Carolina 28640
www.mcfarlandpub.com*

Table of Contents

Preface and Acknowledgments   1
Introduction   5

1. The Coal Towns   9
2. The Appalachian Pastime   19
3. The Emperor of Baseball   30
4. Tye Harber's War   43
5. The Boys of the Lonesome Pine   49
6. Moonlighting Bearcats   76
7. A Wide-Awake Town   86
8. Fathers and Sons   94
9. Fertile Soil   104
10. Almost Valhalla   113
11. The 1951 Hazard Bombers   128
12. The Choices We Live With   136
13. Bob Bowman   144
14. Vince Pankovits and the Mean Season   153
15. The Old Man of the Mountains   163
16. The Women in the Stands   170

Epilogue   187
Chapter Notes   191
Bibliography   195
Index   199

Preface and Acknowledgments

This project began when I came across a pictorial history of Lee County, Virginia, that featured photographs of local semipro and professional coalfield baseball teams dating back to the early twentieth century. As in photographs of baseball teams anywhere, the young players looked alert and excited, but the coalfield players had an added hunger about their eyes, an edge that was almost palpable. As a longtime baseball fan but a new arrival to the region, I found the photographs intriguing and began to do some research. To discover that the entire southern Appalachian coalfield region had avidly supported baseball for decades—and throughout the convulsive changes in the coal industry—was remarkably interesting. And a little research made it readily apparent that the combination of coal mining and America's pastime produced a different animal from the game as it was played elsewhere. But it also showed that information on the game in the Appalachian south would be as hard to locate as the ruins of the most remote mountain coal camp.

Southern Appalachia is an area long misunderstood by the outside world. Its mountains have served for centuries as an effective fortress for keeping its own people in and strangers out. Many Americans have never heard of coal camps; those that have generally regard them as alien cultures at best and, at worst, medieval institutions. In this work, I have attempted to demystify the Appalachian coal camp, to show that, in many ways, it was like any other little American town except perhaps for its salty, dynamic personality, bred of the dangerous work that was its lifeblood. The unusual ethos of the coal camp, where being alive could never be taken for granted, engendered a distinctive brand of baseball, as tough and lively as its players and fans.

As many similarities as a coal community might share with any other American town, there were differences. Baseball played by mineworkers, for instance, was not just a relaxing diversion but a desperately needed physical and emotional release for athlete and spectator. For the coal companies, baseball in the early days could be wielded as an anti-union tool, and throughout the years it was a lucrative corporate enterprise, with huge amounts of money—from gate receipts and gambling—passing between the hands of operators and on to hired ringers.

Other differences between the coal camp and the average American town were more profound than those regarding baseball. While towns from every region of the country dealt at some point with the effects of war, unionism, and segregation, those issues in a mining community were far more complex and I have touched upon them. I have not attempted in-depth analyses of these topics—each is important in and of itself and is far better covered by experts in the field if one seeks a comprehensive study—but I have presented them in the context of baseball, as each issue significantly affected the game locally. I have also included some major league success stories to show the caliber of players produced by the coalfields, and, lastly, have attempted to introduce the reader to local baseball's most stalwart fan base, the women of the camps.

In the many historical surveys of American baseball—even those of the industrial leagues—the sport in the southern Appalachian coalfields has been sorely neglected. Considering the dearth of information, it is fortunate that there are a few excellent articles by regional experts like Stuart McGehee, Bill Archer, and Paul Nyden. William Kashatus has written an invaluable survey of players from the anthracite fields of Pennsylvania. Each was a valuable resource. For the bulk of my research, I relied on local and regional newspaper accounts, which, in the early pre-sports page days, were limited in scope and frequency. Fortunately, with the second boom of coalfield baseball after World War II, newspaper accounts became more common. Without a doubt, though, the most important resource was the former players, their relatives and their fans. They were located through word of mouth and by appeals through newspapers and social organizations. These people gave tirelessly of their time and memories; I am deeply grateful to them all. Because so much of the text is in the form of quotations from them, I have spared the reader the confusion of notes. Each speaker is introduced and identified in the text and is listed in the bibliography by name with interview dates.

This project would never have happened without the entire staff of the Lonesome Pine Regional Library in Wise, Virginia, especially Linda Smith and the remarkably patient Hazel Jessee. Thanks also go to the staff of the Mountain Empire Community College Library in Big Stone Gap, Virginia. Of immense help were Dr. Stuart McGehee of the Eastern Regional Coal Archives in Bluefield, West Virginia, Phyllis Sizemore of the Kentucky Coal Mining Museum in Benham, Kentucky, and the historical societies of Bell County and Van Lear, Kentucky (with special thanks to Danny and Trevor Blevins), and the historical society of Wise County, Virginia (with special thanks to Paul Kilgore and Gladys Stallard). Likewise, I am indebted to Phil Smith of the United Mine Workers of America, the Jesse Stuart Foundation, Martha (Mrs. Alan Pollock) and her illustrious family, and Eric Hicks for his patiently rendered technical support. I would never try to estimate how many hours R. Tim Gilley spent sleuthing on my behalf but I know they were plenty and I'm immensely grateful to him.

Nothing enhances a rich baseball history better than photographs. Virginia photographer Chuck Clisso deserves the highest praise, not only for his painstaking reproductions but for his contemporary portraits of the former ballplayers. He captured each man's spirit and nobility in a way that I feel no other photographer could have and I am very grateful for his contribution.

Many people have been helpful in tracking down players and stories. They include Sterling Brickey, E. C. Mullins, Hoppy Hopkins, Luke Stewart, Walter Dick, Delores

French, Carolyn Sundy, Bennie Massey, Darrell Helton, Rachel Mickey, Clarence Owens and the Central Baptist Church of Beckley, West Virginia.

On a personal level, I am indebted to Mark Gardino, Belinda Winn, Janice Barrett, Alfred Stites, Lottie Robinette and the entire Grillo family. Thanks go to my family— David Sutter, Thomas Harding, Isaac and Everett Sutter-Harding and especially my sister Cindy Sutter; it was from trying to be like her when I was young that my love of baseball took root. Special thanks go to my dear friend Salty, who has made the stories so vivid for me. And my profoundest gratitude goes to T, for unflagging strength, support and belief.

Introduction

Since the first time human eyes regarded them, the mountains of southern Appalachia have been considered intensely, mysteriously beautiful. What makes them so visually enthralling is also what has kept the area so isolated through the centuries. They may not be the tallest mountains in the world, but they are closely spaced and steep, with hollows that remain in perpetual shadow. Long, unbroken ridges make for difficult travel. Forests are dense and silent except for the occasional rushing stream. This "dark and bloody ground," as it has been called, has bred unique children, proud and independent, with a dash of melancholy that is perfectly conveyed in the despairing lyrics of the Carter Family. It can be a mournful place, its inhabitants historically exploited and its resources exhausted by unscrupulous outside entrepreneurs. Yet the people of Appalachia cling tenaciously to their cultural heritage, and it is beginning to pay off; the world that formerly mocked them now comes on pilgrimage to a place that offers unique American music, art, and folklore.

The cachet that the name Appalachia now carries is indeed attracting visitors. They flock to craft fairs, where the artisans bask in the new respect afforded their traditional arts. Lovers of mountain music and bluegrass tap their feet to a Ralph Stanley CD as they drive rental cars along the Crooked Road to his museum in Clintwood, Virginia. And the vistas of the southern Appalachians can still make the heart skip a beat. With all that the mountains can offer a tourist, few visitors, if any, are coming to investigate the rich history of baseball in the region. Yet it existed and was played with a vengeance in the coalfields by the anonymous men who supplied the resource that fueled this country, providing the public and private sectors with energy. With the first warm days of spring, these men emerged from the rigors of the Appalachian winter to play on ball fields from northeast Georgia to southwest Pennsylvania. Like that of other industrial leagues, baseball in the coalfield was a seriously competitive game and spawned many a major leaguer. Northeastern Pennsylvania coal communities can claim dozens of native sons who made it to the big leagues. And the heart of southern Appalachia—eastern Kentucky, southern West Virginia and southwest Virginia—also had its major league success stories. Many a local boy who grew up with coal dust under his nails eventually cracked the show, usually after paying a measure of his dues on semipro coal town teams.

The story of coalfield baseball in the Appalachian south begins with two contempo-

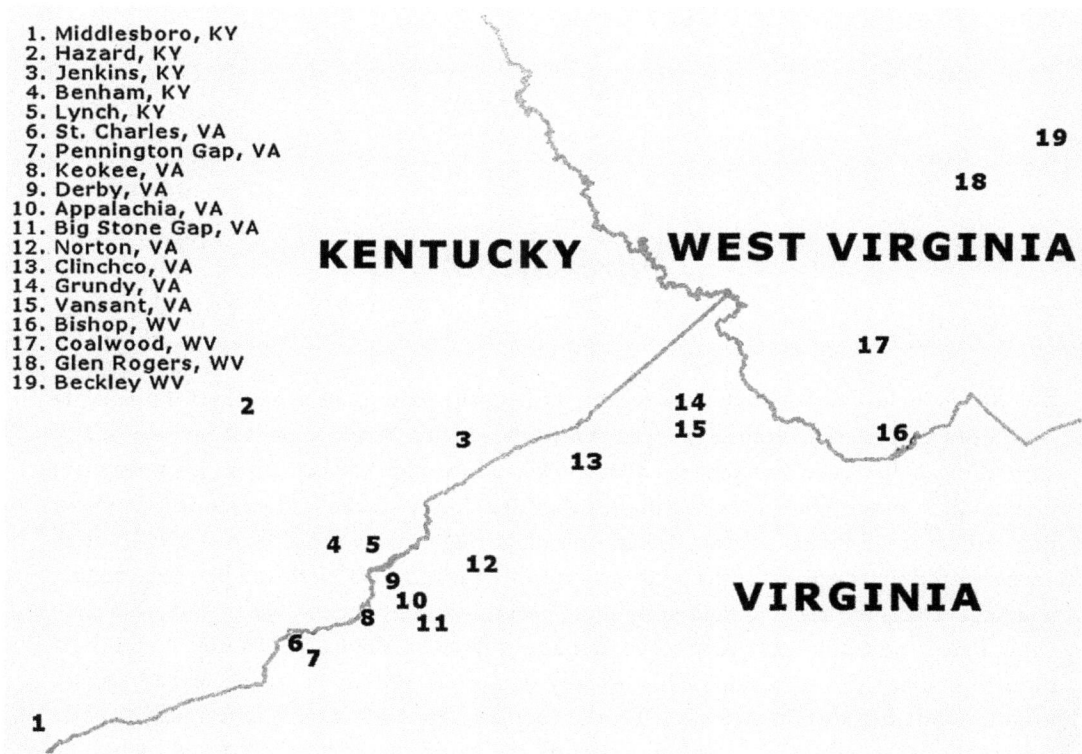

Map by Eric Hicks

raneous late-nineteenth century phenomena: the growing mania for baseball in this country and the birth of the coal camp. The first will be familiar to any fan of the game. The second is probably unknown to most, unless they have grown up in, or read about, an industrial company town. Various industries used the company town as a means to attract workers by offering the advantages of housing and public services around or adjacent to the workplace. The coal camps, from their meager beginnings as shanty towns built around the mouths of mines, would eventually grow into complete communities, some with populations of several thousand people. Row upon row of cookie-cutter houses were built, in between mountains and up the sides of them, with larger public buildings—company stores, schools, hospitals and churches—the only structures to break up the architectural monotony.

When cars were a rarity and mountain roads were frequently impassable anyway, a miner and his family had few means to leave the camp, where their entertainment options could be limited. Some of the wealthier companies provided recreational facilities, including movie theaters, skating rinks, or dance halls for their workers. But the one luxury common to all camps was the baseball diamond. It was the focal point of coal camp life each summer, with games played every weekend and fans sometimes numbering into the thousands. Leagues formed throughout the coal camps and independent coal towns within a county or over several counties, some eventually crossing state lines.

It has been suggested that in the early days of the coal camps, before the unions had gained solid ground, coal company owners and operators found competitiveness between the teams an effective means of keeping labor agitation to a minimum. Certainly the major coal companies found it in their best interest to keep the union out of their mines and were prone to try anything to keep it that way. The belief prevailed that promoting a ball team and supplying new uniforms and equipment, like any good little league parent, would stoke competitive feelings towards other camps. If a furious rivalry existed between two teams, it was less likely that the opposing players, or their fans, would engage in brotherly shoptalk between double-headers. It was one of many tools employed by paternalistic company management to keep the word of the union from seeping through camp boundaries.

For the miners themselves, baseball meant the same thing that it meant to any other player or fan in America. It was an all-consuming passion, played and watched with as much heart as any major league game but by men who rarely, if ever, managed to go to a large city to see one. The worker, who spent long hours in the mines, blasting, picking and loading coal, or who inhaled black dust all day on the tipple, found renewed energy when he washed off the day's work and headed to the ball field in the evening for practice. For a talented few, their prowess on the mound or behind the plate won them work above ground, perhaps in maintenance or a machine shop and, happily, a padded pay packet. And many a high-octane ringer was hired by the company to improve a team and usually given nominal work above ground or a bulk payment in cash for merely showing up at the diamond.

For the fan of the game, baseball is beloved as much for its atmosphere as for the competition. An afternoon game is a few hours of warmth and ease, punctuated by the anxious moment. It is the joy of watching grown men playing a kid's game in sunlight and open air. This gives added poignancy to the game played and cheered on by coal miners. For most people, the very idea of being underground for even the shortest amount of time is unbearable, invariably evoking an intense visceral reaction. Add to that the bleak reality of countless fatalities in the history of American mining and the specter of black lung, and the job usually falls at the very bottom of the list of desirable occupations. But in the heart of Appalachia, it was typically the only work to be found and, to this day, one of the few jobs in the area that pays a living wage. To feed his family, the coal miner was forced to leave his fears at the mouth of the mine and descend deep into the earth. His colleague above ground, working in the preparation plant or on the tipple, faced serious dangers as well. For a few hours every week, for a few months out of the long year, a handful of these men provided for themselves and every resident of the camp a respite from the darkness. It is small wonder that baseball meant as much as it did to these men who rarely saw the sun.

Chapter 1

The Coal Towns

The Appalachian Mountains begin in Quebec and run in a southwesterly direction for roughly fifteen hundred miles before they end in central Alabama. The chain is from one hundred to three hundred miles wide, and is divided into a series of ranges. Some of the oldest mountains in the world, the Appalachians were formed some 480 million years ago in a slow but violent collision of Africa and North America to form part of the single giant continent, Pangea. The force caused the colliding edges of these land masses to thrust upward, creating a chain of high, jagged peaks similar to the Himalayas in the center of Pangea. Through years of erosion—from flooding, freezing, thawing, and sliding—they were eventually worn down to the mountains we see now. The eventual separation of the African and North American continents divided the mountains, leaving part of them in northwest Africa (Morocco's Anti-Atlas mountains), the other part of them in eastern North America.

But it is what lies beneath these graceful ridges that fuels this tale, and that is coal, the by-product of a swampy soup of decaying organic matter subjected to intense pressure and heat from the earth's core. The story begins in the tropical heat of three hundred million years ago, when the marine sea that covered most of North America began to shrink. As fresh water mixed in, great swamps were formed, their waters stagnating as organic matter decomposed in them. The weight of layers of sediment, combined with high underground temperatures, transformed these peat bogs into coal, seams of which range from a couple of inches to hundreds of feet in thickness. The coal of southern Appalachia is bituminous, which is soft and dirtier than the older, purer coal called anthracite. Bituminous coal is closer to the surface than anthracite, and thus easier to reach. It is smoky but ignites readily, and is primarily used to generate steam for electricity.

In pre–Columbian Appalachia, Indian tribes including the Cherokee, Shawnee and Tuscarora hunted buffalo and elk, now long disappeared from the region. Once Europeans had established settlements in the east, and the colonies began to expand, land-hungry settlers looked westward only to find the southern Appalachians blocking further expansion like a vast, forbidding sentry. In 1750, Thomas Walker, doctor and explorer (and the first man to discover and use coal in Kentucky), found and mapped an ancient hunting trail that led from Virginia through the Cumberland Mountains into the frontier of Kentucky and Tennessee. Twenty-five years later, Daniel Boone would widen the Cumberland "Gap," opening the west to settlement.

Most of the people who chose to settle the Appalachians were immigrants from the British Isles, predominantly Scots-Irish who had fled the economic distress and burgeoning populations of their native countries or the yoke of indentured servitude in the American colonies. What they found in these mist-shrouded mountains was inaccessible and rugged terrain, difficult to farm but, because of that, less expensive than land to the east and north. The very inaccessibility of the area appealed to the independent frontiersmen as it ensured that neighbors would be scarce and visitors even more so. The grueling life of a pioneer, coupled with a lack of interaction with the outside world, made for isolated pockets of people who clung tenaciously to their own cultural traditions.

Chances are the world would have maintained little or no interest in Appalachia (except as a gateway to greener climes) or its inhabitants but for the industrial revolution. The area was thick with the resources needed to drive that revolution, a veritable paradise of timber and minerals, most in the form of bituminous coal. Transportation and industry were creating a never-ending demand for the stuff and the homes that sheltered millions of people worldwide depended on it as well. Starting in the 1880s and continuing for seven more decades, coal was the leading source of energy produced in the United States. The first commercial mine in what would become the United States was opened near Richmond, Virginia, in 1748; the first commercial shipment followed a decade later. Once discovered in Appalachia, the rich fields of coal proved too strong an enticement to British and American industrialists to be ignored. For this enterprise to succeed, the industrialist banded with the railroad magnate who by the 1850s had pushed across the Appalachians with the Norfolk and Western. Starting in what is now Roanoke, Virginia, the N&W crossed the mountains to Cincinnati and, by the turn of the century, the Chesapeake and Ohio, Norfolk and Western, Louisville and Nashville, and Southern railroads had moved across the heart of the Appalachian coalfields. Connecting branch lines and spurs to individual mines meant that tracks spread across the hills like a spider web.

After the resources had been mapped, the venture capitalists needed large unbroken tracts of land and acquired them for pennies from the mountaineers whose families had worked them for generations. Some of the wealthy investors convinced themselves that there was benevolence in the land grabs; after all, they reasoned, the mountaineers were ignorant, their squalid lives completely bereft of the benefits offered by the civilized world. Any ethical qualms they might have had about what they did were banished by the idea that they would be improving the lives of these unfortunates. So their representatives entered Appalachia with wads of cash, which they waved under the noses of people who had known only the hardest of hard-scrabble lives. The desperation of poverty induced many a small landowner to sell either his property or its mineral rights to the gentlemen from the outside.

> Interlocking interests of coal and steel led the captains of American industry and banking to purchase mineral rights over vast stretches of the region for a pittance. Their investments established patterns of absentee landownership that would endure into the twenty-first century. Among the industrial capitalists whose agents acquired fortunes in coal deposits from unsuspecting mountain families were J.P. Morgan, Henry Ford, and H.H. Rogers, a principal associate of John D. Rockefeller.[1]

In the 1880s, as more and more land was accumulated by venture capitalists and more mines were opened, the Appalachian version of the company town was introduced. Once a rich vein was discovered, labor was the first immediate need, for transporting equipment, building and manning sawmills, sinking the mines and then extracting the coal. The capitalists who bought the small farms and other properties from the locals padded the purchase with the offer of jobs and housing. The one-time farmer and landowner now found himself employed by, and soon living under the nose of, the coal company. The company town was not a new phenomenon, nor exclusively American; it had been a fixture of the coalfields of England since the first half of the nineteenth century. Company towns had been springing up across this country to house industrial laborers ranging from steelworkers to salmon-canners. Some of the industrialists who founded these communities may have been in absolute earnest in wanting to provide utopian living and working conditions for their employees. Others, however, considered their human workers less valuable than the mules that pulled the coal carts and installed their workers in camps that were little better than feudal compounds.

The earliest coal camps were exactly that—camps—with miners and surface laborers living in tents or shanties. While the miners bore deeper shafts into the earth, the workers above ground built sawmills and ovens for coking, a process by which bituminous coal is baked into fuel for blast furnaces. Because transportation for these men was severely limited, essential goods were made available to them at the company store. There, the miner could purchase his boots and his tools, including a carbide lamp for light and blasting powder to dislodge great amounts of coal.

For the sake of consistent, large-volume output, companies realized the necessity of keeping a steady supply of miners and reasoned that a single man would be far less inclined to be completely loyal to his employer than a man with dependents. So after housing was built (not free but low cost) and the company store was up and running, more public services were provided in the hopes of attracting the family man. Once the advantages of a home, stores, schools and doctors were provided for his loved ones, a man would have to think long and hard about quitting his job.

Most family housing in the camps was built from kits or tightly-controlled architectural plans, hence the rows and rows of identical dwellings. In some camps, substandard housing was given to African American and immigrant families; in others, equal housing was the rule. While model towns provided well-built homes for families, a few with indoor plumbing, others offered shacks that let the mountain winter in through the cracks in the floor and the walls. In most of the camps, housing was provided for teachers and white-collar workers, multi-roomed residences were offered for visitors, and rooming houses were offered for bachelor workers. As the towns grew, palatial homes were built for administrative bigwigs and their families; these homes were usually perched on a ridge overlooking the camp, conveniently above a good deal of the noise and dust. Model communities of the twentieth century, like Derby, Virginia, were committed to keeping the unions out and, to this end, built management housing in the thick of the camp. This enforced the understanding that the corporate "father" was always there, with one ear sympathetically turned to the worker and the other glued to the ground for any hint of union rumbling.

Derby, Virginia. The sturdy, attractive architecture of this coal camp has landed it a spot on the National Register of Historic Places. Each of these buildings housed two families (courtesy Chuck Clisso).

While entertainment options were limited in smaller camps, almost all, even the meanest, had a movie house or a structure that doubled as one. In a small camp, the experience could be a doubtful one as described by a persnickety visitor to Wad, West Virginia.

> It should be noted that the movies are a commercial undertaking with profit as the chief consideration and not to provide wholesome, stimulating recreation for the miner. The screen is very poor and streaky and the sound reproduction is equally bad. The seating arrangements are extremely bad and the seats are most uncomfortable. Instead of padded seats with springs, long wooden benches or folding chairs are used which are removed after the movie.[2]

Wad was a poor camp; wealthier ones offered a dizzying array of amenities to keep the community engaged, including theaters with movies that were probably just as unwholesomely entertaining as those in Wad, but with considerably plusher surroundings.

But the beating heart of any coal camp was the company store. In its heyday, it carried virtually anything a mining family could need, from toys for the kiddies to the latest couture to kegs of blasting powder (the miner had to buy his own). Not only were the company offices housed in the store but the post office was too. It was a gathering spot, a place to socialize as much as to conduct business. In the early years, company stores enjoyed a complete monopoly, as outside merchants, sometimes even peddlers, were not allowed on company property. In some camps, the "disloyalty" shown by shopping elsewhere could get a miner assigned to shifts in the worst parts of the mine. While its prices were generally inflated, the store (sometimes called "the company sore" or "the pluck-me") was nothing if not convenient and good for offering a large variety of goods. There were, however, negatives involved in the company store. One of those was scrip.

Early on, because of the difficulty in getting the large amounts of cash required to pay the workers, companies began to issue scrip instead of United States currency. Sometimes scrip was the only legal tender accepted at the company store. In the 1800s scrip was paper chits, but by the twentieth century it was also issued in metal tokens, unique to each company and therefore useless outside the camp. In the rare instance that scrip could be redeemed for cash elsewhere, it was never an even exchange. When a miner ran out of precious cash or scrip for necessities, he could borrow against his future pay. Add to the scrip system a pay schedule that often deferred one month's pay until the end of the next month and the mining family could easily spiral into debt. At its best, the scrip system was always convenient for the company and sometimes for the mining family. At its worst, it was part of an ingenious system that could keep workers indentured to the company, often for life.

For every few coal camps dotting the mountains, there was always an incorporated community somewhere nearby, a nexus of railroad tracks for the seemingly endless strings of coal cars coming from the various mines. They were usually settled by a mix of coal and railroad men, bankers and merchants, and while they were officially independent and incorporated municipalities, virtually every lump of locally-mined coal, and every coin earned by its sale, made its way through them. As the mines produced, so did the towns, growing busier and richer during boom years. Banks and hotels sprang up, attempting to outdo one another in the grandeur of their architecture. The streets were crowded, filled with people until the wee hours. Starting in the 1940s, many of the commercial centers established bus systems which ran a circuit of the camps for the mining families who wanted shopping alternatives. While the scrip system was still in use, mining families could use theirs to purchase goods in town, although the rate of exchange was poor. Recreational opportunities abounded: the betting man had gambling joints, and the person in search of something to wet his whistle had his choice of barrooms. Bordellos were popular places to spend money although it would be hard to say if they accepted scrip.

By the end of the nineteenth century, mining in Appalachia was widespread, producing two-thirds of the coal in the United States. In a bid for desperately-needed laborers, coal companies from across the nation sent representatives to meet central and eastern European immigrants as they stepped off the boat, luring them to the coalfields with the promise of a bright new future. This flow reached a high point by 1900, then gradually slowed to a trickle. The onset of World War I saw many young immigrant men returning to Europe to fight, and local native-born miners joining the armed forces. Mining companies began sending operatives, or "transportation men," southward in search of African Americans, whose post–Civil War dream of a better life had amounted to worse than nothing. "One company agent, remembered by the name 'Limehouse,' was legendary in his ability to sneak sharecroppers away from white landowners at night by hiding recruits and their families behind stacks of vegetable boxes on his truck."[3] Tragically, many of these workers, like the immigrant workers before them, were shipped into areas in times of strike, not aware that

they were being brought in as scabs. Once in the coal camps, both groups of newcomers, African American and European, were given housing in neighborhoods built specifically for them, the structures frequently inferior to that given the white families. Often, the hollows and ridges of a camp provided natural boundaries for ethnic enclaves. In the town of Dante, Virginia, which was originally called Turkey Foot because of its topological layout, each "toe," or hollow, was home to a different minority. In other, flatter camps, the division of races was carefully planned, with black families typically getting the smallest houses closest to the mines. Camp schools and churches were segregated as well.

Separate residential areas went hand-in-hand with unfair practices in the pre-union mines. Black miners were often given the more dangerous jobs underground and fared poorly in any attempts to advance. "While the white miners did not seem to mind working beside the black miners underground, they severely resisted any attempts to upgrade the Negroes to higher skilled positions."[4] Although his life in the mine and the camp was arguably better than it had been in the sharecropping South, the black miner could suffer the same racism that plagued the rest of the country.

Yet despite the obvious negatives of coal camp living, many former inhabitants, including minorities, remember their days in the coal camp as happy ones, although most are not old enough to vividly recall the pre-union years. Before the union came into an area, the mining family was absolutely at the mercy of the company, which owned everything in the camp, including, thanks to the scrip system, most of the family's household goods. When the union began to have a voice in local communities, and the paternalism of the past could no longer silence it, some company owners and managers responded harshly. A miner and his family could be immediately evicted from their home at the slightest hint of agitation. The camp and the roads into it were tightly controlled and company thugs often patrolled the streets to prevent union proselytizers from entering company property. Egregious conditions in commercial mining led to the establishment of the United Mine Workers of America in 1890, which won an eight-hour workday for its members in 1898. Despite furious warfare waged by mining companies against it, and a campaign to frighten the general populace by equating it to Bolshevism, the UMWA survived. Great gains were made in 1933 when the National Industrial Recovery Act gave workers of all industries the right to organize and bargain collectively, a move which eventually spread the union through most of Appalachia. A third victory for miners came in 1946 when union members were granted health and retirement benefits.

The Fair Labor Standards Act of 1938 decreed that minors couldn't go into the mines to work; while reducing a family's potential income, it also relieved parents of one of their

Opposite, top: Stonega, Virginia, is also on the National Register of Historic Places. This was the African American neighborhood, situated nearest the mining activity. All of the houses were two-family dwellings. The reflective triangles on the house in the foreground are for the benefit of coal truck drivers who hurtle down the road at surprising speeds (courtesy Chuck Clisso). *Bottom:* The former African American school and lodge in Stonega. The proximity of most coal camp structures, including houses, to the road helps explain the constant pall of dust. This structure is old and in poor condition, but its hue is due primarily to the coal dust thrown by trucks coming from nearby mining operations (courtesy Chuck Clisso).

Coalwood, West Virginia, was designed as a model camp and boasted a variety of architectural styles, including Tudor style apartments. This once-handsome structure, replete with gothic arches, was the high school (courtesy Chuck Clisso).

This Baptist church was built early in the twentieth century and served the African American community in Dante, Virginia. It was also used by the Methodist congregation of the camp (courtesy Chuck Clisso).

worst fears and allowed their children a chance at childhood. In many ways, the social environment of the camp was ideal for children, thus the golden memories of some former residents. What is remembered most vividly by former residents is an extremely tight-knit community where each family looked out for the one next door. If a miner was injured or killed, his family could depend on assistance from other families and, occasionally, real sympathy from company officials. Some supervisors, even those adamantly opposed to unionization, were much-beloved father figures in town, taking an active interest in the lives of the workers. Before individual churches could be built, the camp's different denominations typically shared one building. While the company store was the main gathering spot for years, eventually small entrepreneurs opened restaurants or soda shops, complete with jukeboxes and dance floors. Wives kept vegetable and flower gardens while they battled the constant pall of coal dust covering every surface—horizontal and vertical—in the camp. In the Hungarian camps, routinely referred to as "Hunk Towns," women baked bread in traditional beehive ovens.

While in some ways this coal community lifestyle had its advantages, there remained the ever-hovering specter of disasters underground. The inherent dangers involved in mining coal are familiar to everyone who has ever read a newspaper. For every one hundred men who avoided being killed in the mines, there are dozens of stories of those who were killed, or were permanently disabled. A quick look at the statistics compiled by the Mine Safety and Health Administration shows that from 1900 until 2006, the national tally of miners killed in on-the-job accidents was 104,621.[5] To paint a clearer picture of coal mining in the heart of Appalachia, there is this devastating statistic: from 1996 to 2006, out of a total 366 mining fatalities in the United States, 106 were in Kentucky and 115 were in West Virginia alone.[6] This does not take into account the number of people who have been ravaged by black lung disease or crippling arthritis from lifetimes spent in small spaces. No, the dangers involved in and around mining are self-evident; it is, quite simply, one of the deadliest jobs there is. What in the world, one might ask, could ease a miner's lot, could joyously counter that kind of awful daily grind and give him something to look forward to? The answer was right there, its enduring symbol laid out in the middle of every Appalachian coal camp.

Baseball.

CHAPTER 2

The Appalachian Pastime

Winter is an inhospitable time in Appalachia. The hollows are so deep and narrow, their walls rising so steeply, that many an acre of ground stays in shadow from October to April. Because roads have been built on former hunting trails, and those built on former buffalo trails, they are not only twisting but perilously banked. A mere dusting of snow makes driving on them a gamble with one's life. On rock faces lining newer roads, those passages blasted from the hills, frozen waterfalls make opaque sculptures, subtly tinted from minerals in the rock. Snow will cling to the north side of a hill despite a string of sunny days. Mountains are gray brown except for the occasional evergreen and the mountain laurel which keeps its waxy leaves year round. Jagged outcroppings of rock have lost the invisibility brought on by summer and are on full display.

Then suddenly, in the tangle of dead trees and vines, the sarvis, or serviceberry, trees begin to bloom. In past centuries, their flowering was a sign for the circuit preachers to leave their snug cabins and head out for weddings, christenings and long-delayed burials. On the mountainsides, the clusters of white blossoms are almost indistinguishable from the mists that rise like wraiths out of countless caves to tangle in the treetops. In a few weeks, the white flowers of the sarvis yield to lavender as the redbuds come into their glory, their blooms balanced on gracile black trunks. Gradually, entire mountainsides will take on a green so luminous it's almost pink. Spring has arrived.

In the late nineteenth century, starting with the balmy, lengthening days of spring, baseball madness swept into every corner of America and mining towns were no exception. In 1898, in Coxville, Indiana, a three-fingered third baseman by the name of Mordecai Brown started with a semipro team of miners. An injury to the starting hurler gave Brown an unexpected opportunity to pitch a 9–3 victory and take his first step toward immortality. The great Honus Wagner began playing in 1891 for the St. Luke's club of Carnegie, Pennsylvania. And at about that same time, Hughey Jennings, one of the most engaging players ever to be elected to the Hall of Fame, climbed out of the mines on the other side of the state in Moosic, Pennsylvania, to play for $35 a month.

Among all the industrial workers who formed baseball teams in the United States, coal miners may have been both the best- and worst-suited to play. Their strength was legendary, especially in the pre-mechanization days, as illustrated by this simple mathematical calculation.

Assume that a miner swings his shovel five times a minute and that the average weight of a shovelful is 20 pounds—or 100 pounds a minute. Multiply that by fifty minutes per hour (allowing ten minutes in each hour for the necessary tasks of checking the top, blasting, moving cars in and out, and laying track) and then by six hours, and you have 30,000 pounds, or 15 tons (the traditional 16 tons requires still greater effort).[1]

And they had endurance to match. An obituary of a coalfield player tells of his ability to do a day's work in the coke yards, shoveling coal into furnaces, by lunchtime, then pitch a game that afternoon.[2] At the same time, the terrible working conditions sometimes faced by miners, and the toll those conditions took on them physically, would seem to count miners out as athletes. In a *United Mine Workers of America Journal* article, a former player describes the challenges. "'It wouldn't have been so hard if you could've worked at a normal stance. But we had to kneel to shovel. We got 89 cents a ton, and that was for clean coal—no rock—loaded by hand. But we lived to play baseball. After the game, we'd wind up at the gas station and play it all over again, maybe get home around 10 o'clock and be up at 5:30 to go to work again."[3]

It's impossible to know the name of the first team of southern Appalachian ball-playing coal miners or when its men first took to an empty field. The history of the first company town teams, their scores and statistics, are lost to time. Team records were rarely kept, except perhaps to molder in an attic or to be swept away in one of the region's frequent floods. But it is safe to assume that, as soon as enough mines were operational and there were at least eighteen employees at each, baseball mania gripped the local coalfields. One of the earliest ballgames on record was played in Perry County, Kentucky, in 1889.[4] A longtime writer for the *Post* in Big Stone Gap in southwest Virginia recalled seeing his first local game in 1899.[5] Clearly the sport had taken on utmost importance by the turn of the new century because, two years later, the *Post* printed a fairly heated letter to the editor demanding appropriate adherence to the rules of baseball in the upcoming year.[6] There is mention of the coal camp of Keokee, Virginia, having a team as early as 1901[7] and nearby Dorchester having a team by 1903.[8]

In the days before the Model T, transportation of teams to and from competing camps was an issue. But a look at the layout of mining camps across southern Appalachia shows that they were close together, some separated by a single ridge. Movement between them was substantially eased by the network of railroad spurs that entered each camp.

As the camps began to field teams, so did the nearby incorporated communities. For the most part, these teams were composed of men who were given jobs at nearby mines, arranged for them by team sponsors. Packed as they were with the best players money could buy, both camp and town teams were frequently potent threats. Railroad shops often organized teams to compete with their mining counterparts; in the southwest Virginia coalfields, one of the best baseball diamonds was at Andover, a railroad camp set in the midst of the mining communities.

In coal camps and incorporated communities alike, baseball became much more than just a game. West Virginia historian Stuart McGehee aptly describes where the game fell on a coal town's list of priorities: "You can tell a lot about a society by its land utilization. In southern West Virginia, people live on 45-degree-angled slopes. So how you use what

The proud Dorchester team in the aftermath of an uneven victory over Big Stone Gap, ca. 1910. Players are unidentified (courtesy Gladys Stallard).

little flat land there is tells you what's important. And what they used it for was a baseball park."[9]

The fans poured into the stands and onto the field, having arrived by car, by flatbed truck, and on foot. The preponderance of railroad lines meant that, for especially important games outside the camp, hundreds of fans would travel by train to attend. The supporters were a hardy lot, willing to endure sometimes primitive seating (or none at all) under the merciless summer sun when there was no grandstand. Or, unpredictable mountain weather could mean the occasional discomfort of an early winter. During one foggy, frigid championship game, some enterprising Virginia fans helped themselves and the players by building fires along the baselines.[10]

Often heightened by betting and liquor, passions ran high among fans. Murder was not unknown in coalfield baseball games. In West Virginia in 1933, a player struck and killed a first sacker after accusing him of blocking the base.[11] Fights in the stands were common occurrences as well; in 1934 pandemonium broke loose among the spectators when "'Happy Jack' Elkins, the rip snortin' dinky tootin clown" hired to cheerlead for the St. Charles, Virginia, team was asked by a policeman to be seated.[12] But it was the umpires who could suffer the most when fans' baser passions were aroused; it was common throughout the coalfields for umpires to require police escorts off the ball field and out of town

The Dorchester superintendents seemed particularly interested in documenting their teams. Existing photographs of that camp's various teams are still fairly easy to find, as was this shot of the 1909 team, though the players' names are not given (courtesy Elaine Downing).

after a tense game. In 1950, the Middlesboro, Kentucky, team was fined a whopping $500 when a fan slapped an umpire. Umpires were frequently influenced by the crowds; more than one former player, and more than one fan, has stated that rulings were often made according to who shouted the loudest. In the smaller camps, umpires were frequently recruited from the grandstands, which could mean ending up with men scarcely qualified for the position. Herb Scott of the Dante, Virginia, Bearcats recalls one named Jim. "Jim couldn't hardly see no way. They throwed the ball and Jim never did say nothin'. A minute went by. Finally somebody said, 'Judge it, Brother Ump.' And Jim said, 'Too close to call.'"

As the Appalachian coal communities became increasingly riveted by the sport, it was just a matter of time until leagues evolved. By 1911, a Captain Fitzhugh Stephens was attempting to organize a league of five coal towns in southwest Virginia, an effort gushingly lauded by a local newspaper: "The columns of the Wise County News are open, without money and without price, to help push and further the movement. While there are those who oppose the playing of the game, there are countless others who regard it as the greatest pastime pleasure in all the catalogue of American sports."[13]

The early leagues that sprung up in the coalfields were often overlapping amateur and semiprofessional ones that would morph continually over the next four decades in southern Appalachia. Like the leagues in the major league farm system and affiliations, they were

Top: The triumphant Stonega team of 1912. It is highly likely that, in addition to enhancing overall camp pride, these men had just added to the personal wealth of company brass. *Back row, left to right:* Wells, LF; Tate, C; Wampler, 2B; Murrin, 1B; Davis, SS; Richmond, pinch hitter; Holston, RF; Hall, P. *Front row:* Baily, Capt. and P; Baker, CF; Dr. Claude Bowyer, Mgr.; Engle, P; Taylor, 3B; Duffy, mascot (courtesy Elaine Downing). *Bottom:* A later Stonega team. While the uniforms have changed and most of the 1912 players are gone, the team has kept the same manager (camp doctor, Claude Bowyer) and mascot, Duffy (courtesy Elaine Downing).

fluid, with individual leagues adding teams here, releasing them there, limiting themselves to one state, or sometimes incorporating mining towns from across state lines. Both West Virginia and Virginia boasted a few suitably-named and short-lived "Coalfield Leagues." The United Mine Workers of America often sponsored teams and leagues; the slogan for a 1934 Virginia local was "Baseball and More of It!"[14] An industrial league operated dur-

The 1924 Dorchester team. *Back row, left to right:* Joe Griddonak, Rufus Robinson, Roscoe "Cy" Young, Jim Mooney, ? Cobble, Opie Horn. *Front row:* C.F. Connelly, Dean Osborne, Roslin Reed, Howard Shanks, Fred McLaughlin; George Turner. Mooney went on to pitch for the Giants and the Cardinals (courtesy Gladys Stallard).

ing World War II around Charleston that combined chemical, steel, and coal interests. In that state's southern coalfields, where camps crowded the mountains, teams scrambled for the obvious advantages offered by a spot in an organized league. In the late 1920s, when a local newspaper announced the formation of a local league, so many teams wanted in that two divisions had to be created, an "A" League and a "B" League.[15] In 1937, the Mountain State League formed in West Virginia, a venture into Class D ball that would (like its similarly-named neighbor to the south, the Mountain States League) serve as both launch pad and crash site for a number of big names.

In the late 1940s, leagues were formed at a dizzying pace. In southwest Virginia alone, it was an embarrassment of riches for local fans who could choose from among the amateur Clinch Valley, Stone Mountain or Tri-County leagues, the semipro Lonesome Pine League or the professional Class D Mountain States and Appalachian leagues. The latter, begun in 1911, expired a few times, only to rise phoenix-like from its own ashes to eventually gain permanence as a rookie league. Pillars of the Appy League include Johnson City, Kingsport and Elizabethton in Tennessee, Bristol in Virginia and Bluefield in West Virginia, whose affiliation with the Baltimore Orioles is the longest in major league history. The Appalachian League produced one of the greatest moments in baseball history, major or minor, when in 1952 a tall, skinny nineteen-year-old right-hander pitched a 27-strikeout, no-hit game against Welch, West Virginia. Ron Necciai, who was playing for the Bristol Twins, established a record as the only hurler to ever strike out that many men in a nine-inning professional game and he did it while wracked with bleeding ulcers. A ball from that game is rightfully enshrined at Cooperstown.

Every league in the coalfields was different but each had set schedules and rules. Some adopted a divided season, the winner of the first playing that of the second at the season's end. Others employed the more stirring Shaughnessy playoffs, a four-team, two-round system, the obvious advantage being that even a dark horse could forge ahead to win the championship if they could just eke out a berth. All-star match-ups and championship series were huge affairs that could easily draw crowds of thousands. In 1933, the exuberance surrounding the local Mountain Empire Series championship in Kentucky was aptly described by a reporter who, days later, still sounded slightly pixilated.

> To Corbin on the special was wild and woozy for many of the fans while many took it more quietly than they did last year when on the Pineville trip, the ten coach train to the doubleheader baseball game was crowded plenty with about three times the number that the Lonesome Pine special carried to Pineville last year. The St. Charles Band which accompanied the baseball club on the choo-choo did their part in supplying the music both on the way to, and returning.[16]

Black coalfield teams were playing each other by the early 1920s but rarely formed leagues or set schedules. Even into the 1940s, individual games were arranged via correspondence between individual teams. Don Griffey of the Harvester Sluggers of Benham, Kentucky, says that it was up to the secretary of the club to write ahead of time to set a date. Often games were scheduled with ball-playing relatives in other coal towns. Miners' work schedules could interfere with games. Says Griffey, "Sometimes all the men couldn't get off work to come and play with them, then they would go to some of the neighbors and get enough players to fill in and make a team." Some African American teams, denied sponsorship from the coal companies, got financial support from black businesses in nearby incorporated communities. Most relied solely on hat-passing to pay for uniforms, equipment and gas. Some mining towns didn't employ enough black miners to form teams. As a result of these disadvantages, the existing black teams were forced to cover a much wider geographical area than their white counterparts. And although the white teams received the distinction of being called semiprofessional, even the company-sponsored black teams were almost consistently referred to as amateur. While cash-poor, these teams were rich in loyal and enthusiastic fans. What baseball played by black players gave to the local black populace is inestimable. "These teams provided entertainment, unity and a sense of pride for the working-class communities. Moreover, these teams provided a sense of self-worth to black ball players. Blacks claimed a certain symbolic *and* real power through identity as baseball players."[17] Black teams competed against white teams in benefit or exhibition games in the spring and fall, but that was typically the extent of integrated games. There is never any mention of racial tension at these match-ups.

In southern Appalachia, it was not just the homegrown heroes who tore up the fields. In the days of barnstorming, every kind of team made its way through all but the most isolated camps. At one time or another, fans enjoyed seeing their hometown boys take to the field against such diverse touring celebrity teams as the House of David, the Bloomer Girls and the Zulu Cannibal Giants. Major league teams, at either end of their professional season, stopped in many a coalfield hamlet for exhibition games. A lingering Appalachian loyalty to the Cincinnati Reds stems from the frequency of that team's visits to the coalfields and the intrepid spirit that carried the players into some of the most distant hollows. In 1924, Hall of Famer Edd Roush and his colleagues went up against the McDowell County, West Virginia, All-Stars who won 4–3. Publicity photographs taken at the time show the Reds in their uniforms sporting guns and holsters, allegedly to protect themselves from the wild mountain men. Their weapons must have done the trick because the All-Stars were thoroughly thumped in the next day's game.[18]

In Lynch, Kentucky, Gean Austin recalls seeing his local coal team play Negro League teams four to five times a summer. The Lynch Grays commonly went up against the likes of the Birmingham Black Barons, the Detroit Stars and the Kansas City Monarchs in the mid–1940s. And an exhibition game between almost every coalfield team, black or white, and the ubiquitous House/City of David was a regular event. But West Virginia was surely

The Bishop State Liners of the late 1940s. One of the most formidable teams of the coalfields, they were frequent competitors of the legendary Raleigh Clippers. Note the mix of races among attending fans. *Back row, left to right:* Nathaniel "Eagle" Wooley, unidentified, Curtis "Sonny Jim" Mott, John Mallory, Willie Lee, George Burl. Middle: Sherl Owens. *Front row:* unidentified, Herman Simmons, Wade Spikes, Wayne "Dump" Spikes (batboy), George "Sug" Montgomery, John Hawkins, William Bennett (courtesy Frank and Ethel Bennett).

the most fortunate of all the coal states in the rich diversity and frequent visits of famous barnstormers. In Charleston in 1937, fifty cents could buy an afternoon's entertainment watching the Homestead Grays compete against the Pittsburgh Crawfords. A lucky few remember seeing some of the greatest names in baseball as they barnstormed through the region. Frank Bennett, of the Bishop State Liners, from a camp that straddled the Virginia/West-Virginia border, still speaks with awe about seeing the immortal Josh Gibson play in Welch. And in 1952, the *Charleston Gazette* announced a game between the Kansas City Monarchs (featuring player-manager Buck O'Neil at first) and the Indianapolis Clowns (with a young, shining shortstop named Hank Aaron).[19]

Less famous teams also toured the coalfields frequently. One Virginia native remembers seeing a barnstorming black team come through the Stonega camp to take on the local black club for a weekend exhibition. On Saturday, the local nines had a great day of it, winning an embarrassingly easy victory over the visitors. That evening, it was suggested that the Sunday game be made a little more interesting. Bets were eagerly placed with few noticing that the visitors wagered heavily on themselves to win. Sunday's bout was a slaughter, the local fans falling prey to one of the oldest short cons in the book.

From left: Wade Spikes, George "Sug" Montgomery and William H. "Babe Bush" Williams (Ethel Bennett's grandfather) of the Bishop State Liners prepare to board their bus for an away game. The camp of Bishop straddled the boundary between Virginia and West Virginia. Photograph not dated (courtesy Frank and Ethel Bennett).

Baseball in the Appalachian coalfields thrived for the first four decades of the twentieth century. It had begun as discrete pockets of players in home-sewn uniforms, walking or riding a local coal train to a nearby camp for informal tilts. By the 1930s, it had become (for the coal operators, at least) a business—strictly organized and carefully tended. The public appetite for it was insatiable, and more and more towns began to dream of professional ball clubs. But by the late 1930s, the world was changing dramatically and local baseball would take several hits, large enough to bring it to its knees. During the Depression, coal demand had fallen sharply and use of the mining machinery that made human hands obsolete was on the rise, with predictable results in terms of layoffs. The start of World War II found the world once again clamoring for coal, enough to give the industry a needed boost. But Pearl Harbor meant that the American miners who would have benefited from that boost were forced to don the uniforms of their country and ship out. As for baseball, if the teams survived at all, they were made up of the few men left behind. Most of the leagues came to a grinding halt. The Mountain State League of West Virginia, which in 1942 had become Class C, shut down altogether, but the Appalachian League managed to struggle through the war years. Most of the semipro leagues expired. A few, like the Lonesome Pine, held themselves together with little more than Scotch tape and grim resolve,

A game played at the Glamorgan camp of Wise County, Virginia. The throngs hugging the baselines were typical of coal camp games and the attire of the umpire suggests that he was drafted from the crowd (courtesy Gladys Stallard).

their teams comprising remaining miners, American Legionnaires, employees of local businesses, and teenage boys.

With the war's end and the return of the men, coalfield baseball was revived. The larger coal camps and commercial centers began playing almost immediately, although most of the smaller camps never again fielded teams. Appalachian baseball was given a rich, if short, second life and lived it exuberantly until the early 1950s. But by then, some of the same ills of the earlier years resurfaced. With the war over, demand for coal fell yet again, signaling the end of the coal camps as the many of the mines closed for good. With the exodus of the companies and the workers, the camp houses were sold to the few families left behind. The buildings not purchased were left empty—silent, deteriorating landmarks to what would never be again.

There were other bells tolling for coalfield baseball as well. The ready availability of automobiles meant that what few workers remained were freed from the necessity of living within walking distance of the mines. A miner could now leave the immediate area of his work and build his family a little home, miles away from the noise and the constant cloud of coal dust. Soon, there were no players or fans left in the ghost towns that had once been busy camps.

More insidious was another threat, a bulky box with a small screen, showing up in living rooms across America. It showed fuzzy images of characters with names like Lucy and Ricky and Uncle Miltie. Soon enough, names like Casey and Yogi were added to the daily broadcast schedule. From that box came the sounds of a big league stadium heard in the background of the lulling banter of the play-by-play. The cry of joy from a fan in Appalachia could commingle with the cheers of the thousands of fans in Cincinnati or Boston. But best of all, as bad as the reception might have been or as often as the rabbit ears needed adjusting, one could still make out a batter at home plate and—almost, maybe, just barely—follow the trajectory of a ball as it sailed out of the park. For the Appalachian fan, as for everyone else in America, the Sunday afternoon baseball game was now filtered through electromagnetic rays, tubes and speakers. Viewers could be comfortable and slightly disengaged, watching a game played by men they'd never met.

CHAPTER 3

The Emperor of Baseball

There are at least three things that a real live town needs: one or more good churches, a good public school and a good, bad or indifferent baseball team. There ought to be in each of these towns enough inhabitants who have sufficient sporting blood in their veins to get behind a proposition of this kind and support a representative baseball team. St. Charles has spoken, the News approves, who will be the next man to bat?[1]

With those words, the editor of the *Powell Valley News* in 1922 was giving voice to an opinion, an opinion that was enthusiastically held by much of his readership, that for the good of small-town America, there must be official baseball teams belonging to leagues. Independent teams of miners and their haphazard pick-up games might be fine for the smaller coal camps. But organized leagues meant fixed schedules and playoffs, handsome uniforms and loving cups, everything that a boomtown wanted. And St. Charles and Pennington Gap, Virginia, were boomtowns with a passion for baseball that bordered on madness, holding the residents of both towns in a vice grip for decades. The teams of each town would alternately battle each other, and then band together to battle others teams in sporting wars that kept both populations captivated.

Through the years, the various teams of Lee County could claim some of the most interesting baseball players ever to hotdog on green grass. A traveling circus stopped once in Pennington, only to lose one of its clowns to the local baseball aggregation as a shortstop. In between plays, he thrilled the spectators with his backflips.[2] Clay "Cowboy" Barker, a pillar of the Lee County teams, showed more talents than just with a bat; at a 1933 game, he graciously agreed to pull a tooth for a suffering fan between innings.[3] The St. Charles Miners were famous for many years because of their manager "King Tut" Stapleton, who was known for his ear-splitting war whoops as his boys began to hit. And the hot-headed Pennington Gap club was once forced to forfeit a game to Middlesboro, Kentucky, when the umpire tossed enough of its players in the first inning to stop the game in its tracks.[4]

Lee County sits in the shard-sharp southwestern tip of the state, puncturing Bell County, Kentucky, its western neighbor. It is the home of the Cumberland Gap, one-time gateway from the known world into that of the unexplored west. Approaching Lee County from the east or south, there's no evidence of coal; in fact, all but the western edge was, for years, tobacco country. Pennington Gap, with a population of about two thousand, is a picturesque little town surrounded by softly-undulating hills. But a short five mile drive northwest into the tightening mountains takes one to the virtual ghost town of St. Charles, a once-booming commercial center in the thick of the coalfields. As mining operations have ground to a halt, so has the life of St. Charles, the population of which now sits at roughly one hundred and fifty. At one time, Pennington Gap and St. Charles were dynamic towns with shops and theaters, restaurants open long into the night and parking always at a premium. To this day, the two towns, and the county seat of Jonesville, are the only incorporated towns in the county.

When information on Lee County is needed, one naturally goes to its unofficial historian, Larry Fish. Besides being an authority on local history, Larry is a peerless storyteller. The timbre of his voice, his impeccable vocabulary and drawling delivery leave the listener feeling slightly intoxicated. The fact that he profoundly loves his home county and its collection of characters doesn't mean that he fiddles with the truth. A few hours with Larry and one comes away with a clear but colorful portrait of Lee County, warts and all.

The first issue addressed must necessarily be the psychological differences between the agricultural, Old South gentility of Pennington Gap and the hectic, hardscrabble mentality of the coal town, St. Charles. "There was always a roughness to St. Charles. And they felt the difference," says Larry. "But part of it was that they enjoyed being different. While you always had animosity between coal camps, they all banded together against an outsider."

Born into blue-collar St. Charles in 1906 was the man who would spend his life trying to keep baseball fans in Virginia, Kentucky, and Tennessee whipped into an absolute competitive frenzy. In the annals of Appalachian baseball, no man will live as vividly as Virgil Q. Wacks, father of the Lonesome Pine League and president of the 1948–1954 Mountain States League. A man of preternatural energy and a seemingly endless talent for promotion (of others and of himself), his shadow loomed large over every aspect of the sport in the region for twenty-five years. No contract was inked, no bat swung, no bet placed on balls and strikes but Virgil Q. Wacks knew of it and had most likely influenced it. He successfully married his three great obsessions—baseball, cinematography, and journalism—to become the area's most notorious mover and shaker. "He was simply marvelous and one of the most fascinating people to talk to. Well, you didn't talk to him, you listened. He did all the talking," Larry says.

Larry Fish suggests that Virgil, having been born in a coal town to a mining family, might have felt a subtle sense of social inadequacy. Finding a lifelong friend and fellow baseball fan in a wealthy young Penningtonian named Perle Stewart might only have enhanced his desire to transcend the black dust of St. Charles. Good-looking, well-dressed and well-educated, Perle was everything Virgil wanted for himself. "By nature of the family he was born into, Perle was automatically accepted into the social groups around St. Charles and Pennington; he didn't have to prove himself," says Larry. But Virgil did, and he faced the task with the zeal of a Horatio Alger character.

After college, which he attended on a baseball scholarship, and after earning a cinematography diploma, Virgil Q. Wacks threw himself into journalism, first with the local *Powell Valley News*, then with different regional newspapers as a stringer. He covered every kind of story, a perfect job for him as he could advertise his own endeavors via his official role as journalist. One of his earliest self-promotions appeared in 1928, in an article from St. Charles (presumably written by Virgil, as that was his beat) announcing that his motion picture, featuring a local drug store and funeral home, would be shown at the theater there.[5] At points in his career, according to the *Powell Valley News*, he was variously a Universal Newspaper Newsreel Motion Picture cameraman for Universal Studios in Hollywood[6] and producer of Hearst Metrotone Newsreels.[7]

Early in life, he developed a few interesting eccentricities, such as a certain reluctance to spend money. Larry Fish describes him thusly: "Thrifty, frugal—some people would say downright stingy." Virgil was well known for turning off the ignition and allowing his car to coast down the steepest, knottiest mountain roads, sending passengers into a paralysis of white-knuckled terror. At the bottom, he would inform his victims just how much gasoline had been saved, conveniently converting that figure into cents.

Virgil's reserve of ideas was as inexhaustible as his energy and ambition. "Even standing still talking, Virgil would have to be busy with something else. He was like a whirling dervish and ideas kept pouring forth," says Larry. "He'd come up with ten ideas. Nine of them wouldn't work, but one would." Throughout his life Virgil would take on such tasks as promoting tourist sites, county fairs and festivals in the area, and creating films that touted local businesses and relocation opportunities, sometimes slightly enhancing the facts to paint a more interesting picture. In the late 1940s, several major magazines and wire services carried his account of snake handlers and other religious oddities in Lee County, sending a frisson of discomfort through many locals. When the television age began in the 1950s, he launched his own local program, a showcase for his own peculiar short films, haphazardly tied together with his own disjointed narration. He once responded to criticism of his show by replying, "You've got to keep it down to our hillbilly level."[8] Larry Fish laughs, "Back when those things were originally on television, I thought, 'Oh my God, everybody from everywhere is going to think we're a bunch of congenital idiots.' It was hokey but it sold."

Virgil Q. Wacks, the energetic and eccentric genius behind coalfield baseball in three Appalachian states. He was twenty years old in this photograph (1929) and already busy as a journalist and promoter (courtesy Larry Fish).

But for all of his promotion in other venues, covering baseball was his overwhelming passion and, like a seasoned carnie, he squeezed as many superlatives as he could into every sentence he wrote. The leagues he promoted were always the fastest, had produced the most professionals, and offered the biggest championship pot. Larry Fish feels that Virgil's exaggerations could be chalked up to product packaging. "He was doing this because, if you're going to grab somebody, you don't talk about the five-inch fish, you talk about the twenty-four-inch one."

Baseball had always been big in Lee County; a 1921 photograph of the Pennington team shows a bedraggled group of men in mismatched uniforms, some with the letters apparently written on their shirts and more than one in a railroad cap. This was not good enough for Perle Stewart, influential young gadabout, who in 1922 laid plans for a proper team, going so far as to solicit the local ladies or "fannettes," as he called them, to donate food for a fundraising dinner.[9] He had ambitious plans, including a large park with grandstands. Soon he was about the business of finding players, starting with a catcher from Tennessee who allegedly had "a record of using an awfully mean pole and pushing a wicked peg."[10] For the first season or two, the Pennington team played close to home but in 1924 started crossing county lines to face stiff competition from the camps and coal towns of neighboring Wise County. At the Dorchester camp, for instance, the team repeatedly suffered at the hands of future New York Giants pitcher Jim Mooney. By 1925, these teams coalesced to form an inter-county league that played happily for five years, periodically straying over state lines to play in Kentucky and Tennessee.

In March of 1932, a group of gentlemen (led by Perle Stewart) representing several coal towns and camps from Lee and Wise counties met to formulate a plan for a new league which was to be called the Lonesome Pine. The meeting must have been most exciting as the men were addressed by Frank Calloway, formerly of the Philadelphia Athletics, who had earned his stripes playing for the old Coalfield League of Wise County in the early 1920s. The consensus of the Lonesome Pine organizers was for a "strictly amateur league, using home talent exclusively."[11] In the final rules, the boundaries stretched to include a nearby county but the amateur status was to be zealously protected. These men were familiar with coalfield baseball and knew the temptation to stack the teams. "Any team found guilty of using a payed [sic] player automatically forfeits all games in which the paid player participated."[12] The season was to be split, the winner of the first half playing the winner of the second. The teams that made up the league were Dungannon, Appalachia, Norton, Derby, St. Charles and Dryden.

By the middle of May, the Lonesome Pine League was already a smashing success (although the roster of teams had shifted already) and fans were flooding the stands. Perle Stewart, as manager of the Pennington club, was in his element. To put the icing on the cake, Virgil Q. Wacks began writing a regular front-page column in the *Powell Valley News* in what would become his unmistakable journalistic voice. Here he recaps a recent game between St. Charles and Pennington: "The game from the first to the ninth inning was like a drunk man going down a street, first to one side then to the other. There is no doubt but what this was the most thrilling and interesting game played in the league this season. One man was seen trying to drink his cigar and at the same time try [sic] to take a puff from his coca cola bottle."[13]

But it took only a few weeks for the rules of the new league to be broken. By the end of June, the readership of the *News* got their first whiff of righteous indignation, something that Virgil did very well. It seems that the Derby coal camp team had brought in a pitcher, a

Mr. Hollingsworth, from outside the designated boundaries and, to add insult to injury, suspicious minds suggested that he had been paid. With this brazen disregard of the rules, the young journalist's days of wide-eyed innocence ended. For such infractions of the Lonesome Pine rules, no one from managers to league office holders was spared a verbal blistering.

> When the noble and sincere rules and regulations were made by the officials of the Lonesome Pine League it was just like the little boy's mother telling him not to go in swimming—didn't mean a thing.... I know there is something putrid in a portion of Scandinavia—that's wording it modestly.... [Hollingsworth], fine fellow he is ... the longest he ever lived in Lee, Wise, or Scott counties was about nine hours and that was while he was passing through.[14]

By the next April, Virgil was trumpeting the second season of the Lonesome Pine League—only now no longer just from his typewriter at the *News*. He was a stringer for the Associated Press and the *Knoxville News-Sentinel*, and working that position to its best effect. Although lacking an official title in the Lonesome Pine, he was now in the thick of the organization, "present to negotiate all necessary league arrangements for completion."[15] It was Virgil who was now laying down the rules for the season and drawing a line in the sand about the practice of importing "foreign" players. He was also adamant that no teams from outside the league boundaries should play. And the team list would be permanent; there'd be no more of this dropping in and dropping out nonsense. This was an exciting time for him to assume some authority, particularly as St. Charles and Pennington Gap had combined their teams to create the Lee Smokies,[16] which featured some of the best local talent. From this exalted perch, Virgil spent the season typing furiously. Whether it was a eulogy to a player killed by a wild pitch or an attempt to reclaim the attention that had been lost to a new league that was successfully promoting itself with a banner-dragging airplane,[17] he kept his readers absorbed by the Lonesome Pine.

For unknown reasons, as his day-to-day dealings with the Lee Smokies increased, Virgil's fastidiousness regarding rules went southward. Not only was the infamous pitcher Hollingsworth hurling for the team on a regular basis but, for the championship game at the end of the season, the Smokies brought in a really big gun in the form of Claude Jonnard, former twirler for the New York Giants.[18] Not surprisingly, they won. To cap a successful season, Virgil announced plans for a motion picture to be made about the Lonesome Pine League. *Stars of '33* was to be shown in theaters throughout the region to what he suggested could be record-breaking audiences. To ensure such, he dangled this bait: "Quite a number of the best looking girls of Southwest Virginia and Eastern Kentucky will add the romantic flavor in the bonquet [sic] scenes in the final shots of the picture."[19]

At the first of the next year, Stewart and Wacks seemed keen on the idea of getting the Lee Smokies into talks about the soon-to-be-revived Appalachian League. But getting into the league would mean having to build a park that could pass professional muster, and plans began to take shape for a field that would have the admiration of the entire country. In a burst of civic pride, a few dozen locals pooled their resources (about $100 each) and purchased fifteen acres of land. A bit of smooth talking got them enough used lumber for the grandstand and fencing. The result was Leeman Field, listed by the Library of Congress for twenty-five years as world's largest enclosed ball park. Virgil Q. Wacks was beside himself with glee and it showed.

The Lonesome Pine League's 1933 champions, the Lee Smokies. The gentleman in white on the front row is Perle Stewart, Virgil Q. Wacks' partner in the high stakes business of baseball. Tye Harber is standing in uniform, fourth from right, and his brother, Walt Harber, is on the front row at right (courtesy Ty Harber, Jr.).

> We want good ball and we demand it, say the men who have the quarters to back it with, and brother, I am with you, lets [sic] have good fast ball or either quit and forget about it and let the whole three years accumulations drift into darkness where pessimist and believers think everything is destined to go. I am an optimest [sic], and I believe to the fullest that this will be the greatest year for baseball we have ever had, when opportunity knocks, why in the heck don't we grasp it. We are and don't you doubt it.[20]

Although nothing came of the professional league dreams, Lee County, with its new field, hurled itself back into the Lonesome Pine League with what Virgil colorfully referred to as "razzusiasm" which was "boiling over and splattering all over two tone shoes" in St. Charles.[21] The United Mine Workers of St. Charles added their weight in sponsorship. Former University of Tennessee football star Beattie Feathers joined the roster. The Smokies sailed into the thick of the season with the primary promoter at the helm, informing his readers that the Lonesome Pine League was now considered by many to be "the fastest amateur circuit that has ever existed out side of professional loops."[22] Despite this outward support, within a couple of seasons, it was apparent that the league's biggest boosters, Stewart and Wacks, were beginning to chafe under that amateur status and were staring forlornly at the heavenly realms of professional baseball. The hiring of a former major leaguer Johnny Gooch as manager (he never showed up to his new job[23]) and a visit to Perle Stewart from Branch Rickey's scouting brother Frank had fans joining Stewart and Wacks in thinking larger thoughts.

To add fuel to the fire, Virgil Q. Wacks was now rubbing elbows with officials of the Knoxville Smokies of the high-ranking Southern Association. Swept away by his new friends and new status, he seemed suddenly bored with the Lonesome Pine, and began to report on it with a slightly contemptuous sniff which sometimes grew to nothing short of a mean streak. After announcing that he, as the official representative of the manager of the Knoxville Smokies, would be picking the players for the Lonesome Pine All Star game, he made clear that he was "interested only in young talent and not grand daddies who are playing now on what they've previously accomplished in past years."[24]

When the Lonesome Pine League lost its twelfth player to a major league contract in March of 1936, Perle Stewart and Virgil Q. Wacks were again spurred into action, making plans for a revival of the old Appalachian League. Thwarted in their attempts, the two impresarios reluctantly turned their attention back to the Lonesome Pine, which without diligent supervision had wandered far from its original course. They floated the idea of turning it into a chartered professional league but finances made that impossible. But there was certainly too much money flying around for it to be called "amateur" with a straight face, as Wacks baldly admitted, pointing out that individual salaries often exceeded those of Class A players and team salaries were often more than a thousand dollars a month.[25] Money had so imbalanced the experiment that the purists in the organization decided to return the league to a strictly amateur standing, with all the original rules re-instituted, including the one regarding the exclusive use of local, unpaid talent. But, in a repeat of the league's beginning, within two months, those rules had been trashed and the Lonesome Pine was, yet again, semi-professional, with players earning as much as $50 per week. And as the playoffs approached, it was taken for granted that the coalfield managers would be trawling the minor players of the major leagues, searching for that one man who might put their team on top.[26]

In late 1937, Perle Stewart and Virgil Q. Wacks realized their fondest wish when the Pennington Gap team was accepted into the recently re-established Appalachian League. New parents couldn't have been more proud, and Virgil began promoting the team, christened the Lee Bears, with all of his considerable talent and energy. He giddily started advertising Pennington Gap as "the smallest town in the nation playing professional baseball."[27] With Virgil and Lee County marching proudly into a bright future, the newly-orphaned Lonesome Pine League was cast aside. Without leadership, support, or boostering, it soon faltered and failed, leaving the local coal camps and towns, Kiwanis clubs, WPA and CCC workers to stitch together an unremarkable and short-lived league to fill the void.

As for the Appalachian League, this pre-war chapter in its history was one of skullduggery, plots, coups and scandals of Shakespearean proportions. The maiden season was almost called off before it began, what with the league only able to attract four teams and not all of those with decent facilities. The sports editorialists were pessimistic about the financial implications of professional baseball, given the last failed incarnation of the league. Added to this was the likelihood that the Tennessee cities (home to three of the four teams) would probably not agree to Sunday games. Still, the league was launched and the Lee

Bears went into the fray with the backing of the St. Louis Browns and did all right for themselves in the first season (with four teams, it would have been difficult to do really badly). After a few late-winter squabbles, the Appalachian League began its 1938 season with six teams. On opening day, Virgil arranged for Miss United States of 1937, clad in the same bathing suit she had worn when she was crowned, to throw out the first pitch. At the end of the 1938 season, the Lee Bears found themselves competing for fourth place. Virgil and the Lee County promoters threw themselves into the final series festivities with abandon. Western star Ken Maynard and "his famous horse Tarzan" entertained the crowds at Leeman Field with "about 30 minutes of stunting, riding, shooting and roping." Virgil Q. Wacks encouraged attendance by slyly suggesting that the event, and therefore the spectators, would be immortalized on film.[28] Presumably that reel of film did not contain footage of the irate Pennington fans, who, after their team lost, flooded the field with the intention of harming the umpires, nor the ensuing police intervention.[29]

The Browns pulled their support from the Lee Bears when the season ended and December brought a rumor to the effect that, because of the fans' behavior, the team wouldn't be able to return for another season. Virgil's anger could have singed the reader's eyebrows.

> The flashing headlines of Hitler and the ever changing disturbances across the sea has [sic] taken back page in Pennington Gap, over Lee County and in towns directly interested in the Appalachian League baseball since the great war broke out Friday night ... President Guy A. Kaufman, Business Promoter Perle Stewart and Financial Promoter C. F. Connelly put out their chin today and said "Where the hell do they get that stuff, we are not going to play ball, the Bears will be in there again next spring if there is a league and financial difficulties are not bothering us and haven't bothered us."[30]

But the team was indeed in deep financial trouble and not able to rally the fans. This column was more than just a case of Virgil being in the dark or whistling in it. It was the beginning of a lifelong habit of glossing over fatal problems within a team or league.

In November 1939, the Lee Bears were unceremoniously booted from the Appy League because of debts, only to be readmitted within a few weeks thanks to the backing of a very potent sponsor. The newly-reorganized team from Lee County was named the Lee Miners and for a very good reason: King Coal was the force that had stepped in to save the day. Rather than lose the franchise, a corporation composed of big coal operators, a handful of local businessmen and five thousand United Mine Workers was formed to get the team back on the field. The board of directors was a little like the House of Lords (coal company superintendents) and the House of Commons (representatives of the UMWA locals). Virgil Q. Wacks, "the man with a 1,000 jobs," was made business manager of the club.[31] With several thousand miners at his back, Virgil seemed to lose any lingering feelings of his old coal camp self-consciousness and attacked his new position with almost religious fervor. At year's end, when the league dumped the Miners yet again (this time because of a reduction in the number of teams), he reacted like John L. Lewis, accusing the Appalachian League board of "a personal attack upon labor and the union-owned team." He even made a not-so-veiled threat, saying that he had been told by the Lee County union locals that if the Miners were not re-admitted, the Appalachian League venues would be picketed throughout the upcoming season "since they had coldly booted out the league's only labor-owned team."[32] In January 1941, Virgil announced plans to appeal to Major League Baseball commissioner Kenesaw Mountain Landis.[33] Given Landis' temperament, it is reasonable to assume that even Virgil eventually thought better of the idea. His wounded pride and hatred of the Appalachian League would gnaw at him for years to come. He later quoted the powers of the Appalachian League as having told him, as they shut the door on his dreams, "You have to be cold-hearted as hell to play baseball."[34]

By the opening of baseball season 1941, a wobbly Lonesome Pine League was going with the fully-restored support of Virgil Q. Wacks. He seemed to have partially recovered from the Appalachian League debacle and once again was broadcasting games and advancing brainstorms like his Queen of the Lonesome Pine beauty contest. But the coalfield teams were already losing men to the military at a trickle, an augury of the loss that was soon to come.

The war years kept Virgil Q. Wacks busy. In early 1942 he applied to become a foreign correspondent, and, while waiting for a response from Uncle Sam, he seemed to have appointed himself to the job of keeping spirits up in Lee County. Besides writing his regular columns and articles boostering baseball, he branched off into an ever-widening circle of entertainments. In 1942, the front page of the *Powell Valley News* announced a performance by "the Great Virgil" at the Pennington high school auditorium. It must have been a packed house because even the most disinterested would have succumbed to copy like this.

> You will ask yourself: "Are they humans or demons," these strange people who seem to have the unbelievable power to change their bodies at will and pass through solid walls. The Great Virgil claims to present any kind of spirit manifestation and has a standing offer of $1,000.00 to any spirit medium, fraudulent or otherwise, who can present a séance that he cannot duplicate by scientific means.[35]

He also stayed busy with his filmmaking and productions featuring very minor Hollywood types. He enlisted in the naval reserve, but was at home for most of the war, filing stories, trying for assignments overseas and even doing a little pitching for the St. Charles Miners.

When the war finally ended in 1945, the first real baseball season in years began with an embarrassment of riches for the Lonesome Pine. Men were returning in large numbers to the coal camps and each team manager luxuriated in his packed rosters. Virgil Q. Wacks began banging his drum in early April 1946, the league having laid down the law that all fields must be enclosed, which meant an end to cow pasture play. Officials promised to hire professional umpires and Virgil was already touting the number of scouts that Perle Stewart had arranged to look over the players. Once again, professional players were barred and a rule stated that weaker teams would not be allowed to quit when they knew they couldn't make it into the pennant race. And every game would be broadcast on the radio by Virgil Q. Wacks. These might be called the glory days for the Lonesome Pine. Ample numbers of strong competitors, thrilled to be alive and at home, played their hearts out for the next five years.

Despite the heartache of the Appalachian League experience, professional ball still sang its siren song to Virgil and Perle Stewart. In June 1946, a plan was made to merge the Lonesome Pine with another semipro loop in Virginia to form a Class D league. It had the full backing, of course, of Virgil Q. Wacks who at this point began to refer to Stewart in every column as a major league scout (he was probably more of a bird dog) and as a member of the Baseball Hall of Fame in Cooperstown (which he decidedly was not). The culmination of these plans also turned out to be the culmination of Virgil's baseball career: the Mountain States League, Class D, professional. It was admitted into the National Association in March 1948, becoming the fifty-seventh league to enter the ranks; six teams represented Virginia, Kentucky, and Tennessee. Virgil Q. Wacks, in surely his most shining moment, was named president of the league.

No league starts out without wrinkles and the Mountain States certainly had its own. Publicity and press coverage in the first year were extremely poor. And it's never a good sign to have the second season start out with every team receiving a presidential dressing down for loafing and griping.[36] None of the clubs did well financially. By that season, one of the thorniest issues faced by the league was the increasingly fractious relationship between President Wacks and some local sports editors. Many found him to be something of an absent parent, rarely speaking to managers and officials, difficult to find when needed, and high-handed in his dealings with everyone. Julian Pitzer of the *Middlesboro Daily News* was one of the first to voice anger at Wacks. He lambasted Wacks for the suspensions of two players who had been openly critical of the president on a minor matter.

> Anyways, it seems it is now a crime—at least in this section of the country—for a person to air an opinion. Many of the soldier boys thought that was part of what they fought for a couple of times.... Perhaps the mistake that the suspended players made was in saying it to the face of the person rather than to his back. The truth does hurt, at times, doesn't it?[37]

Despite more and more grumbling from the press, Virgil Q. Wacks, albeit somewhat distractedly, attempted to oversee the league as it made its way through the sometimes choppy waters of the minors. The Mountain States faced the never-ending problems of money, crowd support, allowable team sizes, and maximum number of veteran players permitted. It successfully integrated in 1951 after a couple of stalled attempts the year before and tried to fend off the corroding effects of televised major league games. And all the while, Virgil continued his colorful adventures in promotion. It was he who was the brains behind the "Queen of the Minor Leagues" pageant, with which he attempted to catapult a winsome, baseball-loving lass into a full-length movie opposite none other than Bob Hope.[38] It seemed that nothing much could rattle him—except, perhaps, for umpires.

Virgil had long been plagued by his umpires. As early as 1949, he wrote an article for the *Kingsport Times*, in third person as he often did, explaining why he had fired an umpire. Apparently, the gentleman had a fervent desire to break his contract and go home to New York; he wanted to see to his girlfriend and also wished to attend radio school. The president had given him a number of chances to straighten up and had received promises to the effect that he would, but to no avail. The umpire bolted shortly before the opening pitch of an important game. Virgil defensively reported, "An hour later, with three umpires already on the sidelines, and Wacks scrambling everywhere for an immediate replacements, Stein boarded a bus for the Bronx, leaving the league flat and taking with him unowned gear of another umpire."[39] Before the 1953 season started, Virgil Q. Wacks decided to fire an entire staff of umpires and start fresh. But a few of the new ones brought unfavorable attention, and on a national scale, to the Mountain States before the year was out. One very nearly reignited the Civil War.

Charlie Anderson, a rookie umpire from New Haven, Connecticut, was new to Appalachia. He wrote a letter to one of his hometown buddies, commenting on the fear that area residents inspired in him. What young Anderson didn't know was that his friend would send the letter to a local paper where it would be forwarded to the major wire services and run across the country. The *Knoxville News-Sentinel* ran the complete text, including the final paragraph, the subject of which was eastern Kentucky: "One town, Middlesboro, Ky., the fans come to the game with guns and we are all complaining to the president as we feel that one of them nuts will take a shot at us."[40] The people of Middlesboro and Appalachia at large, perennially the butt of hillbilly jokes and ancient stereotypes, were appalled. The *Daily News'* general manager was quoted as saying, "The very implication is preposterous. Mr. Anderson is living in a dream world of 20 or 30 years ago. He has insulted Middlesboro with his ridiculous accusations."[41] For his part, Anderson at first denied even writing the letter, and then confessed to it the next day. Area newspapers, particularly those in Kentucky, demanded that the league president issue a public statement on the mess but were left unsatisfied. "Wacks, often elusive at times of stress in the league, could not be reached at his office in Pennington Gap," the Middlesboro paper dryly reported.[42] The National Association was not asked to investigate and the matter faded away. But a few weeks later, another wire service story in which another umpire contributed his two-cents' worth, made the rounds. "Mountain States is the league where one game had to be forfeited for lack of baseballs; where a team once lost its uniforms because of a large cleaning bill; where two teams both use the name 'Smokies'; where an umpire charged fans carry knives and pistols."[43] As damning as the article was, it did include a compliment, paid by said umpire Ed Castellano. "It's part screwball and yet better than most Class D leagues as far as the brand of ball is concerned."

A competent publicity office might have been able to tamp down the flames of the umpire wars but, according to Julian Pitzer of the *Daily News*, Virgil Q. Wacks had abolished his. Until that point, information was easily gathered by all the local media outlets, but by spring of that year, getting the daily scores, let alone any updated information on teams and players, was like pulling teeth. The league offices (meaning Virgil) justified this decision by saying that it cost too much in telephone calls to report the scores. Pitzer was livid; he wrote, "One of these days, the Mountain States is going to wake up in the grave. One of the quickest ways to dig such a grave is to keep doings in the league from reaching the people who pay the freight at the admission gate."[44] Pitzer was not the only person voicing disapproval. Columnist Jack Kiser of the *Kingsport Times-News* addressed the president directly.

> It's good business for the league heads to get together once in a while. That's something I think you've neglected to do. The league hasn't had a meeting since Kingsport, Maryville, and Knoxville were voted in. That's a long time, too long, I think. There's plenty of gripes going to come out at this meeting today. If worst comes to worst, you may find yourself without a league to direct.[45]

It seems that the president had turned off the metaphorical ignition and the league was careening wildly down a very steep mountainside.

This didn't keep Virgil Q. Wacks from starting 1954 with the usual spring in his step, due in part to the fact that the Mountain States had been officially upped to a Class C circuit. He actively bragged that, despite the loss of a couple of clubs, others were reporting advanced ticket sales of as much as $20,000.[46] As good as that sounded, the financial realities were nowhere near as rosy. Long before the first hamstring stretches of spring training began, it all began to implode, almost every team having been completely tapped out. Advancing a class certainly hadn't helped, with higher salaries and league fees. Clubs started folding as early as January. Throughout the entire pitiful saga, Virgil Q. Wacks put on the cheeriest of faces and attempted to spread glad tidings while sports fans and journalists were left to guess at the realities. "The latest quote from loop prexy Virgil Q. Wacks—'steady as a rock'—was extremely optimistic but did little to clarify the picture. Wacks said that only reports from enemy territory were to the affect that the league was shaky."[47] One can only guess to whom the phrase "enemy territory" referred. But with this mysterious enemy and his testy-at-best relationship with the press, Virgil must have considered himself surrounded on all fronts. Still, he would not admit that the league was in trouble.

The Mountain States league had diminished to four teams by July, and its end came on the twentieth of that month when the Harlan Smokies dropped out. The *Kingsport Times* wrote, "The overly optimistic MSL President Virgil Q. Wacks, who said only last week, 'We're solid as a rock,' could not be located at his home in Pennington Gap, Va. for a comment."[48]

Virgil, for his part, refused to admit defeat. After observing a barely-decent mourning period for his defunct league, he announced that he was planning a fresh start for a new one to be created for 1955. The president of the National Association promised his full support but sagely advised Virgil to be certain of the financial readiness of the teams before he made any announcement. The announcement never came.

In the ensuing months, Virgil's participation in the sport he loved was limited to his new fight for the minor leagues, carrying the ponderous title of Chairman of the Anti-Broadcast Commission of Major League Games into Minor League Territory.[49] He tilted at the windmills of televised baseball by furiously denouncing its broadcast into the Mountain States region. That, of course, was a war he could never win and he eventually surrendered. He devoted the rest of his active life to other business interests, like the Lee County Fair, North Carolina's Tweetsie Railroad, and "The Virgil Q. Wacks Varieties Show," which was broadcast from Kingsport for an astonishing twenty-six years.

As for baseball, Wacks had spent decades cajoling, pleading and threatening southern Appalachia into supporting it on all its levels. He'd molded himself from a scattershot young reporter into a businessman who'd helped put his region on the baseball map. He'd used the media to build support for the sport, embellishing on the truth when he felt it was needed. Then, when he was given a league of his own to manage, he marginalized the newspapers by offering only bluster and meager crumbs of essential information. When league crises arose that required a steady guiding hand, he was infamously hard to find. Then, when the Mountain States faced dire financial and attendance troubles, he spiritedly denied that they existed, until there was nothing left but the tattered remnants of the teams.

That said, Virgil Q. Wacks was, for a generation, the face and the voice of baseball in a three-state region and it is no exaggeration to say that, without him, the game would never have reached the levels of success that it did. Every year since the 1920s, he had been the reassuring harbinger of baseball season, announcing it in a flourish of his signature copy. His unharnessable prose matched his own joy in the game, a joy he generously shared by annually awakening the winter-drowsy Appalachians to all the delights that awaited them with the budding of spring.

CHAPTER 4

Tye Harber's War

The story of America's military manpower during World War II was one of ever-increasing need. A man's age or occupation might get him a deferment one week, but he might be drafted the next. The Selective Training and Service Act of 1940 said that men between the ages of twenty-one and thirty had to register for the draft. Pearl Harbor changed that and with the entrance of the United States into World War II, the act was revised to state that all men between eighteen and sixty-five were required to register for the draft, with those between eighteen and forty-five liable for service. In the beginning, deferments for men of draft age were based on dependents and occupation, but even those rules were altered as the extent of America's mission became clearer. By 1942, the draft boards of the coalfields had been informed that there would be no blanket deferment for miners. Each case was unique, and, if a man were indispensable, it was up to him to prove it to the owner of the mining company and up to the owner to then prove it to the draft board. It was up to the board to determine if the person in question was a "necessary man" to the mining operation. Although the people of Appalachia wondered how guns and tanks could be made without steel, and steel without coal, they acquiesced when General Lewis Hershey informed them that men were needed on the battlefields as much as they were in the coalfields. Still, some locals questioned the wisdom of drafting the workers of an essential industry. As the miners headed for war by the hundreds, one regional editor expressed his concerns, pointing out the mining vacuum that forced the British to recall thousands of troops.

> If miners can better bring the war to a successful conclusion by operating machine guns than by driving mine motors, then they should not be deferred. The same goes for farming and all else. But there are many minds close to the coal industry which predict that this country will duplicate the British crisis in coal if miners aren't kept under the hills bringing out the fuel which is THE basic ingredient of war materials.... Miners are as essential as soldiers, if coal is thus a prerequisite to victory.[1]

By 1943, the military was so stretched that the edict came down. Married or single, dependents or not, the only man who could be deferred if he was healthy and of age was an indispensable worker in an essential industry. The ranks of Appalachian coal miners were ravaged. While the sons of Appalachia were dying overseas, their fathers were, quite literally, doing the same in the coal mines. Food rationing and increased mine production meant that men were going into the most dangerous and physically demanding job there was under the disorienting effects of hunger. And in addition to the faceless phantoms of supply and demand, inflation and rationing, there was also a recognizable villain: the coal company itself. As if the wartime coal boom was not enough to feather the nests of coal magnates, some used the excuse of rampant nationwide inflation to gouge their workers at company stores. In 1943, John L. Lewis demanded an exception to the 1942 wage freeze because food prices in company stores had risen roughly 125 percent in three years. When that was refused, talk of strike began to be heard. A worried populace, unaware of the realities in the coalfields, railed at Lewis and coal miners at large, accusing them of selfishness and lack of patriotism.

What that general public didn't understand was that, as dangerous as mining had always been, it had become much more so during this period of increased output at increased speed with increased hunger. "Each week, 500 more were hurt. As of May 1943, when the first of that year's coal strikes began, U.S. armed forces in World War II had tallied 27,172 killed and wounded. During that same seventeen months, mining accidents had claimed 34,000 injured and almost 2,000 dead."[2]

While threatening a government takeover of the mines, President Roosevelt also promised an investigation into the claim of price gouging. The first Office of Price Administration investigation showed numerous violations but prices not substantially higher than other locations around the country. However, Harold Ickes, at that time head of the Solid Fuels Administration, sought a second investigation. It revealed that many company stores were not only overcharging but were selling outdated goods and goods in poor condition.

In the final year of the war, the OPA awarded coal and ore miners across the board extra ration points for meats and dairy products, averting another strike by finally acknowledging that the grueling physical labor involved in the mines called for a much higher number of calories than the men had been getting.

The war altered every aspect of American life, including baseball. Though the game was handicapped by the loss of men, it never stopped completely, either on the major league level or the pitifully scraggly semipro level on which the teams of the coalfields played. No, it probably wasn't the same quality of baseball that the fans were accustomed to; gone were the big bats, along with the merciless fireballers. But what wartime baseball may have lacked in strength and talent, it made up for in heart. No team could prove that better than the 1942 St. Charles Miners.

On Sunday, December 7, 1941, Edward Tyrus Harber was at the home of his fiancée, Edith. At twenty-nine, he had already been drafted and sent to Fort Riley to train with the horse cavalry but was released after training because of his age. Edith Harber, now his widow, recalls that, as they listened to the radio reports of Pearl Harbor, he looked at her and sighed, "Oh, this is gonna get me."

Born in Pennington Gap in 1912, Tye Harber came from a family of railroad workers. His father and uncle engineered the last steam engine to run from Louisville to St. Charles. Generations of the Harber men took advantage of the railroads, jumping the train in Pennington to play baseball in nearby towns. The family was baseball crazy, illustrated by the fact that Tye's parents named their four sons for famous players: Tye for Ty Cobb, and his brothers for Walter Johnson, Harry Walker and John McGraw. Tye began playing at an

Tye Harber while playing and managing for the Detroit Tigers' Troy, Alabama, farm team between 1936 and 1937. He had long played for Lee County and had been a member of the 1933 champion Smokies (in the championship photograph on page 35, he is standing in uniform fourth from the right) (courtesy Tye Harber, Jr.).

early age and he and brother Walt joined the Lee Smokies of the Lonesome Pine League in 1933, helping the team to the championship. Shortly thereafter, Tye was signed by the Detroit Tigers and spent time playing first base and managing their Class A clubs in Panama City, Florida, and Troy, Alabama. His son, Ty, Jr., was born after his father was well into his thirties, so never really saw him play. "Most of what I know about my father's athletic ability came from other people," he says. "He never talked about himself." But from speaking to those who knew his dad, he's discovered a lot about him.

Meeting me in the cool dimness of the Methodist church office in Pennington Gap, Ty is armed with his grandmother Glessie Harber's scrapbook. It is overflowing with newspaper clippings, most of them regarding Tye's minor league career. He is even mentioned in an old *Sporting News* clip, the date torn off long ago. "He was slow but they kept talking about his propensity for scooping up bad throws. He was not a real good hitter but you could always count on him for a hit a game. So I guess he was just dependable. He certainly wasn't flashy." He played his brand of dependable Class A baseball for a few years in the minors, eventually realizing that his lack of speed doomed him from going further. He gave up his major league ambitions and returned home to become a teacher; he was in the first year of his teaching career when the Japanese bombed Pearl Harbor.

In late May 1942, the Lonesome Pine League was cobbled together from the remaining miners, teenage boys, and young men, who, like their coach, were waiting to be called up. McRoberts, Harlan, Black Mountain and Middlesboro made up the Kentucky teams and Dunbar and St. Charles represented Virginia. Tye Harber, now teaching and coaching at St. Charles high school, was plucked from his baseball retirement and handed the reins of the St. Charles Miners. He also played first base. Today, the local legends from the time are gone. Most names are not recognizable and the war years were more than likely their only shot at glory. Tye Harber was given this makeshift baseball team and, due to a delayed season start, no time even to practice before the first game, in which the Miners went hitless. In their second game, at the end of May, the Miners lost again but their redemption lay in the fact that the pitching staff, which included Tye, held the enemy to just two earned runs (but they scored six on errors). The Miners began an upswing by winning the next game, in which pitcher Gene Parsons set a league record by holding Black Mountain to four hits and striking out sixteen. Not one to rest on his laurels, in between games Tye Harber was riding herd on his ragtag team, with constant practice. And by mid–June, the changes were becoming evident as the club began to rise in the rankings as reported in the *Powell Valley News*. "Manager 'McGraw' Ty[e] Harber's St. Charles Miners baseball team, who opened the season digging amongst cellarites, are now digging with Dunbar for the league leadership. They are tied for first place with five wins and two losses each."[3] This article is also the first time that mention is made of young Bill Halstead, a player for the Miners. At eighteen, he was nearing his departure time for the navy. When he returned after the war, he became one of the stars of the Lonesome Pine, Mountain States and Appalachian leagues, eventually assuming command of the last.

By the end of June, the coal-mining fans of St. Charles, edgy from the war and tired like the rest of the country, were finding reason for joy. The St. Charles Miners were now routinely referred to as "The Harbermen" after having won seven straight games, the last one in the ninth with a seven-run rally. As the Fourth of July approached, Virgil Q. Wacks (his bitterness towards the regional professional league unabated) announced that the Miners, sitting at 9–2, would play in an exhibition against the Newport Canners, "one of the better teams of the 'Boss Ruled' Appalachian League."[4] (Virgil also took time to advertise a benefit radio show at Leeman Field to help bail out the Miners Baseball Club which had taken a severe financial hit with its ousting from the Appy League. A few of the acts from his hand-picked lineup were the Tennessee Hillbillies, Cowboy Copas and his Gold Star Rangers and Emory Martin, the "world's outstanding one-armed banjo player."[5]) The Harbermen beat the professional team 5–4, but lost the next tilt to the newly-formed Martin Brothers Hardware of Bell County which had stepped in to replace Black Mountain. "They were weakened somewhat Sunday and, too, were overconfident because of ten straight wins, and with the law of averages right at their heels, an upset was due—and true to baseball it came."[6]

Tye Harber called for even more practice, leading the Miners to two more victories, when, to the upset of Lee County, he made the grim announcement that he had been called back to the army. He played his last game against the Middlesboro team and was gone. His managerial record was 11–3 and his team was leading the league by a margin of two and one half games. But his crew was now without a pilot.

On the night before the Miners next game, the team unanimously elected one of Tye's teaching colleagues as manager and carried on their winning streak. But the void was felt and long after his departure, Tye's absence worried Virgil Q. Wacks like a missing tooth; he continued to hearken back to the halcyon days of the Harbermen. In truth, however, Tye was just a symbol to Wacks and his readers; players throughout the league were leaving at a breathtaking clip. Scheduled games were being cancelled for lack of eighteen men eligible to play. By September 1, Virgil announced dates for the playoffs but warned that it was unlikely they would take place, and they didn't. The Miners, the team that would undoubtedly have taken the championship, sitting as they were at 19–4, had been reduced to five players.

At the end of the sad season, Virgil Q. Wacks bade baseball goodbye, and, in a peculiarly honest, unembellished tone, praised the man who had made Lee County so proud. (Included, of course, was the requisite barb at the hated Appy League.)

> Speaking of Ty[e] Harber ... he is now playing first base in a khaki uniform at Fort Oglethorpe, Ga., and with him are several boys that played with Pennington Gap in the dilapidated Appalachian League.... At the close of school, he took over the St. Charles Miners, lost a couple of games before he could get the kinks out of the boys, but then took off like a spit-fire, and when he was called to the colors in July, the Miners were parked safely and securely at the top of the league, which consisted of five other very tough opposing clubs.[7]

Tye wouldn't stay at Fort Oglethorpe long; Patton's Third Army Division awaited him. When he finally came home to stay in August 1945, he saw his son for the first time. Tye Harber taught that son to play baseball. "The fondest memory that I have is that every day, when he came home from work, it would be me and him with a baseball, a bat and a glove. He wouldn't eat supper until we'd played ball," says Ty. "He always had time for me regardless of what was going on. And every year on my birthday, I got a ball, bat and glove. Every year." Both Ty and his mother Edith talk about how much Tye Harber wanted to play in the big leagues. Edith says that, late in his life, she once found him on the porch, deep in thought. When asked about it, he responded by saying how much he wished he'd gotten to play in the majors—just once. But what he had done, many years before, might have been more important. He pulled a bedraggled team to victory when everybody needed it most.

Tye Harber taught school and was a principal for many years. When he and his wife lived at the Pruden coal camp in Kentucky, the school that they both taught in sat across a creek from their house. Every evening, after dinner, they'd walk back to the schoolhouse where she'd prepare lessons for the following day. As she worked at her desk, the sounds of baseball wafted in from the field outside, where her husband was teaching another generation how to love the game.

Chapter 5

The Boys of the Lonesome Pine

Southwest Virginia has the peculiar distinction of never being part of a map of the state. The commonwealth is so wide and oddly shaped that the area is always an inset. It is said that eastern Virginia looks upon western Virginia as a red-headed stepchild. Invariably, when one says he lives in Norton or Big Stone Gap or St. Paul, friends promise to drop by the next time they're in D.C., not realizing that this little detour would cost them roughly eight hours of driving time. A day's drive west from beaches and colonial towns, through the rolling hills and former tobacco plantations, will take them into an alien land. Looking at a map of the area vaguely referred to as "the southeastern United States" will cause further confusion, as the shared borders of southwest Virginia and eastern Kentucky are always maddeningly situated in the gutter of the book. This area is referred to as the Land of the Lonesome Pine, capitalizing on the well-known novel by local John Fox, Jr. A semipro baseball league, with seasonally fluctuating boundaries, but primarily formed of teams from Virginia and Kentucky and sometimes Tennessee, also utilized the name.

From its beginnings in the early 1930s as an amateur league through its second life and sad demise in the early 1950s as a semipro league, the Lonesome Pine kept regional crowds entertained while it periodically attracted attention from upper-echelon nabobs. A certain Ringling Brothers quality was sometimes lent to the league by some of the personalities and events associated with it. And because they were in the coalfields, some of the ball parks were notoriously difficult to play on, so booby trapped with obstacles like tipples and railroad tracks that an outfielder almost always took his life into his own hands when he took the field. A Kentucky newspaper reported in 1941 on a broken shoulder sustained when a player fell into a ditch while chasing a fly.[1] The ubiquitous fogs of the mountains also played a role in final scores; pop flies could easily turn into doubles or triples as fielders tried in vain to find the ball in the mist. Yet, despite the unintentionally humorous aspects, everyone involved took the game and the league very seriously.

One of the six teams in the brand-spanking new Lonesome Pine League of 1932 was from the coal camp of Derby, Virginia, which along with nearby Stonega, is now on the National Register of Historic Places because of its surviving architecture. Both towns were owned by Stonega Coal and Coke and were part of a virtual empire of eleven camps built in the area beginning in 1902 when the company leased the coke ovens and mines of Virginia Coal and Iron. All of these camps were laid out to allow easy access to the independent commercial town of Appalachia.

Derby was the jewel in the Stonega Coal crown. Built in 1923, it was a model community, an experiment in "contentment sociology." The idea was to supply the worker and his family with everything they needed, including morally correct activities and recreation. It was thought that giving a miner a job, home, school and wholesome diversions would cement his loyalty to the company and quash the threat of unionism which had taken over most of Kentucky and West Virginia. And the entire community of Derby, which featured attractive tile houses, with electricity and indoor toilets, was one of the most handsome camps in Appalachia.

When Derby officially opened, at its helm was a superintendent who would stay there until his retirement in 1945. His name was Brownie Polly and he was a baseball man. Born in East Stone Gap, Virginia, Polly grew up playing high school baseball in nearby Appalachia. He was such a Cincinnati fan that, for most of his adult life, he went to the city at least twice a summer to attend three games each time. In the area's mining history, he is considered a hero for saving the lives of 77 men in the Derby mining disaster of 1934.

Brownie Polly's fierce love of baseball gave him a take-no-prisoners approach to a winning season. When the semipro Lonesome Pine League began in 1932, he wanted Derby in it and he wanted the team to be championship-ready; he would do whatever was necessary to make this happen. Polly's son, Brownie Polly, Jr., recalls that his father engaged in a practice common to all ambitious coal company superintendents of the day: he hired ringers. In the late 1920s and early 1930s, Mr. Polly went so far as to give jobs to three University of Tennessee football All Americans. For very little work and decent pay (especially by the Great Depression standards), Bobby Dodd (later head football coach at Georgia Tech) came to play for the Derby Daredevils. Gene McEver (later inducted into the College Football Hall of Fame) added oomph to the roster. He even missed the 1930 Volunteers' 1930 football season because of a knee injury sustained in a game against nearby competitor Big Stone Gap. But the college football player with the longest career in baseball in the Lonesome Pine League was running back Beattie Feathers, brought to Derby by Brownie Polly. By 1934, Feathers saw enough of a future in the sport to try out for the Cincinnati Reds. The outcome of that audition was not entirely happy and within a couple of months he was back in southern Appalachia, this time playing for the Lee Smokies.

Nineteen thirty-four was the year of the Chicago World's Fair. In August, local papers enthusiastically reported that Beattie Feathers had ended his baseball season and was off to Illinois to join the Chicago Bears and play with the team in an exhibition game. But Feathers returned for the 1935 baseball season, enhancing his reputation as a crack player with the Smokies by, among other feats, blasting out four doubles in one game. For his entire life, he successfully balanced his two sporting passions. History records his successes not only with the Chicago Bears but with the National Football League's Brooklyn Dodgers and Green Bay Packers as well. At the end of his NFL career, Feathers returned to the area and to baseball, playing and managing for the Appalachian League in the 1940s.

As powerful a bat as a sturdy football player might wield, what Polly needed most were pitchers with the finesse and firepower to lead the Derby team to the Lonesome Pine League championship. For this kind of seasoned expertise, Polly went for veterans. There were plenty of former major leaguers who would be up to the task but they were outside the area and couldn't always be trusted to get to Derby on their own. So Brownie Polly needed a courier of sorts, someone he could depend on to fetch the desired ringers and transport them safely to Derby for the all-important weekend tilts. Enter Woody.

Woodrow Williams, named for the American president who was in office when he was born, lives in a house filled with evidence of his 94 years. Amid the many photographs and the bric-a-brac (including a railroad clock that chugs and whistles for a full five minutes on the hour) sits Woody. He is a man with an impish delight in all things, particularly administering gentle blows with his cane, an act he refers to as "hitting love licks" (even local elected officials do not escape them). The Williamses were one of the first families to move to Derby when the camp opened. Woody enjoyed an idyllic boyhood there, and by the time he entered high school, had been drafted into the service of Brownie Polly's thriving baseball club.

Woody wore a variety of hats with the Daredevils—catcher (a dramatically crooked little finger bears witness to this), first baseman, left fielder, grounds keeper—but perhaps his most important role was that of courier. He had acquired a driver's license at thirteen, had access to his brother's Chevrolet, and had a penchant for speed ("I was known as a little hot-rodder"). Brownie Polly saw these as definite attributes and from 1928 through 1931, on a weekly basis during baseball season, he sent Woody to pick up the weekend pitchers. In the spring, Woody would be plucked from school for the mission; in the summer, he would be called from his teenage meanderings. "He'd send me as far as Cincinnati or Lexington or Asheville—wherever he could find a good pitcher," remembers Woody, who would be given a $50 bill, a gasoline credit card and strict instructions from Mr. Polly. Woody clearly remembers those given for a certain Ohio ringer. "He'd say, 'Now, Woodrow, he lives in Cincinnati but he's going to meet you in Covington across the river. His name is Hollingsworth and he'll be wearing a red sweater.'" Once he'd gotten his passenger in the car, Woody was to drive straight through to Derby, stopping only if absolutely necessary. The most important command of all was to keep liquor from Mr. Hollingsworth at all costs.

Even on the torturous mountain roads of the 1920s and 1930s, Woody in his Model T could make it to Cincinnati in six and a half hours, no mean feat, as he traveled on two-lane roads all the way. Once he and the pitcher arrived back at Derby, Woody could drop his precious cargo at the local hotel, where the onus of babysitting fell to the woman who ran it; it was up to her to keep the ringer sober until game time. When the Sunday game was over, the pitcher was paid, and, presumably, allowed a well-earned libation. As for Woody, he gassed up the Chevrolet for the long return trip to Cincinnati.

It was another of Woody's many responsibilities to hit up individual miners for voluntary payroll deductions to add the money collected by passing the hat. But extra cash was always needed and Brownie Polly frequently relied on some tried and true fundraising methods. Woody remembers Polly purchasing a new 1929 Model A Ford for $500 and selling 1500 to 2000 chances on it. Tickets were attached to the edge of a circular board which was spun, while a crack shot picked off the winning ticket with his rifle.

The Derby of Woody's youth is long gone but what remains makes for an interesting drive on an autumn afternoon. The existing Nicola Construction Company-built structures are varying shades of red; over the years, the homes' owners have attempted to outdo the original orangey brick color of the tile with varying degrees of success. Some houses are cinnamon, others a brilliant claret. Interspersed between the structures are doublewides, and the yipping of tiny dogs fills the otherwise quiet air. Woody uses his cane to point out the remnants of "Hunktown" and his parents' house and the back road where he learned to drive. "This was a good camp to live in," he says, squinting into the sun that is setting on the ruins of his hometown.

Terry "Salty" Smith also grew up in Derby, or in a tiny camp on the outskirts of it called Crossbrook. Crossbrook sat near the largest local ball field at Andover and Salty spent his formative years watching the men practice. "I picked up baseball by going down there and fielding ground balls for them guys when they were taking practice. Or by going out and shagging flies in the outfield. They practiced every day," he says. "And everyday, when my father got home from the mine, he'd ask my mother where I was. When she told him I'd been out at the ball field all day, he'd come and pull me off and bust my tail. I'd go right back the next day." Salty well remembers Hollingsworth, the pitching ringer brought in from Cincinnati, although his recollection is tainted. The hurler was brought in for a very important game but only lasted for three or four innings (apparently the ringer delivery man who was sent for Hollingsworth that time didn't follow Mr. Polly's explicit commandment regarding demon rum).

Salty's father was a proud union man and legendary coal loader who once won a $5 gold piece for loading 24 cars in one day. He was one of the miners killed in the 1934 methane gas explosion in the Derby mine; Salty was nine years old. His mother was allowed to stay in her camp house and was given a pension but it was doled out to her in modest increments, never enough at one time for her to escape the shadow of the mines that had taken her husband. When Salty reached adulthood, his mother made him promise not to go underground, a promise he kept. After returning from the war, he worked on the Stonega tipple for a few years, eventually making his escape from the mining industry altogether in 1952. But Salty's memories of his childhood, as a fatherless boy obsessed with baseball, are vivid—sometimes poignant, frequently hilarious.

He clearly remembers all the ringers brought into Derby by Brownie Polly. In addition to Mr. Hollingsworth, he remembers Howard Smith, who was a fearsome slugger. "They all played at Andover and in right field, there was a creek and he used to hit a lot of balls into that creek. When he hit 'em in that creek, a lot of times they'd wash on down. But the opposing right fielders, a lot of them put another ball into their hind pocket. Well, they'd go over that bank like they was going in the creek and they'd wet that ball and come right back outta there and throw it back."

It seems that the right fielders weren't the only ones playing fast and loose with the balls. Behind the grandstand at Andover was a battalion of ball-nabbing boys who waited patiently for a foul to be hit back and over. "They'd foul a ball over that grandstand and them boys would be lined up down there. The one who would catch it would throw it to the next boy and the next, all the way down almost to the camp. The railroad had yards behind that park, where they parked empty train cars. The boys really had a way to hide. The team would send somebody looking for the balls but they never got 'em back."

The Andover field had grandstand seating for roughly two hundred, recollects Salty, but many were the occasions that the crowds numbered in the thousands. He remembers an African American woman called Aunt Jane who would set up a concession stand below the train trestle early in the morning of each game day. "She would fry catfish and sell anything you could think of to eat—hot dogs, bologna sandwiches. And Nehi sodas. But I didn't have a nickel for a Nehi."

Stonega's philosophy of contentment sociology eventually died when the union was voted in, and during the struggle to achieve this goal, even baseball was affected. Salty says there were two teams at Derby when he was a boy, one referred to as the Union team and the other referred to as the Scab. They never played each other.

When Salty returned from World War II service aboard an LST (landing ship, tank), he began his tenure as a catcher with the Appalachia Railroaders of the Lonesome Pine League. In those days, the town of Appalachia was a bustling community that loved its baseball almost as much as its gambling. During the World Series games, businesses kept radios tuned in, writing the scores on their display windows. In one of the local watering holes, where betting on baseball from the local level to the major leagues was common, the Railroaders were especially welcome. "Abie Isaac had a beer joint, the Dugout; it was under the street. He gave out free beer to the players. A single was one or two beers and a home run was about ten. Cherokee Lawson had so many there one time it was unbelievable. Everybody on the team could go down there and drink all day if they wanted to," Salty says. On one occasion, when Salty and a teammate stopped in for one and stayed for several, a local policeman approached them. He reminded them that they had a game to play the next day and warned that if they didn't leave immediately to get rested for it, he'd see that they got their rest in jail.

Because Appalachia was a commercial hub, the ball team was sponsored by local merchants and gamblers. Jobs at nearby mines were arranged for the ringers who were brought in to play for the town. The entire team, although rarely paid in cash, was frequently rewarded in merchandise.

Salty was a utility man but catching had always been his first love, from his early days with the local American Legion team when he was the only kid willing to take the abuse behind the plate. "Oh gosh, those gloves weren't padded like they are today and wasn't as big. You tried to find you a sponge to go in there to absorb the lick." He remembers one Lonesome Pine pitcher in particular. "Jack Kilgore threw so hard that after a game, my hand would be swelled up like a beefsteak." But he grins at the memory, saying, "I was in my seventh heaven." He seems amazed by some of the steps he took to win in those days. "You did a lot of things back then that would be illegal today. One of the things I'd try to do, when the batter'd cock his bat and start a swing, I'd get my glove pretty close up to the bat, you know, kinda touch it, throw him off." The owner of the Kingsport Cherokees of the Appalachian League watched Salty go seven for eight and offered him a contract. "But do you know how much they paid?" rails Salty, still indignant after 60 years.

Those 60 years haven't affected the memory of a childhood spent shagging fly balls for the big guys, or a young adulthood behind the late. One of Salty's best memories is of the 1946 Lonesome Pine League championship, following the first full year of regular play after the war. The season ran well into October. In the final inning of the final game, the Railroaders were ahead by a score of 2–1, when one of the St. Charles Miners attempted to score the tying run from second. He was tagged out at home, the fatal blow delivered by none other than Salty, who remembers that he and his champion teammates celebrated the night away in a juke joint on a dark road between camps, drinking beer and listening to his favorite music, the blues.

As noted, the Appalachia Railroaders' most effective beer-earner was a memorable player who is still the topic of frequent discussion in the area. Cherokee Lawson was one of a handful of players who played so long and so well that he has assumed almost mythical status. Paul Kilgore, who played shortstop for the Dixiana coal team, happily remembers how a little brotherly love helped them to victory over the Railroaders and their star player. Today Paul is a respected local historian but there was a time when he, like all the other young men in the camps, could only think about baseball.

> Now I was a real glove man—I consider myself as good as Jeter as far as fielding, but that's all. I wasn't no hitter. I always batted eighth. Appalachia always brought the home umpire with them and we got to bring the umpire for first and third. Old Cherokee was playing third and my brother Harold was umpiring there. They had the knowledge that I wasn't a long ball hitter so when I came up, the left fielder came in some. Well, I got ahold of it pretty good—for me. It felt good, the sweet spot. It just did get over Cherokee's head but didn't have enough power to roll a long way. So I was fast and I came tearing around first, going to second as they picked up the ball. In those thousand thoughts you have in a second I thought, "To get me at third, it would have to be perfect." And it was. He had the ball waiting on me. I went in with a big old hook slide and my brother said, "SAFE!" Lawson said, "Ump, what'd you say?" and Harold said, "SAFE!" There was a field nearby and Cherokee, disgusted, turned around and just threw that ball over that field. I walked in and we beat 'em one to nothing!

In early 1932, the Derby club of the strictly amateur Lonesome Pine League was lambasted for bringing in hired guns, particularly Woody Williams' frequent pitching freight, Mr. Hollingsworth. Regardless of the fuss, there is no indication that Brownie Polly ever stopped importing ringers. And while he continued attempting to build a baseball legacy in Derby, nearby, another powerhouse coal town was doing the same. With money to spare for players, and no hesitation in bringing them in, Dorchester, owned by Colonial Coal and Coke, had already established a reputation. The Dorchester camp had fielded teams since the turn of the century, making certain that each was photographed. Professionally-shot photographs of the teams from year to year pop up regularly in the area. The Dorchester field was infamous, with a railroad track in right field, a creek in left field, and centerfield backed by several thickly-sown acres of corn. A ball hit into the corn, which should have been an easy home run, was frequently manipulated by unscrupulous centerfielders. One told of the many occasions when he would dash into the stalks and fish out an extra ball he kept in his shirt for just such a contingency.[3] The bleachers at the camp could seat hundreds and were frequently overwhelmed with thousands.

Dorchester's reputation for hiring ringers was as notorious as its field. In the late 1920s, operators at the camp hired a young southpaw from Mooresburg, Tennessee, named Jim Mooney. Mooney shone as a Dorchester Cardinal before being snagged by the Sally League and ultimately signed by John McGraw, who put him under the tutelage of Chief Bender. In 1931, after a remarkable first outing by Mooney against the Pirates, McGraw told the *Sporting News* that "he had never seen a newcomer pitch with more confidence and skill in the National League."[4] By the next season, Mooney's star had dimmed slightly but in 1933, he was with the St. Louis Cardinals and on the roster with the Gas House Gang as the 1934 World Series winners. When his major league career ended, he returned to the area to pitch in the Appalachian and Burley Belt leagues.

Hiring ringers was still a common Dorchester practice after World War II. In 1947, a superintendent who wanted his team in the Lonesome Pine was told by an employee about his brother-in-law, a devilishly good left-handed pitcher currently playing semipro ball in Alabama. After completing a lengthy interview and tryout, Willie "Lefty" Winkles was given a job in the company car shop. An innocent and honest fellow, he believed he'd been hired to repair engines. For him, playing baseball on a good team was simply a bonus.

The union wage for that year was $18 per shift. In his first pay packet, Willie was surprised to find that he'd been paid time and a half for the Saturdays when he hadn't worked in the shop at all but had pitched. He approached the superintendent with what he assumed was an error in accounting and was reassured the problem would be corrected. When the next pay packet turned up the same results, again Willie alerted his boss and was told, politely but firmly, to let the matter drop. He did and rewarded the company with fifteen victories and two losses in the 1948 season. He did well enough that he recalls that the people who'd benefited by betting on him would stuff bills into his uniform on his way out of the park. Willie became so renowned a hurler that, in 1950, when Dorchester didn't field a team, other coal towns fought over him. Coeburn offered him $50 a game but Dixiana won him by offering $40 for a Saturday game and another $40 for one inning's pitching on Sunday. He also supplemented his income with a weekly game at Wheelwright, Kentucky and was able to pay cash for a new 1950 Ford. In 1951, he was signed by the newly-formed Norton Braves of the Class D Mountain States League and played for two seasons. There he frequently found himself dueling with a young Hazard, Kentucky, pitcher by the name of Johnny Podres. "They pitched us together. Every time Norton played Hazard, they paired us up. I couldn't hit him and he couldn't hit me. He come over one day and said, 'Wink, I tell you what we'll do: if you let me get a hit, I'll let you get one.' I said, 'Okay. Let me get the first one.'" Willie says that the two maintained their no-hitting stalemate for the duration of the season.

While playing in Norton, Willie was scouted by the Boston Braves, eventually turning down a chance on their Class AA team. Willie, who was newly married at the time, says, "Boy, I wanted to go. I could've made it to the Braves. I just thought more of my wife than I did of going to the majors." In talking with him, it becomes obvious that this pass on an opportunity was completely in character. He's a widower now, his house a kind of dark and untouched shrine to the woman for whom he gave up a chance at the majors. From his living room window, one looks out onto a derelict coal tipple.

Willie admits that, despite a wicked left-handed delivery, he had one weakness. "I could never throw a straight ball. If I threw it overhanded, it was crooked. The only way I could throw one that wouldn't break was to pitch it underhanded." He speaks of his days as a star pitcher as though it surprises him to remember how good he really was. Put a ball in his hand, though, and it's as if he'd never stopped, easily striking the hurler's preparatory stance.

As great as a pitcher might be, he is nothing without a skilled man behind the plate. Willie Winkles might not have known the success he did without the services of an excellent catcher. During Willie's time at Dorchester, that was usually Roy Flanary. Flanary is a big man still, although he walks with the gait of a veteran catcher. He and his wife, Billie Jean, live in the former camp of Keokee where they grew up and where Roy spent his boyhood plotting out a career as either a baseball player or a cowboy. Whether he would have met with any success on the range is anybody's guess but World War II dampened his hopes for a baseball career. Like a lot of his contemporaries, Roy believes his was a generation that lost their best shot at the major leagues because of time spent fighting. "That Lonesome Pine League, that was a good league for semipro ball and there were some good players," he says, seated at a table in his house. It is December and the room is filled with nutcrackers. "I think there was a lot of boys that had a chance of going up in baseball if the army hadn't took their life away from them."

Roy began his postwar, semipro career catching for the Appalachia Railroaders, and, while there, was discovered by the Chicago White Sox. They sent him to their farm club in Madisonville, Kentucky, where he was shortly bumped back home by the return of a former catcher from one of their Class B teams. After that, he signed with the Chicago Cubs and was sent to their Appalachian League club in Elizabethton, Tennessee. "I went over there and stayed for a while and just got to thinking, 'I'm twenty-three years old. A man oughta be in the majors by twenty-three and here I am, just startin' out.' They didn't pay nothin' but $150 a month so I just told the manager I was goin' home." Upon returning home, he played for and managed the 1947 Lonesome Pine All-Stars to a win over Dorchester. Given his success in that competition, he was happily welcomed when he asked for employment at Dorchester. Like Lefty Winkles, he was given a job above ground, in the shop. "Just piddlin' around," he laughs. "It was light work."

Roy is a man who obviously reveled in his abilities as a catcher. "You'd have to learn the pitcher, different balls he'd throw. Study the batter, see what kind of balls he can't hit and try to fool him every once in awhile. I always kindly looked at their feet to see how they were standing, then kindly pick out what kind of ball to throw—a fastball or a curve or a drop or a slider. Oh, I'd talk to the batter, yeah. I'd ask him what did he want us to throw him, what kinda pitch could he hit." Paul Kilgore remembers Roy well. "He was a heckuva catcher. He could be on his haunches and throw that ball to second and burn your hand when you caught it."

When there was no baseball at Dorchester in 1950, Roy returned to Keokee and played and managed the team into the Lonesome Pine League (they dropped out for the 1949 season); they won the championship that year. He left there "when the miners got to wildcatting all the time" and went to Wheelwright, Kentucky, a mining camp that'd been courting him for some time because of his talent. He describes a ringer's paradise. "They gave me a job to play ball. And they had lights so we played night ball. And if we played at night, we didn't have to work the next day. And the camp paid us our shift. The general manager was a baseball man. He didn't care if there was any coal or not."

But being a ringer did not give a man seniority when the layoffs came and the mining boom of the war years was petering out. Up until that point, Roy had successfully avoided going "inside." But at Wheelwright, he was forced to make the only choice a family man could, one faced by many a person in Appalachia. "So they put me on the inside and I stayed there a little over twenty-eight year. That ended my ballplayin'. Entirely. I didn't play no more after that."

Jim Daniels, third baseman for Dorchester, vividly recalls Roy Flanary behind the plate. Jim says Flanary was known for being reluctant to stray too far to chase balls ("He'd always let me chase his down," says Jim). In one game, a batter popped one up between home and third base and Jim, as usual, raced from his corner.

Roy Flanary, Dorchester Cardinals, in 1948 or 1949. Flanary was a much-sought-after catcher; this photograph hints at both his strength and his natural athleticism (courtesy Roy and Billie Jean Flanary).

On this occasion, however, Roy went for it too. At the point of collision, Roy wrapped his arms around Jim and hoisted him up to make the catch. When he had been returned to earth, Jim looked at Flanary and yelled, "Roy, you big son of a bitch. Where the hell'd you come from? That's the only time you've ever left the catcher's box."

Jim was a talent in his own right, but these days he's the small town guy known for his quiet wisdom—the one everybody goes to for advice. Everyone for a hundred miles knows and admires him. A widower, he lives quietly with two cats upon which he dotes. Having returned from the war in 1943, he was one of the original postwar Dorchester Cardinals. "We'd all been in the service. We came back and we knew each other but we'd never played ball together as a team. It kindly mushroomed a little and it was a little better brand of ball than I was accustomed to growing up. I always knew that Dorchester had a ball team but I was too young to play with them." He talks about his years playing third base: "Well, I had a strong arm. I want to believe I knew how to play the position. Maybe with the team structure, I just fit that position." Unlike the other Cardinals, Jim didn't work for the coal company but was self-employed in a business unrelated to mining. This gives him a unique perspective on work and play in the coal camps. He clearly remembers the ringers, including Winkles and Flanary, saying that hiring them was a common practice of coal companies, including one of Dorchester's fiercest competitors in the Lonesome Pine League, Coeburn. An incorporated town roughly fifteen miles away, Coeburn imported college baseball players every summer in its yearly bid for the championship. "They got real energetic by bringing those young college people in to play against a bunch of old men that were working every day," recounts Jim.

Because of his reputation for honesty, Jim is a logical person to ask about the spirit of play in the coalfield leagues. "Oh it was polite ball. I didn't want to hurt someone or see someone get hurt for the simple reason it would take away their livelihood," he says. But with a grin he adds, "Now we played hard. We didn't give any quarter. Every now and then I'd tell Wink, 'You know, you might need to put the ball in that guy's ear.' They'd hit him hard and I'd say, 'You're getting too soft. You've given him something good to hit and he's crowding the plate on you.' We played hard but we played clean." Indeed, coalfield players seemed as unwilling to rumble as they did to slide with spikes up or throw bean balls. "Every now and then we'd have fights at the games but it wasn't so much the ballplayers as the spectators." When asked if the players would clear the benches to support their fans, Jim laughs, "No, no. They were on their own. They started it, they could finish it."

Jim says that scouts were not that uncommon in the stands of the coalfield. "There's no doubt that they showed up at different times. The problem that you had all over the coalfields, where you had organized leagues like we had, was that from time to time you had ballplayers that could have gone into professional ball, but you couldn't keep them out of the area. They'd go somewhere and be back before they got there. They [the clubs] couldn't keep 'em." Jim attributes it to the difference in environment or a profound homesickness. "But there's been numerous people here that had enough talent to turn professional."

Surely one of the most telling details about the value that coal companies placed on their teams was the small percentage of players that actually worked underground. Jim remembers only one of the Dorchester Cardinals working underground. Although he eventually had a career elsewhere, in his early years, Jim worked in the mines during the summers. His father was a coal loader and Jim joined him to help support the family. "Maybe he'd only get three cars a day by himself, but if I was in there with him, maybe he'd get six." A few summers in the mines convinced him that that wasn't where he wanted to be. "I never was comfortable. It was frightening. A miner gets accustomed to it and it's just a day's work. But I could hear every noise. I could hear a rock fall. Daddy couldn't." Like war veterans, miners like Jim's father were reluctant to talk about the horrors they had witnessed underground. Jim said his father refused to give any details about mining disasters he'd seen by saying, "That's kindly the miner's own secret. Let's just leave it be and talk about today."

The commitment of coalfield baseball players to their sport is evident by the grueling schedule they happily kept: usually two games on the weekend and, in Dorchester's case, five evenings of practice. Far from considering it a burden, the men thrived on it and Jim

Daniels was no exception. When asked what his fondest memory of baseball was, he smiles and says, "Just playing. Just looking forward to the weekend. You worked all day and you was tired but you stayed out 'til dark just practicing. And practicing. And practicing."

When Jim Daniels said that Coeburn was Dorchester's biggest threat, he is proven right by a brief study of its teams over the years. A commercial center, Coeburn was one of the independent islands in a sea of mining towns, a boomtown when coal was king. And like the coal company bigwigs, the successful entrepreneurs of Coeburn wanted a winning baseball team and put the money out to get it. Two of Appalachia's most successful major leaguers played there early in their careers, along with others who went up in the minors.

Playing for the Coeburn Blues beginning in 1948 was Darius "Dave" Hillman, a right-hander, who signed a Cubs contract while at Coeburn and spent four years with the club in Chicago. He also played for the Red Sox, the Mets and the Reds. Born in Dungannon, Virginia, he remembers as a kid watching down-and-out former major leaguers play for the local camps. He was discovered by the Coeburn Blues in 1947 while he was pitching for his hometown; they persuaded him to join them, promising him a job at the local Chevrolet dealership. The scarcity of postwar jobs made this offer irresistible. He joined a team that was already famous for buying the best. He recalls the team management bringing in the entire Milligan College baseball team to play for Coeburn, securing them summer jobs with local mining companies. "They'd just, well, they'd just put in the time," Dave laughs.

From the beginning, Coeburn fans were impressed with Dave's stuff. It wasn't long before they'd christened him "Fireball," and were taking advantage of his reliable pitching to line their own coffers. Dave enjoyed the occasional boon from the gambling in the stands. He remembers one instance in which a family member's keen betting sense paid off. "We were playing Dante and my brother was in the stands; he was up there with his girlfriend. So there was booze and he was betting on balls and strikes and hits throughout the whole game. After the game was over, he staggered out of the gate and gave me eighty dollars."

And although Coeburn was a little town in the sticks, a rumor of scouts interested in Dave soon began to spread in the Lonesome Pine League. In those days, local sporting goods store owners or someone with any affiliation with a major league team could scout their areas. If a party they had scouted was signed, they collected commission. Local newspapers devoted ample space to Dave and the scouts that followed him from field to field. But he claims to have been oblivious to the newspaper chatter at that time, declaring, "It was good copy, but unbeknownst to me."

Finally, a scout showed up who rushed Dave Hillman like an avid suitor and pinned him down to a contract. He'd first seen Dave playing against St. Paul, Virginia, and watched him engage in a pitching duel with their man. "The catcher I had—they didn't have those big gloves then, just little ones with not much padding—well, I was nothin' but throwing smoke. Every time I threw a fastball, he'd back up a step. Then the umpire, he kept backing up. Anyway, we beat 'em that night and word got back to me that there was a scout from the Cubs in the stands and he was saying, 'I'm gonna sign that boy if it takes everything I got.'" Dave tried to bargain for $2,000. The scout, Tim Murchison, who had pitched for the St. Louis Cardinals, offered $200 and Dave declined. Murchison came back with what he suspected might cinch the deal. He offered $200 and a Class A contract. "I signed," chuckles Dave, "and my wife left me. She didn't want me to play ball and she moved back home." In fact, his wife Ima Jean just moved into a home a little closer to her family, where she and Dave lived comfortably in the off seasons, during which he worked in a men's clothing store six days a week. He laughs and says that each time he came home after the season ended, Ima Jean would look at their two children and, shaking her head, say, "Oh Lord, there's your dad."

Everyone who played or witnessed coalfield baseball agrees that there was considerable talent around. And many a young player was offered a contract to play in the minor leagues. So why didn't more local boys sign? Many believe it was something akin to "reservation syndrome," that the larger world was simply too alien and unkind a place for a mountain boy. For some, it is thought, leaving a wife or family behind was an impossible proposition. Dave Hillman, from experience, boils it down to the bottom line. "They didn't take the contracts because they didn't pay anything. They could make more in the mines than they could playing baseball. I was making three hundred dollars a month my first four years. I was just dumb and stupid and loved baseball so much I just went on. I knew I had to make the sacrifice."

More sacrifice was to come. On August 10, 1961, while Dave was pitching for Boston, Billy Bruton fired one toward the mound and Dave went after it with his bare hand. His thumb was broken in four places. He is philosophical about it, saying, "A pitcher, when he releases the ball, becomes an infielder." It was his last start in Boston. "I could still throw," he says, "but I couldn't throw a curveball." After that, his major league career wound down with the final seasons spent in New York and Cincinnati.

Watching baseball today, Dave says, "tears me all to pieces" and a pitching bible penned by him would undoubtedly set many a young slumping hurler back on track. "All they want to do is get up and throw the ball. They have not a bit of perspective as to what they're gonna do. I had pitches as much as three innings ahead," he says with exasperation. "You pitch ahead. You think about the future, make him hit your pitch! Don't give into him and let him hit his! Make him hit yours! And I was taught that when I was wet behind the ears." He also wonders at the number of injuries sustained by young pitchers. "You look throughout the whole league and see how many of them are gonna have Tommy John surgery or surgery on their shoulders, whatever. There's something wrong." Dave Hillman is of the school that says a pitch that hurts is one to avoid. "If it don't come natural to you, forget it. You're putting a strain on your arm every time you throw." He pauses and looks at a picture of himself in a Red Sox uniform. With a wry smile he says, "Great game if you don't weaken."

Looking back at his early teammates from the coalfields, Dave says that they were extremely fine athletes and courageous men. "Those fellows had to be huge, strong people to endure what they did in the mines. Because every time that they walked back in there, they were looking death in the eyes."

The Coeburn Blues produced another notable name, that of Tracy Stallard, who, as a rookie pitcher for Boston, threw to Roger Maris for his record-setting sixty-first home run in 1961. After three seasons with the Red Sox, Stallard played for the Mets and the Cardinals. He also spent a number of years in the Mexican league.

Tracy is witty, a tall, lean fellow with a head of white hair. But talking to Tracy means having to track him, mostly from golf club to golf club. Then, when he's cornered, he seems reluctant but resigned to talk about baseball. It's easy to understand why. He's been badgered about that infamous pitch since the ball left his hand. But he looks back on it without regret or embarrassment. He is the first to point out that it landed him in the record books, plus it's earned him many a free round of golf.

No, Tracy doesn't really like to talk baseball and one of the reasons is that his major league career doesn't strike him as any big deal. "I was never impressed with being a ballplayer and I certainly never thought it was a disgrace not to be one," he says. He was raised in the little mining community of Tom's Creek outside of Coeburn where he grew up poor, the son of a miner (and a much-sought-after local pitcher) who gave forty-four years to a job he sincerely liked. "You could have probably given Daddy a job in New York making a hundred thousand dollars a year and he wouldn't have come out of the mines." Unlike his father, however, Tracy couldn't picture himself in the same line of work. "I've been in one time and it scared the hell outta me and I've never been back in. I don't know how far in I went but you had to duck walk to get there," he recalls.

Something of a hellion as a child, he broke his left arm several times and, although it was his dominant side, because of the trauma his right arm grew longer and stronger. To this day, he does everything left-handed but pitch. By the time he was in high school, Tracy was known as a hard-throwing right-hander, so much so that Boston Red Sox scout Mace Brown came to see him play during his sophomore, junior and senior years, during which he was also playing for the Blues. He signed for four thousand dollars. "You can imagine what four thousand dollars sounded like to a kid who couldn't get a nickel to buy gum. I think I got a $2500 check and the rest was salary for that year. First thing I done was buy a $3700 car," he laughs. "A Buick, big as this building." His entrance into the minors did little to excite his tepid attachment to the game. "When I was in triple A, I didn't even know who was on the major league team—that's how much I was interested in it. It was just a job."

Although he doesn't remember that much about playing with the Coeburn Blues due to his youth at the time, he can speak with authority on the quality of coalfield baseball, particularly because of an embarrassing game in which he was involved. At the close of his first year of professional ball, he returned to southwest Virginia where he was approached by a local club to pitch for them. Located in the community of Ramsey, just outside of Norton, the club was made up of locals, many recruited from area mines. (Willie Winkles remembers the Ramsey team, with a wince, as "kindly rough.") In those days, the ball field was located on the edge of a river within an eighth of a mile of a bank of coke ovens that belched smoke endlessly. Through the years, the Ramsey team had floated in and out of local leagues, playing brutal baseball against teams of the same ilk. Tracy recalls his debut with the club: "They said they'd pay me a hundred dollars if I'd come pitch for them. I go up there and I don't get anybody out, not the first hitter. They beat me to death. They were a rough bunch of dudes. They'd knock a ball in the creek and you'd have to pitch with it." He shakes his head, smiling. "I never did that anymore. You can imagine how you'd feel: you're supposed to get everybody out and you just get your ass stomped for about ten runs."

Tracy agrees that fear of leaving home might have been part of the reason young players from Appalachia were reluctant to sign contracts, or to finish them out. And he feels like the men who chose not to sign were the ones who showed the most foresight. "If you stick with baseball, it takes the best years of your life, what should be the most fruitful ones. If you flunk out at thirty, you're hurtin'."

Tracy Stallard keeps the tangible remains of his career in a plastic box under the bed. Among the very few clippings and magazines, there are some black and white photographs from his major league years. In the publicity shots, he is winding up for a pitch (looking properly fierce) or standing amidst fashion models or starlets (looking handsome and slightly goofy). One photo shows him crammed behind the sporting goods counter of a department store, signing autographs while throngs of excited fans thrust paper over the glass barrier towards him. In all the images, he looks uncomfortable—a hapless major leaguer. "I just thought it was a job. I went more for the adventure than the sport." But he adds, "It's a great education. More than you could have gotten if you'd gone to four years of college. You learn a lot about people and that's what you gotta end up dealing with anyway, no matter what business you're in."

In the late 1940s, Coeburn's left-handed version of Dave Hillman was Bill Osborne. Now in his eighties, Bill is a man of slight build and still looks as lithe as a cat. His stature must have lulled first-time batters into a dangerous complacency. Many was the pitching duel played out between him and Willie Winkles, each the nemesis of the other. "I had a good curve ball and I could bring it right down. Had control. I walked very few batters. I never did try to hit one but I'd pitch close," he recalls.

Bill went into the navy as a corpsman in January of 1943 and served in a unique locale. "I went to boot camp in San Diego. At that time, the marines were just hitting all of the islands in the Pacific. They was taking a hundred a day of hospital corpsmen. A draft came in for twenty-nine of us and I spent thirty months at Yosemite National Park." Returning to Appalachia after the service, he immediately joined the Johnson City (Tennessee) Soldiers, of the Burley Belt league. While there, he received minor league offers from the Cardinals and the Senators, but felt the same way that Roy Flanary had—that the years he should have spent perfecting his arm were behind him. So after a year, he went to work at the Clinchfield Coal Company's town of Dante, Virginia. The superintendents of Dante, since its beginning, had been dedicated baseball enthusiasts; one had even served as president of the Lonesome Pine League. Bill's obvious ability and semipro experience made the current superintendent, Rush Adams, delighted to sign him. Bill went to work as an electrician for Clinchfield, a job he held for thirty-six years. He pitched for the Dante Miners for two seasons but when new Clinchfield mines were opened near Coeburn, he traded his Dante uniform for that of the Coeburn Blues.

The town of Coeburn and the management of the Blues were glad to get him; they had lost the championship in 1948 to Dante and it was hoped that Bill's arrival might her-

Bill Osborne shortly after World War II; he was a left-handed pitcher for the Dante Miners and later the Coeburn Blues. "I walked very few batters. I never did try to hit one but I'd pitch close" (courtesy Bill and Wanda Osborne).

ald a better season to come. Bill and his wife, who was pregnant with their first child, were welcomed with open arms and material rewards. Wanda, who had grown up in Tennessee, was reluctant to live anywhere near a coal camp, so they were installed in a neat home on a quiet country road. To keep the new southpaw and his wife happy, little amenities were quickly added, including a front porch with a safety railing for the expected baby, a new washing machine and out buildings. And Bill soon proved himself worthy of the deal. As he won more and more games for the Blues, the town came through with additional little examples of what Wanda jokingly calls "payola." "There was a furniture store that gave us twenty dollars in trade 'cause that's where I got the high chair," she says. "And the man that had the little hot dog place gave us ten dollars and I ate it up in chili buns 'cause I was pregnant."[5]

It didn't take long for other coal companies to come courting Bill for weekly pitching, but the only offer he ever accepted was from Wheelwright, Kentucky. He and Wanda would drive over every Wednesday night after work with a teenage Tracy Stallard in tow. Bill would get paid whether he pitched or not and would sleep on the way home, letting Tracy drive.

Bill Osborne quit playing in 1955 when he shattered his collarbone, jumping from a suddenly brakeless company truck that was hurtling down a mountain road. His recuperation lasted for several months and it seemed his baseball career was over. Before he could hang up his glove, however, there was one last obstacle to face and it was a big one: Leo "Muscle" Shoals. Born in a coal town in southern West Virginia, Shoals was often referred to as "the Babe Ruth of minor league baseball." He hit 362 home runs from 1937 to 1955, yet never made it to the majors, undoubtedly because of a bullet he took during a brawl in 1939. Regardless of this setback, he was able to compile some impressive records. He led the Appalachian League in homers five times and in batting three times. He also played in the Mountain States League and Carolina League, hitting 55 home runs in the latter in 1949. In 1953, the *Knoxville News-Sentinel* described a typical game for Muscle.

> Shoals blasted his 13th and 14th homers of the season and added a triple for good measure. His first blow, a solo affair in the third, cleared the right field barrier, sailed over a four-lane highway and landed in a field—a good 490 feet away. His second homer was a grand-slammer in the eighth which put the game on ice.[6]

It was against this Goliath that Bill Osborne threw the final pitches of his career: "We was playing Saltville and Muscle Shoals was playing for them. I hadn't played any that year—I'd just thrown a little bit. In the seventh inning, why, Saltville scored a run, had someone on base and they wanted me to go in. So I did. I struck out the first batter and do you know who the second batter was? Muscle Shoals. And I shouldn't say this but I struck out Muscle Shoals!" Bill's usually serene smile gives way to a huge grin, but he urges it back down and continues his story. "But he came up again in the ninth inning and hit that ball like a bullet between first and second. That's the last I played. I just quit while I was ahead. A winner."

Bill Osborne, Dave Hillman, and the Coeburn Blues had played their hearts out in the 1948 Lonesome Pine championship but lost, in the end, to their very worthy adversaries, the Dante Miners. Dante and its Clinchfield Coal Company sister town of Clinchco are two of the most remote coal towns of the area. At one time, Dante was the northern terminus of the Carolina, Clinchfield and Ohio Railway which would eventually stretch from the seaports of South Carolina to the Midwest.

The superintendents of Clinchfield Coal, from its earliest days, loved baseball as much as they hated the unions. One was Lee Long who served his long tenure at Clinchfield from 1911 until 1944. As hard as he could be on a miner who might be leaning towards the UMWA, he could be just as lenient on a ballplayer with talent. In an interview of Dante residents, author Katharine C. Shearer was told the story of an ace center fielder for the Miners. It seems he had accepted a job away from Clinchfield Coal. Not only did Superintendent Long allow him to continue playing ball for Dante, but also to remain in his house in the camp as well.[7] (Had the same fellow uttered a word of union talk, it is a distinct likelihood that he and his would have been summarily evicted from both house and camp.) Long's interest in baseball and his involvement in the Lonesome Pine League would get him elected to the presidency of the circuit in 1936. And it is illustrative of the Dante dedication to the sport that pay slips from the 1930s feature ten deductions, beginning with rent and ending with baseball, although it was a voluntary one. Existing photographs and newspaper references to the Dante teams prove that they were around by at least the early 1920s. The Dante and Clinchco teams both had spots in the Lonesome Pine League by 1936; it was probably not a coincidence that Lee Long had been elected to the league's highest office in the same year. But a quick glance at both teams' records in the league proves that, with or without the influence of the Clinchfield superintendent, those players had earned their rightful place.

Alex "Ponnie" Sabo played second base for the Miners. He and his wife Betty grew up in Dante but now live in a nearby town in a house perched on the edge of a bucolic paradise. The gently rolling hills are a far cry from the steep mountain walls and deep hollows of their home town. They are both of Hungarian descent, their parents having immigrated in the early part of the twentieth century. Once in Dante, all Hungarian families were housed in Straight Hollow along with the Greek and Italian families. Far different from the local mountain accent, Betty's speech is marked with very pretty, barely noticeable traces of her exotic background. Both grew up speaking Hungarian to grandparents and can still converse in and read a bit of it. One of Ponnie's most vivid memories is of the first time his mother saw him play baseball. After months and months of urging, Mrs. Sabo finally agreed to attend a game. Unfortunately, it was in that particular game that Ponnie barreled into home, knocking the catcher out cold. His mother left the stands in horror when the ambulance arrived. Needless to say, she never attended another game.

Although he humbly suggests that he wasn't a power hitter, his records of base hits suggest that Ponnie certainly carried his own weight and then some. In the Shaughnessy playoffs championship that Dante took from the Coeburn Blues, he drove in the tying run in the first game of the double-header and scored the winning run in the second. When asked if there was some sort of elaborate celebration after winning the championship, Betty shakes her head and says, "Just a lot of crowin'."

Ponnie is one of the rare white coalfield players, and one of only two or three on the

Dante team, to actually work inside the mines. When he first went in, as little more than a boy, tradition decreed that he be taught the ropes by an older Hungarian man, a family friend, to make him more comfortable. He recalls the company giving jobs to some men if they were good baseball players but never thought that players, as a rule, were accorded any special privileges except for game days. If a ballgame was scheduled for Saturday, his regular shift, Ponnie simply didn't go to work. "I know I missed quite a few Saturdays and I was a regular worker. That was about the only time I laid off was when I went to play but they never said anything about it."

Ponnie insists that he was never fearful about going into the mines and it wouldn't worry him today. "I'd be afraid of the non-union mines. But union? I wouldn't have a second thought because the men have got a say-so," he says. Still, his years underground have taken a brutal toll on his health and, like many a seasoned miner, he discovered that the company he devoted his life to was happy to betray him in the end. "I worked in the mines for over forty-one years, in all kind of dusty conditions. When I went to apply for black lung, the lady for the company got up before the judge and told him that my lungs were just as good today, if not better, than they was when I went in the mines." An extraordinarily gentle man, Ponnie gets angry when he recalls the scene in court. "My only regret is, I should have given a little cuss word and told the lawyer she was a liar. That's the biggest lie she ever made in her life."

Larry McReynolds was a batboy, scorekeeper and ardent fan of the Dante Miners. Not a coal miner himself, nor the resident of a camp, he admired the team enough to religiously attend their games. He can attest to the ability of Ponnie Sabo and his teammates. All of Larry's childhood scrutiny of the team paid off; it undoubtedly helped him become the gifted shortstop he was in college and later. While he was in college, he was offered a contract; he turned it down, but he eventually became an ace in the regional Burley Belt League. He describes attending the coal camp games. "In those days, it was like the circus. And you had your local heroes. It was a big thing, much ado. The whole town of Dante would turn out for those Sunday baseball games. They were good players and it was fast baseball. I know that when Dante would play the Bristol Twins, an Appalachian League team, Dante would clobber them—just *clobber* the professional team."

Another Dante Miner was Myers Fox, a right-handed pitcher. Tall and lanky, he folds himself into a chair to talk. His wife, Lela, like many of the wives, helps fill in periodic gaps in memory. He clearly recalls that Clinchfield Coal Company, like the businessmen management of the Coeburn Blues, was not opposed to hiring college ringers. He says, "The company, if they saw good players, they'd give 'em a job. They didn't do nothing but paint or straighten things a little bit. Never did work too hard—just ordinary jobs, outside work—as much as they could get out of them. But they got the same salary as everybody else got." And, while he agrees with Ponnie that the actual full-time Dante ballplayers didn't receive any preferential treatment, he makes the point that other coalfield players, from other camps, have made: "Very few of them worked underground and played ball too." Myers was a tipple operator for the thirty years that he worked at Dante. "Never been underground in my life," he says.

He declares, with some pride, that coalfield baseball players were an elite group of American athletes. "Most of the good players were from the coalfields. Pennsylvania's one of them," he says, at the same time lamenting that there are not as many major leaguers from the southern Appalachian fields. "This place just wasn't on the map. They may not all have made it to the major leagues but the minor leagues are full of them."

Of all the players who served during World War II, Myers' story of returning home may be the most dramatic. He had been with the infantry of the Eighty-third Division and was part of the D-Day invasion. Wounded, he was sent back to England, where he stayed in the hospital for thirty days. He became a file clerk for the Joint Chiefs of Staff, accompanying them to London, Paris and Berlin. He tells of his journey of thousands of miles back home. "When I left Berlin, I had to get a train to get to Paris to get home. They had these boxcars. I looked up and there was a colored man with his head sticking out from one of them doors of the boxcar. And it was a Kincaid from Dante! He come all the way home with me. We came all the way into Boston and got to Washington up here and I said, 'You gonna ride the train home?' and he said, 'No, I'm gonna ride the bus.' And I said, 'Well, I ain't riding that bus,' so I caught the train, he rode the bus. When I come home, I took that picture (while he had his head stuck out of the boxcar) and I took it to his mother."

What is interesting, and poignant, about this story is that Myers and his traveling companion were, for the most part, segregated at home. While there seems to have been a good deal of mutual respect between Dante's inhabitants, white and black, there were also very clear boundaries, even in baseball. Clinchfield Coal supplied the Dante Miners with their equipment and uniforms. Sadly, the same cannot be said for the African American ball team in Dante, the Bearcats. And while the Miners and the Bearcats shared the same field, and while black fans came to see white teams and vice versa, there was no real fraternization between the two groups except in passing. Larry McReynolds, a committed fan of both teams, comments on this "separate but equal" relationship between the races, one that was oddly cordial yet certainly not close. He says, "I do know that two separate rivers can flow side by side and eventually become the same river. They never saw skin color in Dante."

The same tacit rules of segregation existed at Clinchco, Dante's sister camp which was also built and run by Clinchfield Coal. Bill Patton was one who grew up in Clinchco and for him, segregation was an offense he took personally.

Bill is tall, built like a pitcher, but he spent most of his career catching. He was the third generation of his family to live in Clinchco and he comes from a long line of dedicated union men. His grandfather witnessed the Ludlow Massacre of 1914, in which a company-backed militia, with help from the Colorado National Guard, was responsible for the deaths of over twenty people, mostly children, when they attacked a tent colony of striking miners. He later worked the mines in Kentucky, then moved eastward into Clinchco. There, he became justice of the peace, a thankless job in any scenario, but worse when it came to breaking up a still owned by a camp boss. Even though he'd been warned to ignore the moonshining operation, Bill's grandfather insisted, as he broke up the still, that no one was above the law. Immediately fired, he was also evicted from his home that same night. He spent most of the rest of his life in exile from Clinchco, and was only able to return as an elderly man.

Bill inherited a familial sense of justice. As a child growing up in Clinchco, he remembers the company setting up machine guns against union organizers. Not only is he a lifelong member of the United Mine Workers of America but was also a voice of strength and reason during the Pittston Strike of 1989–1990. In that strike, miners in Kentucky, Virginia and West Virginia protested against unfair labor practices by Pittston (which now owned controlling stock in Clinchfield) including the discontinuation of medical benefits to pensioners, widows and disabled miners. Bill Patton and the other striking miners practiced a non-violent approach in their struggle against the company.

But before he was a champion for workers' rights, Bill was just a kid, growing up in a coal camp that was nuts about baseball. Each summer, he was able to watch former major leaguers, who'd hit the skids, playing in Clinchco. The camp superintendent, Rush Adams, had been a college player and the sporting rivalry between him and Lee Long at Dante was an intense one, each man trying to best the other with a winning team.

By sixteen, Bill was in school, working in the company store and playing baseball in his off time. Already showing considerable ability, he was urged by a local merchant, who was a St. Louis bird dog, to attend a Cardinals tryout camp in Lynchburg, Virginia. In honor of this event, Bill's father ordered his son's first real catcher's mitt from the company store in Clinchco, arranging to pay for it in installments. Bill seasoned his stiff new mitt by wiring a ball into it, soaking it for three days, then allowing it to dry.

The visit to Lynchburg was Bill's first adventure away from home and his mountain accent caused more than a little confusion.

> When I went there, I'd never had a drink in my life. One Saturday, I decided I was going to go to a nice restaurant for a meal. So I had a hamburger and some french fries. I finished and said to the waitress, "Ma'am, may I have my bill?" In a few minutes she came back with a bottle of beer and set it down. I looked at it and thought, "Well." And I drank it. Then I asked her again, "May I have my bill?" and she brought me another beer. And I drank that and decided "no more." Well, Monday morning, when I got into the field house, they said to come upstairs. The manager said, "Patton, we thought you were the cleanest boy we had but reports show you were beering it up over the weekend."

After his tryout experience he came back to the area to join the Johnson City, Tennessee, Cardinals, a team with the Appalachian League. His baseball career, like that of so many others, was interrupted by World War II. After leaving the service in 1946, he had a short stint with the New York Giants' farm team in Bristol, Virginia, but soon returned home to Clinchco, where he played regularly. As word of his catching and consistently good hitting began to circulate, he was able to farm himself out to other teams of the Lonesome Pine. At one point, he had himself made a bat made of willow. At the first opportunity, he used it in a game. His first at bat sent the ball sailing out of the park with almost supernatural velocity. He poled a second one too far and too fast as well. A few practice bats by the umpire, with the same Babe Ruth–style results, and Bill found his personal bat impounded.

He was at Clinchco when one day he and a teammate were approached by two well-dressed men from Jenkins who'd seen them play. "They walked up and asked us if we wanted to play ball for money. I asked them how much and when they told me, I told them

I couldn't make it on what they were offering 'cause I'd just bought a car. They said, 'Well, we'll pay you the limit over the table and make up the rest under it,'" recalls Bill. He went home, bathed, said goodbye to his mother and joined the Jenkins team of the Mountain States League that night in a rout of the Oak Ridge, Tennessee, club. The next day, the company superintendent took the new players to a meeting of the Jenkins Kiwanis where they were introduced as "the boys who stopped Oak Ridge." When he finally did return to Clinchco to get married and settle into work for the coal company, it took time to appease Superintendent Rush Adams. With Bill's defection to Jenkins, Adams had lost not only a Clinchfield employee but a star catcher as well.

Like the rest of the Lonesome Pine players, Bill Patton has some joyful memories. One of his finest is of facing Tracy Stallard. "I hit him like I owned him," he fairly crows. (When told of this, Tracy just laughs and says, "I have no doubt that was true.") But Bill is also a man with regrets. When asked if he thought he'd lost his best chance at the majors to military service he responds, "Absolutely. I lost the best part of the time I should have been improving. And it was harder back then because there were only sixteen clubs to try to get into." His eyes grow moist. "I'd like to know just how far I could have gone."

But perhaps the more enduring sadness is one that involves his sense of right and wrong. Throughout his entire young life in the camp, one of his best friends was an African American kid named Billy Williams. Like his father before him, Billy played for the black team in Clinchco, one that Bill Patton says was exceedingly good. Clinchco, like all coal camps, was segregated. Most camps didn't build high schools for the black children but sent them to ones in centrally-located towns. Thus, black teenagers had arduous journeys to school and back every day and the kids from Clinchco were no exception. Bill Patton gets a pained look as he says, "I'd sit in class in school everyday and watch the train that took Billy and all the black kids to Dante."

Contrary to what most of the white ballplayers, and a few of the black ones, from Dante remember about company support for the black teams, Bill is adamant that Clinchfield provided no tangible support whatsoever. "No. They [the team] bought everything themselves." And, unlike the ball field in Dante, which was shared equally by the white and black teams, Bill's memories of the one in Clinchco are starkly different. "They could use it when we weren't," he says with an anger that is unabated after half a century.

Despite the obstacles facing Billy Williams, he made a name for himself playing for Clinchco and by 1953 was signed to the Class D Norton Braves of the Mountain States League, the second man to integrate that circuit. Known then as Willie Williams, he quickly became one of Norton's best answers to Kingsport's Muscle Shoals. In 1954, Williams was signed by Cleveland as an amateur free agent and spent sixteen years in their minor league system. He is now the hitting coach with the Sioux City Explorers of the Northern League. Bill Patton recalls visiting his old friend once and being introduced by Williams to Minnie Minoso. Bill says, "Minnie couldn't believe that we grew up together, that we were friends who both played baseball and we never played each other. And we had to tell him, 'That's just how it was.'"

Bill Patton's hometown of Clinchco, indeed all of Dickenson County in which it is located, is one of the most isolated regions in the United States. But the neighboring county of Buchanan is even more remote; its knife-like northern point jabs upward to separate eastern Kentucky from southern West Virginia. The area of the county is 508 square miles and has a population of about 16,400. If it takes roughly 400 city blocks to fill a square mile, a little simple math reveals that, if the county were composed of city blocks, there would be fewer than eight people on each block. Still, Buchanan County proudly boasts both a law school and pharmacology school.

Jim Childress was born in Haysi, in Dickenson County, and grew up playing pick-up games with a rather alarming substitute for a real ball: a paper- and tape-wrapped rock. "Whoever had the baseball and a bat, they were the most popular one," he chuckles. But since the 1940s, he has lived in Grundy, in Buchanan County. He is a congenial man whose face lights up when he talks baseball and his ability to pitch, play shortstop and third base. He grew up playing ball like any kid, then honed his skills playing both baseball and softball in the army. Jim showed enough natural intelligence in the army to get himself into specialist training and was eventually accepted into the air force. But events in Europe would change his course. Along with thirty-six thousand other infantrymen, he was called to take part in what he calls "mopping up," as a member of Company A, Fifteenth Regiment, Third Infantry Division. He proudly points out that Audie Murphy was in Company B.

When he returned from the war, Jim was immediately drafted into the local baseball club. Grundy was a coal camp but its management wasn't interested in sponsoring its team. Vansant was the local commercial center and its businessmen volunteered a certain amount of financial support. Together, they formed the Grundy-Vansant club, which formed part of a league, which included the surrounding Virginia camps. They also strayed from the league frequently to play West Virginia and Kentucky teams. The nearby Harman Coal Company team proved to be Grundy-Vansant's greatest competitor, as it was composed almost entirely of ringers. The playoff game between Grundy-Vansant and Harman in 1946 attracted a crowd of over five thousand (Jim hit the winning home run in the tenth).

Usually, however, the crowds were a more manageable size, with most Sunday afternoon games drawing a few hundred spectators. Many would park along the highway and watch from chairs placed on their flatbed trucks. And, as in other coalfield parks, an assembly line of small boys, beginning with a brazen captain on the field, spirited away a wealth of baseballs. "He'd throw it over the fence to one of his partners who'd either run through the creek or throw it up to somebody up on the railroad track. And they'd get away with it," Jim remembers, still amazed at the audacity. With an enclosed park and a loyal fan base, the Grundy-Vansant team produced enough in gate receipts to install lights on their field, an amenity that increased their crowds dramatically.

One of the most ardent fans of the Grundy-Vansant team was from a neighboring camp. "Doctor Daniels was the doctor down at Big Rock and he liked our team. And many times he would sit in the dugout with us. He would have bets with two or three other people, probably fifty or a hundred dollars. But he would tell us, 'All right boys, a quarter for a single, fifty cents for a double, a dollar for a home run.' That encouraged us and we liked him. Most of the time we won. So he would collect from those two or three people, then he'd tell the team, 'Meet me downtown and we'll have steaks for dinner.'"

While he often played shortstop and preferred covering third base, Jim's strong throwing arm caused him to be called in as a relief pitcher for the first time in a game against the Miners of Bishop, West Virginia (at one time piloted by former Yankee Nick Cullop). With ten pitches, he struck out three men, cementing his reputation as a player of strength and versatility. "I think my success in baseball was primarily deception. I was 5 feet, 6 inches tall and weighed 135 pounds. So opposing pitchers would look at you and think, 'Oh, let's throw one right down the middle.' I didn't hit too many home runs but I hit a lot of singles and doubles. And even in my childhood, one of my favorite things was throwing rocks at anything that moved so I developed a fairly strong arm. So same thing: when opposing batters would come up, I could throw faster and harder than they figured I could. So deception, there, was in my favor."

Jim could also play through injuries, including the fortuitous one he received in a 1946 game that sent him to the hospital where he met his future wife Barbara, the nurse who treated him. She was a fan of the game and, in fact, gave birth to their second son within hours of watching her husband finish a game. Jim's dedication to the game and Barbara's dedication to him has not come without suffering. He tells a story of waking up one morning to find her sleeping on the couch. Apparently, at some point in the night, he had raised his arm back to make a somnambular throw, bellowing, "Get him out at third, Porterfield!" and knocked her out of bed.

Inevitably, Jim's abilities drew attention from outside the league. When Clinchco wanted to enter the Lonesome Pine League, they went shopping for players in Buchanan County and found Jim. The by-laws of the league stated that a player had to live within twenty-five miles of the team he played for. Grundy was a hairsbreadth over twenty-five miles from Clinchco but Vansant sat slightly within the boundary. So Jim and two other players officially declared themselves residents of Vansant and joined Clinchco. "We started off with a double-header and I pitched one game and Frank Porterfield pitched one and we won both games. So we got in good with the fans and we played that year for them," recounts Jim. By this time, Jim was working in auto repair ("I never worked in the mines. My father did but I never did. Didn't have any desire to. I would have worked around it as a mechanic or other things but I didn't have any desire to go inside," he says) during the day and playing for Clinchco in the evening. They treated him well, he says. "If you won an important game, you'd find a little extra money in your uniform and that happened pretty well throughout." But, as the team played across a broad area, it was common to work a full day, play a game in another town that night, only to return home at three in the morning, facing the prospect of another day's work.

Passions ran high enough in the legions of coalfield baseball fans that even familial ties could be easily disregarded, as Jim found out when he and the Clinchco team played a game against its bitter rival Clintwood, which happened to be his father's hometown. When it was announced over the public address system that Childress was coming to the mound for Clinchco, someone asked Jim's father, who was seated in the stands, who it could be. His father feigned ignorance as to the identity of the mysterious Childress.

In 1948, Jenkins, Kentucky, applied for and was accepted into the newly-formed Class D Mountain States League and they approached Jim. Their standard offer was one hun-

dred and twenty dollars a month and expenses

Clockwise from top left: Woody Williams, Terry "Salty" Smith, Willie Winkles, Roy Flanary (all are courtesy Chuck Clisso).

Clockwise from top left: Jim Daniels, Dave Hillman, Bill Osborne, Alex "Ponnie" Sabo (all are courtesy Chuck Clisso).

Top, left: Bill Patton, *right:* Jim Childress, *bottom:* Myers Fox (all are courtesy Chuck Clisso).

away from home. For Jim, they upped it to $135. But he was married with a small child. "Had I been single, I would have starved to death to go on and give it a try. But also I realized that they needed somebody bad right then. A month from now, there's some seventeen-year-old kid they'd bring in to replace you. I realized those things. When you start out in Class D, you've got seventeen- and eighteen-year-olds. At twenty-two, you've got two chances: slim and none." So he stayed in Buchanan County, with Barbara and his children, three boys who have all stayed close by. He eventually left auto repair and made a name for himself as a businessman.

Jim played until 1950 when he was sidelined. "When I got hurt, I was coming in from third. The catcher from Red Jacket, he blocked the plate. He weighed about 240. I tried to unblock him. He won." So while he gave up the game, he keeps the memories. In 1980, as Major League Baseball avoided a strike by a splinter, his local paper aptly summed up Jim's feelings on coalfield baseball versus the game at higher levels.

> Those teams don't play anymore and baseball in Buchanan County is essentially just a memory. But it is a good memory and one that will always be present in the minds of the people who were involved with the sport when such things as major league strikes were unheard of, and the game itself was reason enough to play.[8]

The Lonesome Pine is perhaps the perfect model of a coalfield baseball league. Commercial coal towns, model camps, and not-so-model camps combined to create a circuit that operated successfully, and almost uninterrupted, for over twenty years. It was a continuous sideshow of personalities: from wily promoters to bumptious coal bosses; from stellar players who had the talent to advance but didn't to the men who were able to add their names to the major league firmament; from the occasional pickled pitching ringer to the wide-eyed boy who studied him closely enough to grow up emulating his curveball.

In the early 1950s, as the deep mining stopped and the camps emptied, the Lonesome Pine was still hanging on, despite competition with the local professional clubs; indeed, when the Mountain States League folded, the boys of the Lonesome Pine were still swinging away. But the geographical boundaries of the circuit kept expanding; in early 1956, the plans for what would have been the final season included teams from as far away as Williamson, West Virginia, and Pikeville, Kentucky. Perhaps, as in the expanding universe theory, there was simply no longer enough matter and energy to hold the league together.

Most of the players are gone now, particularly those from the infant days of the Lonesome Pine League, and they have taken their personal recollections of those vibrant formative years with them. But the men that are left—the post-war players—can remember the final years of the league, and every game, in seemingly impossible detail. For each one of them, the memories are incredibly vivid and rich. Salty Smith, looking back on his time with the league, explains why he and his colleagues played baseball with a special fervor, even for coalfield players: "You have to understand, we'd all just gotten back from the war—we were so happy. We were just overjoyed to be able to play baseball and chase down girls. To me, those Lonesome Pine years were the happiest years of my life. It was glorious."

CHAPTER 6

Moonlighting Bearcats

One price the black players had to pay for the collapse of a tightly organized league was the lack of official records. While everyone knew, for instance, that Josh Gibson had hit many more home-runs in a season than Babe Ruth did, there was no positive documentation. Men were around who had watched him pole four homeruns out of Griffith stadium in one game. But there was no Elias Bureau to guarantee it had really happened. And while spectators who saw them all might agree that Satchel Paige, Bullet Joe Rogan, or Chet Brewer of the Kansas City Monarchs could throw as fast as a Bob Feller or Walter Johnson, the strikeouts were not set down anywhere, except perhaps by the Recording Angel.[1]

The history of African American coalfield baseball mirrors that of the sport at large in the United States, from its nineteenth-century beginnings until 1947. The black players of the coalfields faced the same obstacles that black players faced across the country did, and those were the strict racial boundaries in every aspect of life. For a black player who wanted a life in professional baseball, the options were limited to the Negro Leagues or individual barnstorming teams. In this case, the Appalachian player might have had the slightest of edges. First, like his white mining counterpart, he was probably physically stronger than his nearest competitor because of the nature of his labor. And, despite its isolation, the very proximity of the region to the Negro Leagues mecca of western Pennsylvania meant that some of the most famous of those teams routinely made their way into the Appalachian coalfields, particularly those of southern West Virginia. It is not uncommon to find references to a particularly talented player being asked to ride along with a team. So perhaps it can be said that the coalfields really did serve as the "minor" leagues of professional black baseball. And what a roster of talent was there. Some of the brightest stars in the Negro Leagues firmament came from a mining background. Mule Suttles was a miner in Louisiana, Piper Davis and Dave Pope were both born in Alabama coal camps, and the incomparable Josh Gibson, born in Georgia, began working in the mines of Pittsburgh when he was fifteen. It is an understatement to suggest that the coalfields offered a wealth of talent and the Negro Leagues employed a lot of it.

In the coalfields, although the black teams played as competitively and as often as their white counterparts, although they shared the same ball fields and often wore the same company insignia on their uniforms, they played well under the radar of most sports pages and many a white baseball fan. Search the local weeklies in the first half of the twentieth century and the white leagues are thoroughly covered. Even in the *Charleston Gazette* of West

Virginia, which as early as 1938 ran a syndicated column by Westbrook Pegler in which he compared baseball's treatment of blacks to that of Hitler's treatment of the Jews[2], coverage was largely limited to the barnstorming Negro Leagues. Local African American teams received little more than short announcements of upcoming tilts and those were usually special events for the Fourth of July or Emancipation Day or, sometimes, pre-season exhibitions between white and black teams.

As the decades passed, regional sports pages began to show the growing political and socioeconomic sway of the local black community by the depth of coverage of its baseball games. Every newspaper of the first three decades of the century discussed black teams in the distinctly condescending terms of the period. And because of the prevalence, and economic necessity, of the often comical shadow ball warm-ups, the games were treated less as events of skilled athleticism than as carnival fare. The papers winked and nudged their white readership toward attendance, extolling the entertainment value. Some sportswriters assured the readers that it was "real baseball" but it was usually secondary to the hijinks and antics that the crowds demanded. By the 1940s, African American teams, especially those of West Virginia, were being given much more actual coverage by the journalists, including details of the games, although there were still no box scores provided. But even into the 1950s, some papers reassuringly pointed out that separate seating would be available for whites.

Oddly enough, the most in-depth look at black coalfield baseball teams in the early years was to be found in the coal company magazines, published monthly by the larger companies and available to residents of the camps. Comparable to small town rags, they were full of local tidbits, supplying everything from obituaries to recipes. Above all, they reinforced the idea that the Company was there, like a dependable neighbor, ready to swap stories or keep one's children distracted for a while. And, like the camp itself, separate but equal was the rule in the magazine as is shown in this description of the Consolidation Coal Company magazine: "Nearly every issue contained a section titled 'Among Our Colored Folks,' which brought readers up to date, via stories or photographs, on the activities of the African American residents throughout the company's mining communities. In this way, the magazine's content and organization was a reflection of real life for the black miner—segregation was something to be encountered at every turn, even in the employee magazine."[3] Because it was usually a monthly publication, the company magazine wasn't always up to date on all the games played; in fact, its reporting was often limited to short biographical sketches of the team in the spring and an overview of its season come fall.

The rare clues about the black coalfield players, found in the form of one line in a faded newspaper clipping or the torn pages of the company rag, are made all the more enticing by vivid team names—the Quiksteps, the Inkspots, the Black Cats. Unfortunately, tracking these lost teams via a paper trail is akin to hunting the unicorn. And it is no easier to find the players in person, for barely a generation after the huge migration of American blacks from the Deep South, they began to leave Appalachia en masse when mining equipment was brought in to replace them. Beckoned by better opportunities in the Midwest and Great Lakes states, few of the original black miners could afford to stay. The sad outcome of this second migration is the scarcity of African Americans who might recall the teams or have documentation of them. For the remaining African American ballplayers and their fans, the memories of their playing days are sunny ones, peppered with lots of humorous anecdotes and bursts of pride. And for the surviving white fans of the black teams, they recollect the players with respect and admiration. Salty Smith is still thunderstruck by his childhood memories of a black team in Stonega, Virginia. Baseball-loving kid that he was, Salty attended every game he could, thus seeing what many of the local white people never did. Whether he knew it or not, his future as a catcher was probably influenced by the Stonega black team's man behind the plate, a catcher known only as Alfred. Salty maintains that he was the single greatest catcher he's ever seen in his life. "He could be on his knees and throw to second base as hard as anybody I ever saw. And he was singing all the time he was catching." Salty still speaks with awe about the power hitters of an African American barnstorming team he once saw play at the Andover camp. He describes that field as having a creek past the outfield and railroad tracks past that creek. "It amazed me how far they hit those balls. They hit 'em over the tracks and that creek, one after another. And I'd never seen anyone hit balls past those tracks before."

Jim Marsh, who grew up in Capels, West Virginia, remembers as a young boy being taken regularly to see an African American team there. "When people were coming in and the game hadn't started, they were warming up and doing a lot of really fancy things— catching the ball behind their backs, over their shoulders—that kind of thing. You knew they enjoyed what they were doing. But once the game started, it was all business. I'm sure they enjoyed it when they were playing but they knew what the pressure was." He remembers one player in particular, a spectacular hitter, who, when he came up to bat, had the spectators eating out of his hand. "I think they called him something like 'Big Papa.' He would wait until everything had settled down. He'd come walking out, holding the bat underneath his buttocks, one hand on either end of it. He'd go just kind of wandering up to the plate. He knew he was going to be paid attention to. They'd start chanting his name." Apparently, Big Papa was able to whip the crowd into a frenzy with his slow, methodical approach to an at bat. Jim adds, "I don't even remember the name of the team, just that guy and all those people yelling for him. He was a hero."

Even Lee County, Virginia, with its tiny black population, had black teams. In his later years, Tye Harber told a remarkable story of the 1920s in his hometown.

> You could not mention the history of baseball in Lee County without mentioning the blacks in Pennington and Dryden. Earl Lane was to the blacks as Perle Stewart was to the whites. He ran a dry cleaning shop in Pennington and had a team of his own. They played at the Zion ball park. One of the best players I remember was Frank Conyer. He was a catcher and was as good as anyone who ever came out of Lee County.... One of the things I remember is that Earl let me play first base on his team in a game where his first baseman was absent. I guess this was the first integrated game ever played in Lee County, or perhaps in the U.S.A.[4]

In Dante, Virginia, which was owned by the Clinchfield Coal Company, there was no newspaper or company magazine so there is little documentation of the early black teams besides personal mementos. In 1935, the *Kingsport Times* gave a one-line announcement of an exhibition game to be played in that Tennessee city by their local black team against that of Dante. It's doubtful that the Kingsport team ever returned the visit to their competitor's home field because, in those days, Dante was not an easy place to reach. Even now, it hides itself in the dark hills.

A local legend claims that Dante was named by immigrant Italian coal miners who found the mines evocative of the many torments of *The Inferno*. In actuality, the town's name, which rhymes with "ant," has nothing to do with *The Divine Comedy* but was the surname of the treasurer of an eastern railroad company. Today, those Italian coal miners are gone, along with the Greeks and the Poles, and, of the handful of Hungarians that are left, most rest in the overgrown cemetery built for them outside of town. In 1930, at the end of the boom days, the population of Dante was almost four thousand. Now, it claims around fourteen hundred residents. Colorfully-named neighborhoods like Cigarette Holler or Bear Wallow Holler, that at one time teemed with life, are sparsely populated now and derelict buildings dot the sad landscape of a once vibrant community. Allegedly, the Dante ball field is also a graveyard, infield and outfield covering the bones of anonymous immigrants who died in blasts while building the tunnels for the Carolina, Clinchfield and Ohio Railway.[5]

Most of the people who grew up in Dante have moved away, some to newer communities nearby. For every inhabited house, it seems there are two that are empty. But an early November morning finds James and Lillie Mabry at their house in Sawmill Holler. James is a jovial man, full of self-deprecating wit. He sits in a chair where he can keep an eye on the front door. It's difficult for him to get around these days. "I thought I was a big man 'til I come to find out about rheumatism and that old bad cousin of his, Arthur-itis," he jokes. It's also black lung that keeps him in his chair most of the time, as he is easily winded. He was advised to quit mining in 1977 because of it, but had two children in college so continued to work underground. Lillie, a tiny, quiet woman, is wearing a pink and white baseball cap and industriously packing away what appears to be an entire street's worth of Halloween decorations.

James' father brought his family to Dante from Spartanburg in the great influx of black workers who came to the coalfields in the first quarter of the twentieth century. James says his love of baseball began eighty years ago when he was six years old, playing in the street with a ball made of silk stockings and tape. He began his tenure with the Dante Bearcats as the team secretary until they, as he puts it, got tired of hauling him around and him not playing. He was given third base to cover. When it is suggested to James that his throwing arm must have been a gun to play that position he laughs, "Yeah, but I didn't know what I was shootin' at sometimes. Couldn't throw straight at all." In fact, throwing wildly wasn't his only problem. In his early days on the team, his rookie status proved to be a greater handicap than a wild arm. "They was runnin' over me on third," he says, until Papa Charlie Saunders, a veteran shortstop, decided they should switch positions. "He was an older player than I was. He was experienced, knew how to get out of the way. He was just taking care of a young boy, I guess." By all accounts, Papa Charlie Saunders was a ballplayer of formidable talent. And although James laughs about it today, he must have been horrified to see, within minutes of swapping positions, a runner slide into Saunders at third and break his nose.

James admits that, through the years, many of the best Bearcats had been ringers, brought up from South Carolina to work and play for Clinchfield Coal Company. Although most of the Bearcats worked underground, he says that a few of the ringers were given lighter work but not better pay. Lillie, from her perch amid the controlled chaos of orange and black, recites a list of some of the southern ringers, even though she claims not to have been a great fan of the game.

The Dante Bearcats, like other black teams, were forced to range far and wide into neighboring states to play and occasionally competed against some big names. James remembers a rare occasion when the Bearcats had the home field advantage in a game played against North Carolina's Charlotte Black Hornets of the Negro Minor Leagues. Far from it being a rout of the mining team, he remembers it as a level match up. "At that time, we had some boys that could hit a ball as far as the Black Hornets could. There was an old tree on the other side of the ball park and that's how they would mark how far it went. One of the Charlotte players could hit the ball over the top of that tree. Now Ed Williams— I guess he played with some of the first Bearcats—he'd hit it out past that, past the school house and that was in the five hundred range. Some long balls were hit out there but nobody could prove it."

Some of the longest long ball hitters were the Scott brothers, Melton (called "Bo"), Herb, and their brother Robert who is now deceased. The two remaining Scott brothers left Dante long ago to move into a neat suburb of Castlewood, down the highway from the former camp and the deep hollers in which they grew up. Indeed, the view from their back doors (they are neighbors) is so bucolic, the verdant hills studded with cows, that it makes the forested bleakness of Dante seem very far away. The two brothers sit on a sofa in Bo's home; in between them sits Bo's wife of 54 years, Elizabeth, a vibrant former teacher and ardent baseball fan. It is a comfortable home, a happy place; it radiates the good humor of its owners.

Like James Mabry's father, Bo and Herb's father brought the family from South Carolina. Bo, the eldest at 84, played shortstop and Herb third base. Their late brother Robert had been a pitcher, once breaking his arm mid-throw; Herb compare the sound to that of a shotgun blast. The surviving brothers started playing as kids and honing their skills during their service in World War II. While Bo was a navy man, Herb was in the army, playing on a team managed by Joe Black, well before he became a Brooklyn Dodger and 1952 Rookie of the Year. When they returned to Virginia and the mines, they were well-prepared to play the type of ball that the mining teams were known for. What James Mabry calls "head up baseball" was a merciless caliber of play that required each Bearcat to maintain a batting average of at least .300. "We didn't hit a lot of home runs but we didn't worry about it. All we wanted to do was keep that batting average up to get in the ball park. If you weren't hitting .300 or more, by God, they wouldn't even let you in the ballpark, let alone play ball," explains Bo.

And echoing James, Herb says that ringers were no less common with the black teams than with the white. "A lot of those people from South Carolina, they played ball here. They—Clinchfield Coal Company—gave them jobs to come and play ball." Bo agrees, adding, "They took care of all the ballplayers. They brought them ballplayers here just to play ball but they'd give them a job in the mines. I believe that just one or two people had come here, then they started telling them about how good the ballplayers was and I think that's how all that came about." While it is noteworthy that Clinchfield Coal brought in black ringers, it must be stated that, while white ringers (indeed, most of the members of the Dante Miners) were given work above ground, the black ringer worked in the mines along with his teammates. There is also some discrepancy of memory as to whether or not the company sponsored the Bearcats financially. The Scott brothers believe that a voluntary payroll donation existed for the team at that time and Herb maintains that if the white team got new uniforms, the Bearcats would receive them as well. James Mabry's recollection of the system is that the Bearcats at first had to supply their own uniforms but that if they needed equipment, they could ask Clinchfield for financial help.

Bud Miller, left-handed pitcher for the team, remembers otherwise. He says that his brother-in-law, the team manager, purchased the Bearcats uniforms. Bud is a big man with a menacing scar across his nose; he sits at the table in his kitchen, which is spotless. He lives in Coeburn now, miles away from Dante and his former teammates. He warms up when the baseball talk gets started. His history with the Bearcats is a long one, beginning in the outfield when he was thirteen. Despite a clear memory of Clinchfield giving no financial support to the Bearcats, he stresses that they were still treated with respect by the company as the Miners. (Katharine C. Shearer, from her close study of Dante, agrees with Bud Miller on the subject of funding and encouragement for the black team: "I do want to say this: the company supported the white ball team. They gave them uniforms and arranged all the games and everything. The black team was separate. They had to come up with their own support."[6])

Even though the two teams only played each other in exhibition games, they shared the field, alternating Saturdays and Sundays. And the fans they drew were black and white, including ballplayers from the Dante Miners. "Oh, yeah, we had a whole heap of white people come to our games," says Bud. "Women folks and men folks too. Oh, yeah. In fact, it looked like one big happy family. They'd come to watch us and we'd go to watch them." Despite the segregation of the town and the ball clubs and inequitable promotion policies in the mines, the black ball players, to a man, remember race relations in Dante as unstrained. "We all got along, I ain't kiddin'," stresses Bud Miller, "'cause we all worked together." As Elizabeth Scott points out, "Color didn't make a difference in the mines."

While there may be differences in memory on some topics, there is uniform agreement on the excellence of the team players. Like James Mabry, Bo speaks of Papa Charlie Saunders with reverence. "I've seen no greater shortstop than Charlie Saunders. I haven't seen nobody that could do like Ozzie Smith except for Charlie Saunders." The reputation of Bearcat pitchers Elijah Hardy and Pete Dowd was such that several hurlers from the white team were tutored by them and Dowd's brother still has a devoted fan in Elizabeth, who says, "Now Ike Dowd could catch—oh, honey! I don't care if it was the wildest pitch." Herb agrees with his sister-in-law but reminds her that Dowd had his shortcomings. "He was a good catcher, he just couldn't throw. But he could bluff you," he says. As for his own abilities, Bo says, "I thought I was good in them days. Nothin' didn't get through there, that's for sure. We were all good players." Although he's quiet concerning his talent, Herb's record speaks for itself as he and another Bearcat, Eugene Barron, were the first black players to integrate the St. Paul Saints of the semipro Burley Belt League in the mid–1950s.

Bud Miller credits a lot of his skill to his manager and brother-in-law, William Adams, who demanded nothing short of excellence from his players, even if they were relatives. He describes Adam's tough-love approach to coaching. "My manager used to get me *down in the country*. He talked pure-dee trash to me and I'd be doing my best. And you know what? He'd make the best come outta me because he would talk trash to me. The more he talked, the more I'd try to play ball. You'd think you'd be playing your best and he'd tell you you could do better. And everybody liked him." Apparently, management wasn't the only voice addressing the players. "Everybody tried to tell you what to do," Bud recalls. "You'd be playing your heart out and they'd think you should do a little bit better." Bo Scott agrees, saying, "Oh, the women were worse than the men were."

As for relations between competing teams, they were always, or almost always, cordial. Bo says, "Baseball in our days wasn't like it is now—jumping up and fighting. We were all friends, regardless of where we were from." James Mabry agrees. "When you come to play baseball, they was just as friendly as you want, treat you nice after the game. They'd want you to stay around there and play around at night." Bud Miller remembers generally

Members of the 1951 Kingsport Braves. *Left to right:* Ike Dowd, Bo Scott, Robert Scott, W.P. Reese, William Letcher. These men competed as the Braves one or two nights during the week and on the weekends as the Dante Bearcats. The fact that they managed this on top of forty hours of mining coal is testimony to their commitment to baseball (courtesy Herb Scott).

positive meetings: "We had several little ruckuses we generally settled and went on with the game."

Of course, there is always the exception. Bud tells of a time he pitched to the team from Wheelwright, Kentucky. Their pitcher, when at bat, had a tendency to crowd the plate. "He stood right up on the base and I told him, 'You stand on the base and I'm gonna hit you.' He said, 'You can't hit me.' I hit him three times outta four and he started toward me with the bat. I drawed the baseball back on him and he wouldn't come out to the mound. I know I could have hurt him 'cause I could throw a hundred miles per hour." And accidents will happen. Herb reminds Bo of the first home run Bo ever hit: "Oh, yeah, you won't believe this. I got up there and hit the ball so hard it hit the first baseman in the head and bounced over the fence. And I had to trot around all the bases, all the way around, looking back at that guy laid out there." The first baseman recovered.

It might have been that the Dante Bearcats would have continued to play exclusively in the coal camps if not for an ambitious businessman in Kingsport, Tennessee, by the name of J. K. "Daddy Joe" Joseph. Daddy Joe owned the successful Liberty Café in Kingsport but apparently wanted to expand his empire to include a crack baseball team. So he went shopping for one and found the Dante Bearcats. Suddenly, in the spring of 1951, the Bearcats found themselves moonlighting as the Kingsport Braves. Not only were the men working their weekly hours in the mines and playing at least two games on the weekends as the Bearcats, now they were heading out of town two nights a week as the Braves. And there was no money involved, just sheer love of the game and endless meals at Daddy Joe's restaurant. An announcement of the organization of the Braves in the *Kingsport Times* is accompanied by a large, prominently-placed photograph of Daddy Joe and his newly-acquired team.[7] This was a signal event because running a photo of a local African American ball club was an extraordinary occurrence, even as late as the early 1950s.

Daddy Joe had stellar contacts and a lot of pull because he soon had his Braves coming face-to-face with some big name teams. According to Bud Miller, this was more necessity than choice because it was hard to find local teams that would agree to go up against a team as good as the Braves. He recalls competing against the Charlotte Black Hornets and the Indianapolis Clowns. The Scott brothers say there was at least one occasion when they played the Birmingham Black Barons. And it was at Daddy Joe's Liberty Café that Bo was able to really enjoy his manager's connections when he got to have dinner with Hank Aaron and Billy Bruton.

When the Kingsport Braves hit the road, they found themselves running face-to-face into the legend of another intimidating local club: the Dante Bearcats. While getting off of their bus for a game in Oak Ridge, Bo overheard one of the Tennessee players say to a teammate, "Man, for a minute there I thought we ought to just go ahead and give up because those guys getting off the bus looked just like the Dante Bearcats." Understandably, Bo and his brother howl at the memory but, by all accounts, the reputation was merited. In a rare newspaper article, it was reported that one Virginia team was mercilessly dispatched by the Braves in June of 1951 when Bud Miller struck out fourteen and gave up one hit, a single. Mercifully, the game was called in the seventh inning when the score had reached 27–0.[8]

Clockwise from top left: James Mabry, Melton "Bo" Scott, Bud Miller, Herb Scott (all are courtesy Chuck Clisso).

As good as the Bearcat/Braves were as baseball players, they were, first and foremost, men with responsibilities. Each spent his entire career underground. James Mabry worked in every capacity from hand-loader to section foreman where, in 1977, he saved the life of one of his men in a roof fall. He remembers that, despite the fact that there had been African American section foremen in the 1920s, the practice had stopped during the 1930s and '40s. "Just one of those things," he says evenly. "They had certain whites that didn't want the boss to be colored." Then he adds, "Most blacks gonna be workers 'cause they know they have to live." James is proud of the position that he held until he retired. "When I started in the section foreman's job, I had three men every month come down from Washington to check on me, see how I was getting along. Oh, that made me feel like a man," he chuckles.

Bo Scott began his mining career loading coal but, like James Mabry, spent his last fifteen years as a foreman, with forty to sixty men per shift working under him. Herb's beginnings in the mines were reluctant. "I started with Daddy loading coal and I quit the first day. Wasn't going back no more. Daddy got up the next morning and I did too. Went on back." Both brothers have witnessed terrible things in a lifetime of working inside. And, like James, both have black lung. But they brush that off and return to their memories. Elizabeth says, "You know, if they were playing now, there's no telling how far the Dante boys would have went because they didn't play around. They played ball."

Bud Miller, like the others, did a bit of everything in the mines, beginning at the age of eighteen. And although he has black lung, it was a heart attack and triple bypass that forced him to retire more than thirty years ago. Bud, more than the others, seems to have yearned, at one time, for a career in professional baseball. When asked if he had wanted to go to the majors, his voice becomes barely audible. "Yeah. Bad. But I'm gonna tell you a story. I used to be kind of mean, I guess. Guess you couldn't call it nothin' but mean. Mr. Joe ("Daddy Joe" Joseph of the Kingsport Braves) said a scout came in there and asked about me. Told him to have me down there on a Friday evening 'cause he was gonna take me for a tryout. At that time, me and another boy got into it, and me and him both went to jail. And I wouldn't call Mr. Joe and let him know I was in jail." After a long moment he adds, "I think it was a scout from the Cleveland Indians."

Bud is holding a baseball in his left hand, enjoying the familiar texture of hide and seams. "What do I love about baseball? I love baseball, period," he says. "Any part of it. I wish I could live my life playing baseball. I'd go to a baseball game when I wouldn't do nothin' else. I'd go to a baseball game when I was hungry, I wouldn't eat meat." He studies the ball for a moment and adds quietly, "I'd give anything in the world to do it all again."

CHAPTER 7

A Wide-Awake Town

The matchless Virgil Q. Wacks often referred to Norton, Virginia, as "wide awake," a phrase he applied to man and municipality alike to convey the idea that this entity took baseball very seriously.[1] And during the heyday of coalfield baseball, Norton was always an active promoter, if not always a direct participant, in a variety of leagues and their machinations.

Norton has the distinction of being known as the smallest city in Virginia. Like a lot of towns in southern Appalachia, it is not laid out in a grid or circle surrounding a town square, but in a long line beside the railroad tracks that have always been the arteries of the coal region. Indeed, the town, which was named for Eckstein Norton, president of the Louisville and Nashville railroad, was actually designed by the Norfolk and Western in 1889. By the 1890s, freight and passenger trains were stopping in Norton, giving birth to a thriving community. As stately and not-so-stately homes, hotels and storefronts sprang up alongside the tracks, small independent mines, known as "dog holes," opened in the hills that surrounded the town. Many locals insist that beneath the well-tended neighborhoods, there is a labyrinth of forgotten tunnels and the occasional sinkhole bears this out.

Like other incorporated towns throughout the region, Norton is a municipality independent of the surrounding coal companies but has historically shared a symbiotic relationship with them and the camps they built. In the peak days of the nearby coal towns and their ball teams, the Hotel Norton, right across Park Avenue from the train tracks, was a convenient gathering spot for promoters to thrash out the rules for a new season, a new team, or a new league.

While the city may not have been one of the earliest townships to jump on the baseball bandwagon, when it did field a team, it managed to pull in some imposing talent from outside the area. The Norton team of 1920, a member of one of the many regional "Coalfield Leagues," had three of its players go on to major league careers, the most recognizable being Mose Solomon, alternately called "the Rabbi of Swat" and "the Jewish Babe Ruth."[2]

For one season in the early 1930s, Norton had a spot on the newly-formed Lonesome Pine League. When it came time to lure the town back into the bosom of the league in 1936, Wacks enthusiastically encouraged Norton and every native son with his own inimitable writing style: "Attorney John McCoy of Norton will head a delegation from that wide-awake town who should and will possibly do so by all means, put a club in the circuit again."[3] To no avail. Besides fielding occasional teams for smaller, less-publicized circuits, Norton was forced to ride the pine for another fifteen years.

In March of 1948, eight teams were organized into the Mountain States League and admitted into the National Association of Professional Baseball Leagues as a Class D circuit, with Virgil Q. Wacks as president. In February 1951, an agreement was reached between the Norton Booster Club and the vice-president of the league, Hobart Ford, who had recently purchased the Newport, Tennessee, franchise, to transfer that club to Norton. The city had just spent $75,000 refurbishing the old athletic field, which was situated downtown in a basin between the railroad tracks and a dramatically-sloping hillside. It was a natural amphitheater. The city also agreed to raise a few thousand dollars in advertising and season ticket sales. For his part, Mr. Ford would run the club, get players, buy equipment and see to general details. He also claimed to be in contact with "an experienced baseball man in Philadelphia"[4] whom he would hire to guide the novice team through the uncharted territory of professional ball. Jack Reider, a scout for the Boston Braves, was made president of the club and, as such, exercised some president's prerogative and christened the team "the Norton Braves." With tongue firmly in cheek, the local *Coalfield Progress* newspaper suggested that the reason behind the club's name was immensely practical.

> A certain amount of sentiment is attached to the name, since Reider served as a scout for the Braves during the past five years. Of course, another reason might be that the Braves gave Reider a bargain buy on some of the uniforms and Reider saved a lot of money by using the nickname and not having to have another nickname lettered on the uniforms.[5]

When it came to the person who would actually coach the new team, in what can be called nothing less than a coup, Norton landed a rather infamous former big leaguer as player-manager. While the name Bob Bowman may not be immediately recognizable, a piece of equipment that came about because of him certainly is.

Born in the coal camp of Keystone, West Virginia, in 1910, Bob Bowman made his pitching debut with the St. Louis Cardinals in 1939. In 1940, after a pre-game fracas in Brooklyn with Dodgers Leo Durocher and Joe Medwick, Bowman was heard to threaten them both. Later that day, in the bottom of the first, Medwick came up and was beaned by Bowman's first pitch to him. While Medwick lay unconscious at home plate, the Dodgers cleared the benches and the Cardinals followed suit. In the end, Bowman was escorted from Ebbets Field by the police for his own safety and Joe Medwick was hospitalized with a severe concussion, never completely regaining his prowess on the field. Distraught Dodgers manager Larry MacPhail, after meeting with resistance to his call to bar Bowman from the sport, took what action he could.

> MacPhail, not forgetting the incident, contacted George Eli Bennett, professor of orthopedic surgery at Johns Hopkins School of Medicine, and the two devised a protective helmet for players. Bennett recalled that MacPhail got a jockey's protective cap from Alfred Gynne Vanderbilt and they took it to Dr. Walter Dandy, a neurosurgeon at Johns Hopkins who was working on a protective helmet for boxers. Just before he died Bennett gave full credit to Larry MacPhail for the use of protective batting helmets in the major leagues.[6]

Bowman stayed in the majors until 1942 and then he gradually worked his way down through various minor league clubs to end up back home in Appalachia and, eventually, into the open arms of the little coal town.

The club was a mix of locals from regional leagues and imports from as nearby as the West Virginia coalfields and as far away as the Caribbean. Southpaw Willie "Lefty" Winkles was lured away from the Dixiana team. The menacing Big Bill Slemp, with his intimidating "roundhouse" curveball, was also an early signer. (Referred to by at least one scarred batter as "the meanest man I ever saw in my life," Slemp had started working underground at the Glamorgan camp in his teens only to be been pulled out by company bosses to protect what was already recognized as a singular pitching arm.) Some of the other Braves were rookies from farm teams, sent to Norton to hone their skills. In a new regional trend of breaking culture lines, Cuban players were being signed to Mountain States franchises in droves; the Braves managed to sign two—a catcher and a first baseman. It was enough of a gathering of outsiders to make housing an issue and every spring season, with the return of the robin, the air reverberated with appeals to local residents to offer rooms for the boys.

So, in the spring of 1951, after a few exhibition games in the area to get their blood pumping (including the requisite match up against the House of David, which the Norton nine took 6–5), the newly-minted Braves looked forward to their first game of the season in Jenkins, Kentucky. After that, they returned to Norton to be met with all manner of festivities, including a parade. Virgil Q. Wacks, president of the Mountain States League, was there along with local notables from the town council and the baseball advisory board, the American Legion color guard and the high school band.

They were off to a grand start—or sort of. They had won the opening tilt in Jenkins but, with their first home game, immediately began to encounter the kind of odd mishaps that plagued the team throughout its short life. After the homecoming celebration had ended, Norton began its tilt with the team it had walloped just a day before. The weather couldn't have been worse. A portent of troubles ahead, in the seventh inning, with the score tied at eight, the new lights at the Norton field blew out and the game had to be called. The Braves stumbled in the next series they played, against Morristown, Tennessee, with skipper Bowman assuring the fans and sponsors alike that the young players were just trying too hard.

After a month of professional play, during which Bob Bowman resigned and then reneged on his resignation, the Braves were in fourth place in the league with thirteen wins and fifteen losses, a mediocre, but not outrageously bad, standing. But morale under Bowman was apparently deteriorating and it showed in the quality of play. Willie Winkles recalls that, during one game, he was ordered by Bowman to "knock the next batter down." Lefty, as gallant a southern gentleman as has ever existed, indignantly refused and was removed from the mound. The next pitcher refused the order as well, leaving Bowman no choice but to pitch the rest of the game himself, presumably beaning as many batters as he pleased.

On May 30, the first African American player in the Mountain States League handed Norton a disaster it would never forget. At Middlesboro, Kentucky, the Braves met that town's Athletics, whose ace was a black hurler who, ironically, was also named Bob Bowman. The night before, in a game against Pennington Gap, the A's had set a record for themselves of 26 runs. In the game against Norton, the A's not only broke their own record set the night before, but Kentucky's Bob Bowman struck out seventeen Braves. After five and a third brutal innings and giving up twenty-two runs, Norton's pilot Bob Bowman relieved his pitcher and went onto the mound himself. Newspaper accounts don't say how many innings the Bob Bowman versus Bob Bowman duel lasted, but within three days, Norton's Bowman had been relieved of his position with the Braves for good, as had Jack Reider, the president of the club.

Whether it was general bullying by Bowman or poor coaching that plagued the Braves, when he was replaced by outfielder George Sifft in early June, the team improved considerably. The sports editor for the *Middlesboro Daily News* remarked on it after a thrashing of his home team, saying, "The Norton team that played last night was a far cry from the one which appeared here two weeks ago. A person hardly would have recognized the same players." His praise continued: "Sifft came along to take over and the Braves have played an improved brand of ball ever since. Probably one of the big reasons is the hustle of Sifft himself in centerfield. In fact, we never knew he could move as fast as he did last night for the seventh and ninth innings."[7]

In early July, with a new player-manager at the helm, the fortunes of the Norton Braves had improved a bit when they set a Mountain States League record of their own (in what must have been a satisfying twist) against the Middlesboro Athletics. In the first six innings of the game, the Braves successfully executed four double-plays and one triple-play, a feat which garnered them a notice in the pages of the *Sporting News*.[8] Unfortunately, they still managed to lose the game 13–3. Within a few days, however, the boys redeemed themselves by sweeping a two-game series against Max Macon's league-leading Hazard Bombers, a Brooklyn Dodgers affiliate.

But Sifft couldn't stop a slide that had begun in July and he was replaced with the third manager of the year, George Motto, who piloted the team to much greater success in its last few weeks. Indeed, the club won an incredible sixteen of its last twenty games. Despite that, the Braves ended their first season in sixth place at 53–72, painfully far behind the champion Hazard Bombers.

By March of the next year, the Norton Braves had a new president, a new general manager, James Johnson (who wrote a local column under the moniker "Mr. Baseball"), and a renewed contract with manager-player George Motto. As Johnson bird-dogged for new talent, several of the past season's players returned to try their luck again. But, at the end of April, catastrophe struck when a fire swept through the Norton town hall, where the Braves' equipment and uniforms were kept. Four thousand dollars worth of essentials went up in flames, even as Mr. Baseball himself, a former fireman, helped battle the inferno. The players awoke on Monday with a game scheduled for that evening and nothing to play with or play in. The Mountains States' club in Big Stone Gap lent uniforms for that night's game and George Trautman, president of the National Association, did his part in securing donations from other teams in the minor leagues.

In addition to the woes caused by the fire, a $2000 stock sale fell far short of expectations, the club was still in debt from the 1951 season, and had suffered the financial loss of two rained-out games. The team was in desperate financial straits. On the morning of May 17, 1952, the discouraged stockholders of the Braves contacted league president Wacks to inform him that Norton was giving up the ghost. Wacks, aware of the team's problems, was not surprised by the decision. He called the franchise owner, Dr. Ford, and they both agreed to move the team back to Newport, Tennessee. All that remained was a formal vote by the board of directors to end Norton's brief attempt at professional baseball.

But at the eleventh hour, a small but lion-hearted contingent in Virginia's smallest city roared into action to save their beloved team. In July of the previous year, a group of local women sponsored a bake sale for the benefit of the ball club; they had managed to raise $63 dollars from the sale of their cakes and pies. Now that that club was packing up to leave, this same group was appalled. "One woman said she would just as soon leave Norton as see the ball club go."[9] They decided that they could—and would—take over the team. While Virgil Q. Wacks and Hobart Ford were ironing out the sad details of the transfer to Newport, this crack team of twenty housewives and mothers descended on Braves president Ed Gardner, the charge valiantly led by his wife, Mrs. Gardner.

> The women got their ducks in a row in quick order and told President Ed if the board would agree to keep the franchise in Norton, they would take over and run the club. They promised to keep the books, do the administrative work, sell and take the tickets, operate the concession stand and sell the concession wares in the bleachers, and police the fence and chase balls if necessary.[10]

Four hours after losing its franchise, Norton had it back again. The new managers immediately jumped to action. Mr. Baseball was the first casualty. Operating expenses were to be slashed; basically any responsibilities besides those of the players would be handled by the women. A former resident of Norton who owned a bus line in Bristol, Virginia, was needled into donating an idle bus to the effort and a plan was put into effect to have all the fuel donated as well. And they would try the stock sale again. "The new management had a good effect on the club, which had won only three of its first sixteen games. The Braves won their first game under the new set-up, whipping Middlesboro, 15 to 6, for their first win since May 6. They repeated the next afternoon, 6 to 2."[11]

Former President Gardner found himself reassigned to grounds-keeping duties. Carroll Tate, former secretary of the club and editor/sportswriter of the *Coalfield Progress*, was ordered to use his connections to get some big talent for the team. He was soon able to report back with positive news from a buddy with the Cardinals. St. Louis would return a couple of players they had purchased from Tate after the last season. The club kept George Motto on as player-manager.

This takeover was a public relations bonanza for Norton and its ball team. The Associated Press and United Press International picked up the story and on the Sunday following the takeover, it was run in most newspapers across the country, along with several radio and television spots. Both *Life Magazine* and *Time* requested photographs. Locally, the newspapers couldn't get enough of the story and published endless pictures of the women brandishing brooms at the former officials and demonstrating correct batting stances to various embarrassed-looking players.

Sadly, this change in management couldn't sustain the team's momentum. Within a month, the Braves were sitting at seven wins and thirty-two losses. But Motto and his bosses did have the vision to hire a young African American outfielder from Clinchco, Virginia, who, though not able to save the team in 1952, would help turn the Braves into a lethal force in 1953. Billy Williams, at that time known as Willie, would bring remarkable speed and dexterity to their defense as well as become an offensive powerhouse.

Near the end of June, Mrs. Gardner released Motto and replaced him with a non-playing manager who was an assistant coach at Norton High School. The Braves lost the first game under his command and he was replaced in July by the second baseman. During this period of revolving-door management, officials were busy offering heady promises to the fans that negotiations had begun with Muscle Shoals for the skipper's job, but it never came to pass. By the middle of August, President Gardner attempted to lure back a disintegrating fan base with bits of gimmickry: in addition to donkey baseball, she allowed the spectators to manage for one game. Fans made out the lineup, selected a starting pitcher and gave all the signs. Something about the formula worked because it snapped a 21-game losing streak. Still, the team limped into the end of the season with a jaw-dropping 30 wins and 88 losses. While one of their own was rated the best fielding pitcher in the Mountain States League for that season, another claimed the most walks (168) and the most runs scored against him (171).

And, to add insult to injury, the National Association reported at the end of the year that, of all the minor league teams in the United States, the Norton Braves had enjoyed the smallest draw of any of them, with only 10,025 paying fans for the season. Granted, the 1952 team had its shortcomings but the sad gate receipts of that year cannot be laid solely at the cleated feet of the players or the feet of the officials. A drive through the town on a Friday night in October these days may help exculpate the Braves, for what was once their diamond is now part of the Norton High School athletic field. Situated as it is in a bowl, it is still common to see spectators outside the fence, watching football games from the comfort of a grassy hillside. It might be that the baseball fans of the early '50s exercised a little of the same "why buy the cow?" philosophy, little understanding the dire effect it would have on their team.

January of 1953 witnessed an enthusiastic meeting of officials and fans, dampened slightly by the treasurer's report which revealed that the club was several thousand dollars in arrears, much of it in back taxes. In February, the women hosted a fundraiser featuring Lefty Gomez, which was undeniably good for additional press, and, hopefully, as good for morale. But by this time, the sportswriters of the *Coalfield Progress* were expressing frustration over the lack of definite information about the future of the Mountain States League itself, not to mention the debt-ridden Braves, and had become openly skeptical each time Virgil Q. Wacks attempted to appease them with assurances that both were "stronger than ever."[12] By April, amid a swirl of rumors that Norton would drop out of the Mountain States League, the new management of the club announced that, contrary to the scuttlebutt, it would be in the circuit. It seemed that at least one dramatic change had occurred since El Goofy had visited; the club had held elections. Although a woman won the office of business manager, all the new officers, including the president, were men. The first issue on the new president's desk was that of the back taxes and the threats coming from the IRS. It couldn't have done much for morale to see a *Coalfield Progress* front page headline on April 16 declaring "T-Men Tell Braves To Get $2600 by April 23 Or Else." While the players delved into spring training, the club was facing the prospect of having the IRS seize the club's $1600 player deposit from the National Association and make the club officers personally responsible for the remainder of the money owed.

In the meantime, the Braves were finally enjoying some good luck in grabbing a new player-manager by the name of Walt Dixon, a first baseman with a solid history in the minors and a lethal bat. The year before joining the Braves, he had played for and managed a team in Alabama; he hit .350 and had 24 home runs.[13] And while Dixon scrambled for players, an unnamed donor pitched in a cool thousand dollars to assist with the tax debt. Although the Braves began the season with some financial shakes, miraculously, they still began the season. Despite some reservations of Dixon's regarding hitting and pitching, by the end of April, the Braves led the league. While they surrendered that position fairly quickly, they remained a force for the rest of the season, thanks to the all-around great playing of Dixon and Willie Williams. A *Coalfield Progress* reporter described one game with enthusiastic, if questionable, writing.

> Tuesday night at Norton, the Harlan Smokies fell before the Braves never say die or quit spirit as Willie Williams, the great Negro center fielder, pulled a Frank Meriwell finish and the high and mighty Smokies fell, 5–4.... Willie found the ball he wanted and drove a sizzling double into left center field as three runs came home to knot the score, 4–4. Smiley then sacrificed Willie to third. Willie unleashed those long, fast legs and stoled the best right under the Harlan catcher's nose.[14]

Throughout May and June, the Norton Braves, while last in fielding, led the league in batting. The team desperately needed its two stars, Dixon and Williams, to counter Muscle Shoals, the man who terrified every pitcher who'd taken the mound in a radius of five states and as many leagues.

Shoals was skippering the Kingsport Cherokees and playing first base. By the third week of June, he had hit a dozen home runs and helped to knock Norton down to fifth place. But the team under Dixon regrouped to such an extent that by early July, it held first (Dixon .441), second (Williams .401) and fifth place (Dick Jennings, right fielder, at .373) in batting honors for the league (Shoals was in third place with .397). The *Knoxville News-Sentinel* noted the averages, saying, "Apparently Walt Dixon, heavy-hitting manager of the Norton Braves, has made up his mind to give a championship to that baseball-minded Virginia town—even if he has to win it himself." The praise went on to include the runner-up: "Willie Williams, who patrols the outfield for Dixon's Braves, must be taking lessons from the boss. He is still in second place with a .401 average, the only other .400-hitter in the league among the regulars."[15] In addition to his impressive batting average, Williams led the Mountain States League with 89 base hits, 22 doubles and 68 RBIs. Through July and August, the whole league breathlessly watched the three-way slugfest between Williams and Dixon for the Braves and Shoals for the Cherokees. The regular season ended with Norton in fifth place, with a 63–63 record, carried that far only by the efforts of their two giants. And, still wracked with financial pains, in August, the penny-wise and pound-foolish management of the Norton Braves sold Willie Williams to the Cleveland Indians for $2000.

The Cherokees easily managed a berth in the playoffs but Shoals and his tribe were defeated by the Maryville-Alcoa team in a rainy five-inning game. In the fifth, Willie Kirkland, a nineteen-year-old outfielder, clouted a two-out, full-count pitch over the fence to break a 5–5 tie. Kirkland was signed by the New York Giants later that year. For Shoals, who never made it past the minors because of a terribly wrong turn in his youth, it must have been yet another bitter pill to swallow. But his average of .427 earned him the batting title and set a record for the league. Walt Dixon, Shoals' late-summer nemesis, followed directly behind him with .415. Willie Williams was tenth in the league with .344.

Early in 1954, a meeting was called to determine the fate of the Norton Braves. Apparently, feelings were mixed. For every voice that called for loyalty to the team, there was one that suggested that it had been a noble experiment that had failed and it was time to admit defeat. Shortly thereafter, another make-or-break meeting was announced and all of twelve people showed up. This was reported in the *Coalfield Progress* with barely concealed contempt on the part of the writer, but it is unclear who he thought merited the largest portion of it, the officials of the club for the money morass or the people of Norton for their lack of support. After pleading and prodding and one final push from Virgil Q. Wacks in the form of a financial plan to keep the Braves afloat, the *Coalfield* published the obituary with this headline: "Wacks Told Norton Will Not Play Pro Baseball This Year, He Is Very Gloomy."[16] That same day, in the *Kingsport Times*, there was another announcement to the same effect, this one in a special column from Pennington Gap, meaning directly from the typewriter of Wacks himself. "The Board of Directors of the Norton Braves told Wacks they couldn't see their way clear to tackle pro ball this year in face of mounting broadcasting and telecasting of major league games in their territory which kept fans from the park."[17]

Of all the beleaguered Braves' many problems, this was the first mention of televised baseball as the culprit that actually brought them down. But even if this claim was wielded, in part, to deflect attention from other issues—including a mismanaged and moribund league—the gist of it was true. And Norton's wasn't the only team in the country to suffer because of the growing appetite for televised ball. Hundreds of little towns lost their teams and were left to nurse the damage to their civic pride. Television was a juggernaut that would reduce the minor leagues to mere nurseries for the majors, no longer legitimate sports options in and of themselves. Broadcast of major league games wreaked greater changes on baseball than the Black Sox scandal, Babe Ruth and the 1947 Dodgers combined. America's pastime, and America's small towns, would never be the same.

Chapter 8

Fathers and Sons

In the film *The Natural*, Roy Hobbs' discovery that he has a son is enough to inspire him to ruin the week of some unlucky stadium maintenance crew. The final idyllic scene shows Hobbs and his newly-found boy playing catch together. There is no dialogue but the point is made: Roy has accomplished what he set out to do and is now settling down to what is even more important. The image of father and son engaged in a game of catch is a powerfully iconic one. Perhaps more than any other, it sums up the experience of the American boy and his dad. And in a world filled with a frequently-excessive adulation of baseball greats, it is important to salute that man in the backyard throwing a ball with his kid, the man who has given up what he thought he wanted most, to become the best father he can be.

In October 1957, West Virginia was as focused on the World Series and Sputnik as any other part of the country, perhaps more so. The hero of the Milwaukee Braves was a native son from Nitro and, in McDowell County, in the southern coalfields, a teenager named Homer Hickam was finding inspiration enough in the orbiting Russian satellite to build and launch a few rockets of his own. The town of Coalwood, West Virginia, would become famous years later because of Hickam and the book he wrote about his early exploits in rocket science. *Rocket Boys* and the movie based on it would put Coalwood on the map and introduce a legion of fans to something that most had never dreamt existed: the coal camp.

From the south, Coalwood can be reached by first going through Bishop, Cucumber, and War, to name a few of the nearby communities. On an overcast spring morning, it's a glorious, if jaw-clenching, drive. Hairpin turns allow one a dramatic view off the sides of steep mountains laced with dogwoods. Every few miles stand the remnants of small coal camps, where ten or fifteen houses, structurally identical but now superficially varied, lie in tight formation. A bar outside of Caretta has an outhouse on either side of the building—one for men, one for women, both clinging precariously to the side of a hill. Upon entering Coalwood, a sign on the highway proclaims it the home of the Rocket Boys and an autographed movie poster for *October Skies* graces the wall of the deli/convenience store that sits at the main intersection of the town. Friendly employees will point out Homer Hickam's childhood home. But the main landmarks of the once-busy coal camp are falling down. Tudor-style apartments are abandoned, as is the massive clubhouse. And perched on a hill is the shell of Coalwood High School; the roof is long gone, allowing the dim gray light to nourish the trees and weeds that grow in former hallways and classrooms. Honeysuckle weaves itself around pipes and girders, and in the boiler room, the huge rusted structures sport luxurious growths of moss and fern. The building is strangely beautiful in its decay. There seems to be no one at home in the houses nearby and the street is silent.

This quiet, dozing village used to be a thriving community, the brainchild of a highly ambitious entrepreneur, George Lafayette Carter. Carter was the founder of the Carolina, Clinchfield and Ohio Railway which, by connecting to other major railways, forged an economic link between the Atlantic and the Midwest. He was a man with many thumbs in many pies. In addition to his railroad empire, he is remembered for his exploitation of natural resources, and journalistic dabbling. He is also remembered as the father of Kingsport, Tennessee.

Carter founded Coalwood but it was molded into a model camp when it was sold to Consolidation Coal Company of Pittsburgh. It was Consolidation Coal that turned Coalwood into a pristine monument to the philosophy of contentment sociology. And, Consol surmised, one avenue to worker contentment was wholesome recreation.

Like most coal companies, Consolidation was keenly interested in seeing its Coalwood Robins baseball team excel; the financial accounts of the club from 1925 to 1927 show that the company expended quite a bit of cash to make this happen. Itemized statements prove that Consolidation ventured far and wide in the pursuit of great players. The bookkeeper who tallied these figures has left a history as rich, and sometimes as inscrutable, as a wall of hieroglyphics. In 1925, for example, Consolidation paid out $8,650.26 in what appears to be, at first glance, predictable expenses including equipment, insurance, and advertising. A quaint item under Miscellaneous is $15.25 spent on "Boys to recover balls Cwd. Park." An umpire set them back $10. But then one is struck by two categories that suggest that Consolidation Coal was perhaps the most brazen of the companies in doing what it took to get a winning team, or at least keeping records of it. No furtive, under-the-table money here, it appears, but outright payment for services rendered by its mining ballplayers. The statement lists $5,084.58 as paid out in "Salaries." A case could be made for those salaries going to managers, secretaries or even groundskeepers except that most of those positions were filled by company employees already being paid a decent living. Even more remarkable is the $393.97 paid out in "Traveling Expenses Securing Players," which lends documentary evidence to the common use of ringers.

Nineteen twenty-six brought more receipts and more expenditures. "Salaries" have gone up (now $5,662.25) while "Traveling Expenses Securing Players" have stayed about the same. The ball-recovering boys have received a raise of $2.25. The price of umpires has risen to a staggering $170. In a coalfield baseball trend, there is the added cost of "Cars for Raffles" ($1,002.54).

The expenditures list from 1927 shows two things: it was an injury-prone year for a couple of players, and Consolidation Coal was still playing to win.

Salaries		8,449.53
Insurance		535.25
Baseball Equipment–		
Balls	$106.51	
Bats	482.59	
Other	41.22	**630.32**
Traveling Expenses Securing Players		172.33
Telephone & Telegraph		57.26
Printing & Advertising		220.63
Guarantee to Other Clubs		846.46
Team Traveling Expense		916.79
Car for Raffle		489.39
Miscellaneous		
Band	8.00	
12 Locks	9.00	
Cleaning and Rep. Uniforms	21.75	
Season Ticket Refund	78.00	
Association Assessment	5.00	
Dr. for Turner	3.75	
Dr. and Dentist for Massey	50.00	
Tickets	21.94	
Boys to recover balls	46.25	
Umpires	182.00	**425.69**[1]

Consolidation was content to spend almost thirteen thousand dollars for one season's endeavors, an exorbitant amount of money at that time.

One of the players that made the Robins a team worth paying for was James Langley Gilley, who had found his first real home in Coalwood. Born in Richlands, Virginia, in 1906, by age three he'd lost his mother and baby brother to an epidemic. He and his sister were separated and shuffled in Dickensian fashion around a circuit of family members until his father was able to reclaim him. Jim's father found work in the newly-opened town of Coalwood, and he and his son went to live there in the boarding house along with other single miners. When his father headed for the mines each morning, at his side was Jim who was employed as a trapper boy (sometimes called a nipper), earning seventy-five cents a day to sit alone at the mine's ventilation doors, opening and closing them for passing coal cars. He attended Coalwood Industrial High School, graduating in 1923 as valedictorian. But as early as his junior year, in 1922, he was playing outfield for the Coalwood Robins, of the Coalfield League of southern West Virginia.

As is the case with most Appalachian coal camps, the Coalwood of Jim Gilley's day lives only in the memories of the people who called it home. Fortunately, there is a fervent group of residents, past and present, who are working to keep the spirit of the town alive. Homer Hickam's successes have helped, bringing attention to and instilling a new pride in the town. One of Coalwood's—and baseball's—greatest fans does his cheering now from Florida. He is R. Tim Gilley, son of Jim, the Coalwood Robin's ace outfielder. In a series of letters and e-mails, he talked about his dad.

Tim describes his father as compassionate and supportive, a loving man who whistled a lot, having picked that up from listening to records of Morton Downey, the "Irish Nightingale." He frequently joined his two small boys and their friends in neighborhood baseball games. Strict when circumstances absolutely called for it, he preferred to leave the discipline of his boys to his wife. He could hold his temper even when his sons committed egregious offenses, such as the time that Tim borrowed one of his father's two prized autographed baseballs. One ball was from the All Star game of 1938. Some of the autographs included those of Mel Ott, Ernie Lombardi, and Leo Durocher; mercifully, it was left on the shelf. But Tim grabbed the other ball, also tattooed with major league signatures which were rubbed off after a lengthy game of catch. If there's anything worse than ruining a signed baseball, it's burning out the clutch on your father's 1949 Ford Coupe. "Dad held his tongue on that episode," says Tim. His father's professional successes in the field of mining are well-known to Tim; from his humble beginnings as a trapper boy, Jim trained for and filled several jobs, including mining engineer, fire boss and foreman. He retired as a Federal Mine Safety Inspector for the Bureau of Mines, Department of the Interior, having served for 48 years. His years as an inspector made him one of the industry experts on coal bursts or "bumps," terrifying geologic events in which literally tons of coal burst horizontally into open sections of the mine. Jim's research undoubtedly saved countless lives.

The 1927 Coalwood Robins. *Front row, left to right:* Grizzle, P; Hughes, 3B; Witry, C; Massey, SS; *back row*: Dunkle, OF and utility; Turner, 2B; Jennings P; Lassiter, 1B; Gilley, OF; Smithdeal, OF; Nidiffer, P. Coalwood, a prosperous model camp, was renowned as a good temporary home for those headed for the show and those on their way back down (courtesy R. Tim Gilley).

But his father's early baseball career has sometimes confounded Tim Gilley. He has spent countless years trolling through newspapers and writing to minor league clubs and historians, trying to get answers to some enigmatic clues left by his father regarding his semipro and professional career. Jim played for the Coalwood Robins intermittently until 1928, breaking up the run with forays into the larger world of minor league baseball. But records attesting to his history are sketchy. His talent was such that he played with the McDowell County All Stars of 1924 when they beat the Cincinnati Reds in an exhibition game. But mostly, other than a few scraps of documentation, all that exists to prove Jim Gilley's skill are the memories of those who watched him play over the years. It was said that he could cover the outfield like the dew. Although no power hitter, he was a remarkably nimble defensive player. Stubby Currence, sports editor for the *Bluefield Daily Telegraph* for over fifty years, was one. When he learned of Jim's death in 1979, Currence paid tribute to him with these words:

> I said I was sad when I read that Jim had died. His death brought back many fond memories of yesteryears. He was a truly splendid baseball player. He had a hitch in the minor leagues but I will remember Jim as a prominent member of the Coalwood Robins, one of the better baseball teams when baseball around here wasn't the national association and when it could really be called "outlaw" baseball because so many players were jumpers or fellows who had been expelled from organized baseball, and many college athletes playing under false names. Jim was a fine center-fielder for the Robins and he could range far and wide and haul them in.[2]

Jim was certainly a ballplayer worthy of notice and further proof is provided by the sheer number of men that he played with who had made, or would make, names for themselves, sometimes notorious ones, in the major leagues. Indeed, along with men who'd grown up in the area camps and honed their skills there, there were some fine future and former major leaguers. One of Jim Gilley's teammates on the 1925 club was the tragic Shufflin' Phil Douglas who'd pitched for the Chicago White Sox, Cincinnati Reds, Brooklyn Dodgers and Chicago Cubs. By 1919, he was with the New York Giants, where his problem with alcohol met with John McGraw's fierce campaign to conquer it. Douglas had already shown that he had tremendous natural talent and, in the 1920 season, boasted a 14–10 record. One of the exempted spitballers, Douglas helped the Giants to the 1921 National League pennant and then a World Series victory. Yet he and McGraw still wrestled violently over his drinking. When McGraw suspended and fined him in 1922, he reacted in dramatic fashion. Drunk, he penned a letter to his buddy, St. Louis outfielder Les Mann, suggesting his readiness to go awol during the pennant race, virtually assuring (he assumed) a loss for the Giants. Mann gave the letter to his boss, Branch Rickey, who had no choice but to pass it on to baseball commissioner Kenesaw Mountain Landis, a man immortalized by his lack of compassion. Phil Douglas' fate was sealed. He sobered up enough to confess his crime and was banned from the game for life. Shortly thereafter, he showed up in Coalwood, but little is mentioned about his stay there, how long it lasted or how he did. Perhaps he only pitched for the Robins in the hottest contests. In 1925, the *Charleston Gazette* reported on a rumor that either Douglas or Eddie Cicotte (another well-known victim of Commissioner Landis' particular zeal) might pitch for the Bramwell, West Virginia, team in an upcoming game predicted to be tight. Douglas, according to the *Gazette*, was at that time playing for Gary.³ It would not be a leap to think that he may have been pitching for all three camps as they are within a radius of roughly thirty miles. It must have been a pitiful scene to witness this character who'd once blazed on the mounds of historic ballparks serving out his exile in the remote Appalachians. In a particularly poignant footnote to Shufflin' Phil's career, in November of 1925, he was arrested in Welch on a charge of being drunk and disorderly. "His arrest was the culmination of a spree which began on Saturday morning and ended when he is said to have attempted to wreck a restaurant. Douglas was employed during the past baseball season by a coal company as a pitcher on a baseball team, and has been making his home at the coal camp."⁴

Many believe that the sentence handed down by Landis was a draconian one. Stubby Currence did. "In a way, I thought it was a bum rap. I always thought Phil was a heavy drinker but in many was he was just like a little boy," he wrote in his column. "I never believed Phil realized what he was doing and probably couldn't have remembered it the next day."⁵

Tim Gilley, who was not born until 1932, has no has no memory of Shufflin' Phil Douglas but he does remember the lengthy friendship between his father and Paul Derringer, who pitched for the Robins before his break into the big leagues. From the historical accounts of Derringer's career, the only certainty is that the future hurler for the Cardinals, Reds and Cubs played for the Coalwood Robins in 1926 when he and Jim Gilley were both twenty years old. Their temperaments couldn't have been more different; although he was still mad about baseball, and had just finished a stint with the Knoxville Smokies, Jim had also finished two years of mine engineering study at Virginia Tech. Paul Derringer, by all accounts, was a poor kid from Kentucky with a lot of hungers as yet unfulfilled. But the two formed a friendship that lasted for many years. It was during the initial stages of it that Derringer got his big break. "Derringer's performance for the Coalwood, WV mining baseball team in 1926 impressed St. Louis Cardinal's scout Jack Ryan, who signed him. The 6-foot, 4-inch, 210-pound, right-handed Derringer pitched two seasons, each at Danville, IL (3IL) and Rochester, NY (IL). Derringer won 25 games at Danville and 40 decisions at Rochester, leading the Rochester, NY Red Wings to two pennants (1929–1930)."⁶

Derringer went on to a long and impressive career. He and the Cardinals won the pennant in 1931 and, with the Reds, he had three 20-win seasons from 1938 to 1940 and went 25–7 in 1939. He led them to two pennants and the World Championship in 1940 and helped the Cubs to the pennant in 1945. In addition, Paul Derringer holds the honor of being the pitcher who started and won the first major league night game in 1935.

But while his professional life was wildly successful, Derringer's private life, which included multiple marriages and bouts of heavy drinking, was a nightmare. And when things were at their worst, he invariably called his old friend Jim. Tim's elder brother recalled that their father received many a distraught phone call from the now legendary former Robin. Tim remembers, as a child, meeting his dad's famous friend. "While living in Jenkins, Kentucky, and later in Welch, West Virginia, we ventured to Cincinnati to watch the Reds play, at which time the Duke was pitching for them. I met him there one time. While warming up, he threw a ball in my direction where Dad and I were standing in the stands. I missed my footing on the steps, lost sight of the ball which bounced into another fan's hands."

In 1926, Jim left the coal mines for another brief stab at professional baseball with the Jeanette (Pennsylvania) Jays. Son Tim wonders what prompted the attempt. "He may have ventured out to try to do it, knowing that there would be scouts in certain areas or teams that would have set up arrangements to try out individuals. How he got up there, I have no idea. But he was single and was able to let nature take its course."

Whatever took him to Pennsylvania didn't keep Jim there for long because 1927 found him again working the outfield for the Robins, ending the season batting an enviable .350. The team itself celebrated a 40–16 season. (One of the additions to the bullpen for that year was Homer Hickam, Senior, who would eventually father the ring-leading Rocket Boy.) The next spring, Jim began with the Winston-Salem Twins of the Class B Piedmont League. But he soon returned home to marry Frances Bragg, a young teacher. The new Mrs. Gilley had worked hard to become a teacher and made it clear that she would not give up her career to follow an aspiring ball player through the mine fields of the professional leagues. Jim got a release from the Twins and played for the Robins again that season while beginning life as a family man (their first son was born a year after their wedding) and advancing his mining career with further study. He was soon promoted to foreman. For a couple of years, there is no evidence that Jim played baseball.

In 1931 Jim appears again, this time on the roster of the Welch, West Virginia, Senators. Far from losing his edge over the two lost years, he seems to have matured into an even more effective outfielder and was now wielding a much more powerful bat. By October of that year, in a double-header against Bartley, West Virginia, Jim was the hero of the second tilt: "Jim Gilley ... was the biggest worry for the Bartley team in the second game. Gilley got four of Welch's 11 hits, including a homerun and a double. He drove in five runs, and scored three times himself."[7]

Jim Gilley played for the Winston-Salem Twins again in 1932, prior to Tim's birth in August. Then he seems to have given up the game until 1934. In that year, he was transferred to Consolidation Coal's Jenkins camp in Letcher County, Kentucky. The superintendent and general manager at Jenkins was B.H. Purser, who was also the pilot of the camp team, the Jenkins Cubs of the Lonesome Pine League. Jim joined immediately. Four of his teammates there were, like him, former Knoxville Smokies; one was 17-year-old Harry Walker, brother of Fred "Dixie" Walker, son of Ewart "Dixie" Walker, and nephew of Ernie Walker.[8] Although little is mentioned of Harry while he played for the Lonesome Pine League, he certainly earned his spot in the Walker baseball empire in later years. In 1940 he debuted with the Cardinals and played with them for seven years. In 1947, ten games into the season, he was traded to the Phillies where he captured the National League batting title with his .371 average. He is the only player to win the title while playing for two teams in the season. His batting title was not the first in his famous family; brother Dixie won the same honor in 1944.

Also playing with Jim for the Jenkins Cubs was Earl Webb who was on his way back down from a major league career. Born in Bon Air, Tennessee in 1897, Webb, like Jim Gilley, started his mining career as a trapper boy. He was prodded into baseball at an early

The Cubs of Jenkins, Kentucky, approximately 1937. Jim Gilley sits on the first row, far left, and on the same row, third from left, is Earl Webb; other players are unidentified. By this time, Webb's major league career was over and he was working as a mine foreman for Consolidation Coal (courtesy R. Tim Gilley).

age by the camp doctor who thought the fresh air would help rid his lungs of coal dust. He started out pitching for mining teams but was soon scouted and signed by Memphis, having to overcome a crippling fear of leaving home before he could join the team. He was purchased by the Giants in 1925 from whence comes one of the most famous stories about the painfully shy mountain kid. When he finally did get to New York (after much cajoling on the part of the scout), Webb immediately became lost in the city and was rescued by none other than Babe Ruth who personally drove him to the Polo Grounds.

Webb was shuffled through the minors and the majors, eventually becoming an outfielder. Only when he was purchased by the Red Sox did he find any real success. And he found it in a big, record-setting way at Fenway. In 1931, Earl Webb batted .333, managed 14 home runs, 103 RBIs and 196 hits. But his greatest accomplishment was hitting 67 doubles in that year, a record which stands to this day. Sadly, he never repeated his success of 1931 and his career wound slowly down. From the Red Sox to the Tigers, from the Tigers to the White Sox, he eventually was sold to the Milwaukee Brewers of the American Association for three thousand dollars and then, in 1935, to the Knoxville Smokies, ending up within one hundred miles of where he'd started out.

When Webb was still with the White Sox, in 1934, the *Kingsport Times* of Tennessee announced that he would be playing in Pennington Gap, Virginia, in a game pitting the Lee Smokies against the Jenkins Cubs, although it is not entirely clear for whom he was playing.[9] The paper reported that he'd be accompanied by a few other heavy hitters including Dale Alexander of the Red Sox. He might have made a connection during that game with B.H. Purser of Consolidation Coal in Jenkins, which would explain the later move there.

The ball clubs of Jenkins had always been fierce, not only in the Lonesome Pine League but later in the Mountain States League as well. In Earl Webb, Consolidation Coal must have seen an able addition to the playing roster. At the 1934 game in Pennington Gap, apparently Webb and Consolidation reached an agreement, for when he left Knoxville in 1937, he went to Jenkins where he played and managed the Cubs and worked as a foreman in the mines. In Tim Gilley's mementos of his father's life, there is an undated photograph of the Jenkins team, with Jim Gilley seated on the end of the first row looking alert and ready to play; Earl Webb sits two men down, looking relaxed but faintly sad.

In her tribute to him, Webb's daughter says that he managed ball clubs in Kentucky and West Virginia into his fifties.[10] In 2002, the West Virginia House of Delegates passed a resolution honoring Earl Webb for his baseball career and "for his size, strength, and expertise in training bird dogs, deadliness of aim with his guns, the violence of his response to insult, and the warmth of his compassion for children."[11]

The Jenkins Cubs of the Jim Gilley era were, apparently, an inspiration to more than one baseball lover. B. H. Purser, the camp superintendent and team manager, also served as secretary of the Lonesome Pine League. In the three years that he managed the club, Jenkins sent thirteen men to professional ball teams and twice won the Lonesome Pine League pennant. In a move worthy of a Depression-era motion picture, Purser resigned from his exalted position with Consolidation Coal in 1936 to become an official in Class B baseball with the National Association, perhaps proving a more extreme devotion to the sport than his fiercest rival, Clinchfield superintendent (and Lonesome Pine vice-president) Lee Long.

In 1942, Jim was promoted and assigned to a position back in Welch, West Virginia. He left the Jenkins Cubs and the game. The rest of his life was dedicated to making mines safer for the men who worked in them and breeding prize bulldogs. He also had a love affair with race cars, in particular a 1967 Porsche. Tim says that he kept himself too busy to pay much attention to the game he had so loved as a younger man. Jim died in 1979. For Tim, there are still questions without concrete answers. He suspects that his father's desire to play professional ball was tremendous, especially having played alongside so many names. "I'm sure that had a lot to do with him wanting to play [professional baseball]—being associated with all that talent," says Tim. "He would have loved to continue playing to see how far he would have gotten. Having played with others who did make the majors was certainly an incentive." He also believes that, as important as baseball was to his father, the time came when family became more important. "What do they say? 'He had a hankering' at times. As for any regrets, I don't think so. He had a chance, he gave it his best shot and was better for it."

Tim's memories of his father are inextricably wrapped around the idyllic ones of his childhood in the coal camps. The Gilleys shielded their boys from any anxiety that they might have felt about Jim working underground. And Tim thinks that his father was too busy trying to safeguard his workers to really worry about his own safety. As for his mother, Tim says that she was always fearful for her husband but never allowed her sons to see it.

Spared adult worries, a small boy could find the coal camp a place both comforting and exciting. Tim recalls well the endless afternoons spent watching his father play baseball, while he drank Orange Crushes with peanuts poured into the bottles. And no urban center could boast a more diverse ethnic mix. He refers to McDowell County, West Virginia, of days past as "a Little New York—a conglomeration of all walks of life." The Cassallis, Dachinkos, Sklepivichs, Del Contes, Subas, Ofsas, Korczyks, Cavallos, Rochchellis, Drosicks, Bellinos, Perpiches, Zaggachinis were a few of the families that made up Tim's world.

As he matured, Tim was introduced to the back-breaking labor of a coal camp worker. During his college years, he worked summers in Gary, West Virginia, a coal camp owned by U.S. Steel. He was spared going underground but experienced the physical challenge involved in work on the outside. His days were spent shoveling "red dog," or mine waste, onto slag heaps and unloading from box cars the seventy-five-pound bags of rock dust used to cut down on methane gas in the mines. It was an international crew that he worked with. "One Italian, about 6'5" tall, really muscular, would pick up two bags—one time he picked up three at one time—and carried them to off-load onto a truck. The rest of us struggled to carry one bag at a time."

Tim's wife Doris was from Richmond, Virginia, and had never been to Appalachia when he brought her home to meet his parents. It was a unique experience for someone from the outside world. "At that time, the mines were in full operation, and [it] was a real eye-opener for her when we drove the back roads.... In doing so, we passed the preparation plants and tipples along the way, with the slate (slag) dumps on the side of the road ... still smoldering and trees denuded of leaves. Had to roll up the car windows in that area, as the air was so acrid."

Once out of college, Tim left the mining camps for good. But like most people who have left Appalachia for better opportunities, he grieves for the land he left behind. The camps of his childhood are long gone. Over the years, strip mining has replaced much of the underground operations, leaving the once-pristine mountains that he loved so dearly scarred beyond redemption. But Tim's still got his memories of it all: a safe, supportive community of rich cultural diversity, a place of unparalleled beauty despite the mines, and, of course, his family. He vividly recalls the baseball games when his father showed up in the nick of time and ran to the outfield, still wearing his mining clothes and covered with coal dust. Tim has a photograph of his father in his work clothes, holding a bat. He looks, in his humble way, like every American dad should: like a hero. Uncelebrated, perhaps, but nonetheless heroic. Responding to a suggestion that his father seemed like an Appalachian Gary Cooper, Tim Gilley simply says, "Nice touch. Fits well."

Chapter 9

Fertile Soil

West Virginia boasts some remarkable names in major league baseball, whether they were native sons, men passing through on their way to immortality, or those on their way back down from the top. Wheeling, in the northern part of the state, was a hotbed of talent, starting far back in the nineteenth century. Jack Glasscock, who was born there in 1857 (when West Virginia was still part of Virginia), played shortstop in the National League from 1879 until 1895 and was the first boy from the new state to crack the show. He was followed by that city's (and the state's) first Hall of Famer, Jesse Burkett. Very fortunate lightning struck twice when another Wheeling boy, Bill Mazeroski, earned his spot at Cooperstown. Born in Bearsville, outside of Wheeling, Wilbur Cooper pitched for the Pittsburgh Pirates from 1912 to 1924. In 1919, John McGraw offered to buy him for $75,000, an outrageous sum in those days, but was refused. Chester, in the Northern Panhandle, was the birthplace of the tragic Win Mercer, who, despite great successes in the sport, committed suicide at age twenty-eight. The area around Parkersburg produced Greasy Neale who hit .357 for the Reds during the 1919 World Series (through what was most likely a combination of skill, luck and the machinations of the White Sox). Harrison County gave the world poor Steve Gerkin who in 1945 posted a 0–12 record with the Philadelphia Athletics. But it also boasted Andy Seminick who in 1950 helped the Phillies to their first pennant in 35 years. The coal camp of Grant Town was the childhood home of Sad Sam or "Toothpick" Jones who, as a child, won the West Virginia Marble Championship of 1937 held in Charleston.[1] His sharp eye and manual dexterity also served him well in his adult life. After helping pitch the Cleveland Buckeyes to the Negro World Series in 1947, he was signed by the Indians, then went on to the Cubs, Cardinals and Giants. In 1955, while with the Cubs, he threw a no-hitter against the Pirates, becoming the first black pitcher in the major leagues to do so. In 1959, after almost clinching the pennant for the Giants, the *Sporting News* named him their Outstanding Pitcher of the Year.[2] But this profusion of talent wasn't just found in the northern part of West Virginia. The entire state has churned out major league players at an admirable rate; in fact, there have been well over one hundred.

In the coalfields of the southern part of West Virginia, one only has to dig a bit to find several famous names, some belonging to men who were wandering through. Along with Paul Derringer, Earl Webb and Shufflin' Phil Douglas were other big leaguers who wound up in the area, finding comfortable temporary homes in the coal towns. Certainly the most recognizable was Stan Musial, who played for the Williamson team of the Class D Mountain State League in 1938 and 1939. Anyone who has ever read a biography of Musial knows about the friendly kid from Donora, Pennsylvania, who signed with the St. Louis Cardinals and was sent to West Virginia to sharpen his skills with the Williamson Colts. In a 1947 column in the *Sporting News*, J. G. T. Spink gave an account of Branch Rickey's first glimpse of the wunderkind, written in a style worthy of any Hollywood screenwriter:

> It was a night game under what the Logan club advertised as "candlelight," and the visibility would have tested the eyes of an owl. But eighteen-year-old Stanley Musial wasn't at the plate for an optical experiment, or to beg a walk or wait for his pitch. He swung at the first curve. There was a sharp crack. Seconds later the horsehide disappeared into the West Virginia night air on a rising line over the right field wall, 350 feet away.[3]

And everyone knows what happened when Musial left West Virginia for Florida, where a fortuitous accident and Dickie Kerr began molding the now-nineteen-year-old into a future legend. Perhaps fewer people know that, in 1938, while Musial was playing for Williamson, Kerr, known as "the honest one," for his valiant pitching in the 1919 World Series, was managing the Huntington, West Virginia, Booster Bees, also of the Mountain State League. By all accounts, Musial at seventeen was not yet showing his potential; his end-of-season averages show him sixty-fifth in the league for batting at .258 and a 4.66 ERA. But Dickie Kerr must have spotted something promising. Besides their relationship as mentor and student, Musial and Kerr shared a friendship that would last a lifetime.

Also pitching that year in the Mountain State League was former Detroit Tigers pitcher Vic Sorrell, who had given that team a solid ten years. Born in North Carolina, he had begun his career in Bluefield, a coalfield transportation nexus located on the border of Virginia and West Virginia. He lived in Bluefield during his off seasons and returned to the city's Blue Grays to play and manage at the end of his major league years. Even at the advanced age of thirty-seven, he obviously still had what it took to win because his first pitching loss of the 1938 season came in August, at the hands of the Beckley Bengals. Although his batting average was ninetieth out of 113 players that season, he had a 1.37 ERA. He stayed with the Blue Grays until the end of the season of 1940.

Helping the Bengals to hand Sorrell that late season defeat in 1938 was Johnny Gorsica who would go on to play with the Detroit Tigers as well. Born in Bayonne, New Jersey, Gorsica made it to the coalfields by way of West Virginia University in Morgantown. The future and former Tigers, Sorrell and Gorsica, were able to team up together for the Mountain State League All Star game of 1938 against the Logan Indians. Something about Southern Appalachia must have appealed to Gorsica because, by the end of his first season with the Tigers in 1940, he had become a resident of Beckley, spending his spare time in the company of his friend Fred "Sheriff" Blake, a Beckley native and retired veteran of many a major league campaign. Gorsica appeared annually with Blake at spaghetti suppers and even old timers' games, even though the rookie was only twenty-five years old. They are buried in the same cemetery in Beckley.

The sons of southern West Virginia's coalfields that made it to the big leagues are many: Arnold Carter, Walt Craddock, Wayland Dean, Earl Francis, Walt Morrison, Bob Bowman and Doc Edwards, to name a few. A few others, often by virtue of their personal eccentricities or fate itself, are particularly interesting. Without a doubt, one of the most compelling was John Milton Warhop, baseball's most famous jinx. He was born in 1884 in Hinton, a community nestled at the confluence of the New and Greenbrier rivers, a major terminal point of the Chesapeake and Ohio railroad which transported coal out of the region. He got his start in baseball playing with the local semipro team sponsored by the C&O. His family name was originally Wauhop but he altered it to Warhop when he joined one of the turn-of-the-century barnstorming teams that claimed to be made up entirely of Native Americans. Slight of build for a pitcher and a constant complainer, he was given the nickname "The Crab" by teammates at some point during his professional life.

His minor league career was nothing short of sensational; he had an 82–20 record over three years at Freeport and Williamsport. He struck out 330 and hurled thirteen shutouts in 1907. Warhop was a submarine hurler and in 1920, William B. Hanna called him one of "the three most poised underhand pitchers of this era of the game."[4] Hanna also said the following, which attests to the skill of the man that thousands of players and fans would denounce as bad luck: "Warhop used to love to catch Ty Cobb napping, and he caught him oftener than any two other pitchers. They [sic] weren't any gamer ones than Warhop." He is also one of only four major league pitchers who twice stole home.

By 1908, he was pitching for the New York Highlanders where he began to amass an impressive collection of bad breaks. In 1909, he led the American League in hitting batters (26) and he did it again in 1910 (18). In fact, he hit 114 batters in his career as a Highlander/Yankee. And he really did seem to suffer from pure misfortune. "Typical was a 1914 game against the White Sox; he shut them out for 12 innings only to lose 1–0 in the 13th on an error, a sacrifice and a single."[5] Hearst sportswriter Frank Menke felt real pity for the little pitcher:

> No pitcher ever stepped onto a mound that got "breaks" that were worse than Warhop's. The subway twirler was really a superb performer, whose average of hits allowed and runs earned was about as good as any man in baseball history. But Warhop's victories were few and far between. If he pitched a five-hit game, it would be his luck to be pitted against a man who pitched a three-hit game that day. If he allowed only three hits in his next outing, some pitcher would hold his club to one hit. And when it wasn't that it was something else. If he allowed only four hits while his club got ten, then his mates would make six or eight errors back of him. Or some freak play would deprive him of triumph.[6]

Of course, Jack Warhop will be forever remembered because of two pitches that he threw in 1915, which gave Red Socker Babe Ruth his first major league home runs.

By 1915, the Yankees, having held on to him long enough to decide that he was indeed a jinx, released Warhop. After six games played and won with the Orioles, owner Jack Dunn released him saying that he had jinxed the team.[7] Warhop wandered around the minor leagues until he ended up with the Toronto Maple Leafs in 1917, their 1918 team ranked by Minor League Baseball as one of the top one hundred teams.

Nineteen twenty found him in Norfolk of the Virginia League, where a local newspaper "proclaims the little under-hander good enough for another trial in the majors."[8] After two years there as player/manager, he joined Columbia, South Carolina, of the Sally League.

"Just recently, Warhop bobbled up in South Carolina. Old as he is, he is showing that he is still great. He allowed only 5 hits. But yes—you've guessed it. Jack's club got fewer than 5."[9]

By early spring of 1927, at age forty-three, he had found his way to New Jersey and the *Sporting News* reported it in this rather poignant fashion: "One of the most interesting members of the Newark squad this year is Jack Warhop, who is trying a comeback with the Bears. He told manager Jack Egan that if he couldn't win at least 20 games in the International League he would retire from baseball. So confident was he that he paid his own carfare to the training camp."[10]

But his tenure with the Newark Bears was brief and by early June he had been added to the pitching roster of Bears of another kind—in Bridgeport, Connecticut—with whom he had a remarkable ride. A 17-inning game, a 13-inning game, a 19-inning double-header and an 11–7 season record all contributed to the new nickname given to Warhop by the city's fans: the Grand Old Man."[11] By October it seemed he would be made manager of the team.[12] But, for whatever reason, Warhop left Connecticut, making brief appearances in Portland and Spartanburg until he disappeared from the sports pages for good. He died in 1960 in Freeport, Illinois, where he'd known such phenomenal success as a very young man, when he'd just been known as "a crab" and not a jinx. Frank Menke said it best: "'If Warhop had been as lucky as he was unlucky,' it was often said, 'he'd have hung up one of the greatest records of any pitcher in the annals of the game.'"[13]

Hidden away in what used to be the Winding Gulf coal field near Beckley is what remains of the once-thriving coal camp of Stotesbury. In 1911, when it was owned by the E.E. White Coal Company, a twelve-year-old boy named Fred Blake went to work in the mines, most likely as a trapper boy. After a year of pitching at a military academy and West Virginia Wesleyan, he returned to the area to play for the team at Glen White, where he began to earn a name for himself and a reputation that spread around the state. It was on a recommendation from Cincinnati Reds hurler Greasy Neale that Blake found himself signing with the Ohio club in 1919 but the Pirates soon got him on waivers. Blake warmed the bench for a while, then tired of it and went back home to play with the mining team in Ward, West Virginia, one of the fiercest in the area. But Pittsburgh called him back to an embarrassing debut as a reliever against the Giants. "My uniform was too big for me and I must have looked pretty bad. It's a wonder I didn't get all our infielders killed. That was in the Polo Grounds and before I knew what happened the Giants had six more runs and I was on my way to the showers. That was the longest 500 feet I ever traveled, with the fans ridiculing me."[14]

He was sent to the minors for some honing and it was at Rochester that he was given the moniker "Sheriff" by the owner of the club, a name that would stick with him for the rest of his life. He left Rochester for Seattle where he stayed until the Chicago Cubs bought him in 1924. He stayed for seven years, enjoying a 17–11 season in 1928 but suffering as the losing pitcher in Game Four of the 1929 World Series against the Philadelphia Athletics. Rallying in the seventh inning, the A's scored ten times to win the game 10–8. The A's went on to win the series. But Blake was always proud of his batting average for the series: he'd gone one for one.

He alternated between the majors and the minors for his entire professional career. In 1937, at an advanced age, he was picked up by the St. Louis Browns. The *Charleston Gazette* poetically honored the local hero's return to the show: "Baseball's comeback artists, ageless, penniless and full of dreams, are descending again on the Major League training camps. The Browns, for example, are taking pitcher John Fred (Sheriff) Blake to camp. The Sheriff is as old as law and order, but there he is in his 38th year, getting another tryout."[15]

He finished with the Cardinals in 1937, did some pitching in Alabama, Texas, and Oklahoma, then came home to the mountains saying, "Do you realize I haven't seen the buds come on the trees in West Virginia since 1920?"[16] In 1941, he managed the Huntington club of the Mountain State League but was released within two months. He then returned to the coal mines of Raleigh County, where he worked until retirement.

Sheriff Blake was an extraordinarily good pitcher. Looking back on his career, he credited his vicious breaking fastball to a double fracture of his thumb as a kid.[17] He might have written a primer on the beauties of simple, pared-down pitching for he had strong feelings on messing with the basics. For him, a fastball, a curve and a change of pace were all that any pitcher needed. To expand beyond those was to court disaster. He explained his beliefs to a writer for the *Charleston Daily Mail*: "If you rely on a good fast ball and curve, you're more sure of 'em and they'll break for you. But these trick deliveries don't break a lot of times and the batters know it. When a screwball doesn't break, they knock it out of town."[18]

Years later, at age 81, he expressed his disdain for television and the effect it had had on coalfield baseball. "I thought television was the best thing that ever was, which it was when it started out. But now I think that television has ruint the world."[19]

In 1938, as the young Stan Musial was sharpening his skills in Williamson, a native from 25 miles down the road was making his way from Brooklyn to Philadelphia to take the mound for the Phillies. Max Butcher was born in the mining camp of Holden in 1910. By nineteen, he was pitching for Logan in the Tri-State loop. In 1931, he was scouted by an agent of the Philadelphia Athletics and farmed out by Connie Mack to York after the southern training trip. Sent back to the A's, he was released immediately. He returned to West Virginia to join the Beckley Black Knights of the Class C Middle Atlantic League. He was a very popular young pitcher in Beckley, earning praise for his talent and versatility from the *Charleston Gazette* in 1932:

> Not only are the Black Knights leading the rest of the clubs but a member of their team is setting the pace among the Middle Atlantic hurlers. It is none other than Max Butcher, a former Beckley boy. So far this season Max has 3 wins to his credit without a solitary loss, besides doing yeoman's work as a relief hurler. Keep it up, Max, we're for you.[20]

In a trial by fire, the Black Knights went up against the House of David in April of 1932 and the young hurler got to test his mettle against Grover Cleveland Alexander who was touring with the long-haired team. Butcher and the Beckley boys fell hard in a 7–0 shutout.

In 1934, Butcher was picked up by Baltimore and farmed out, eventually making it to Galveston where in 1935 he was named MVP in the Texas League. By the next spring, he was in Brooklyn with the Dodgers, his first major league season a disappointment. He was plagued by injuries and illness but, when he was fit, he showed "enough of what it takes to justify considerable faith in the future."[21] When the season ended, he returned to West Virginia and started an off-season routine that he would engage in throughout most of his years in the majors: he kept himself busy playing basketball and on all levels apparently. From the Tigers of the coal town of Man, West Virginia, to a C&O–sponsored team to a professional league in Logan County, he was a basketball dervish. Perhaps this helped to give him a distinct enough carriage to cause one writer to comment, "He pitches with his body poised in an uncommonly erect position."[22]

His luck with the Dodgers began to improve in 1937 when he posted an 11–15 record, the *Sporting News* exclaiming that "Nobody on the pitching staff, with the exception of [Van] Mungo, has more stuff."[23] But Mungo must have been a bad influence on the mountain boy. In April of 1938, Burleigh Grimes of the Dodgers slapped a hefty $500 fine on Butcher, charging him with excessive revelry. It seems that Dodgers management had stumbled upon a lively party hosted by Butcher in a hotel room. This might have been a forgivable offense if not for the fact that Butcher's only mound appearance for the season had resulted in a wild throw, allowing the Philadelphia Phillies a win. In August of that year, he was traded on waivers to the Phillies and finished the season 9–12, and a year later he was traded to Pittsburgh, where high hopes were rewarded. "Including his victory over Dizzy Dean on Labor Day, Butcher had turned in three straight victories for the Pirates, two of them shutouts, and with a little more luck, all four would have been whitewashings."[24] The off season must have done him good because he came into the season of 1940 with guns blazing. The *Sporting News* waxed ebullient in April.

> Big Max Butcher, pride of West Virginia, and the same Max who carries 225 pounds with the grace of a big gazelle, jumped high into the favor of the new Pittsburgh pilot last week while the Buccos were sticking a defeat plaster on the Athletics. Frisch asked Max to travel the seventh-inning route against Connie Mack and the mountaineer responded by going the full distance, Butcher finishing strongly. It was entirely new stuff in March for a Pirate pitcher so far as this long-time observer was concerned.[25]

Hit in the pitching hand shortly after, he wasn't able to start until late in April but by mid-season, he was still considered the Pirate's ace. Nineteen forty-one brought his best record of 17–12 but he was sidelined for a good part of 1942 with a bad arm. The remaining war years brought him respectable winning records.

Sadly, when he arrived at spring training in 1946, the "big gazelle" was no longer so fleet of foot. The *Sporting News* reported that Frankie Frisch was angered over the weight the big man had packed on over the last two seasons and there were issues over his salary as well, as the Pirates had dramatically trimmed his paycheck. He was given an outright release in March and while there was hope that he'd come back to the fold, instead he returned to West Virginia in July to play with the Class D Appalachian League's Welch club. A brief flirtation with the Washington Senators amounted to nothing, as did one with the Raleigh Capitals of the Carolina League.

Having married the postmistress of Man, West Virginia, back in 1940, Butcher settled there eventually and in spring of 1949, an ad ran in the *Charleston Gazette* issued by the semi-pro team of Man, appealing for games. The Man field, it said, boasted both lights and Max Butcher as player-manager. Five years later he was cashiering in a liquor store and attending a few old timers' nights, a sad irony because, when Max Butcher died in 1957, he was only 46 years old.

Perched on the Kanahwa River is Nitro, a town that didn't exist until 1918. In that year, with its entry into World War I, the United States government chose this plot of ground for an explosives plant, one which produced nitrocellulose for gunpowder. "In eleven months, 90 percent of the town and plant were constructed, but the war ended before gunpowder production began."[26] Nitro has continued to be the site for the manufacture of chemicals; it is still best known for its plants, including Monsanto which produced dioxin for years. Thought not a coal town, Nitro sits on the edge of the coalfields and owes its existence to the mines and railroads which initially populated the area.

Eight years after ground was broken for Nitro, Selva Lewis Burdette, Jr., was born there, his mother having hailed from across the county line in a little place with the curious name of Unexpected. He led an average childhood in Nitro, throwing rocks and playing baseball. He picked up the nickname "Frog" in adolescence because of his unreliable, hormone-altered vocal chords. Having tried and failed to interest the American Legion baseball team in his abilities, in 1944 he found a spot with the American Viscose Rayon Spinners. In fact, he had been given a job as a messenger boy at the plant because of his throwing abilities.[27] At that time, Viscose was part of the War Industrial League whose membership included a gamut-running mix of teams from such industries as U.S. Rubber, Carnegie, Carbide, DuPont, Monsanto, American Fork and Hoe and the town of Highcoal, representing bituminous miners. Burdette started the season out very well, a June performance labeled "dazzling" by the *Charleston Gazette*,[28] and ended his premier season as a Spinner with a 12–2 record. After a year in the service and a year of college, he was given a tryout with the Yankees ("I wasn't going to go. Heck, I couldn't make my American Legion team in Nitro when I was 17."[29]) and entered their labyrinthine farm system for a five-year stay, pitching only twice, in relief, for the team itself at the end of the 1950 season.

His reputation as being somewhat troublesome began almost as soon as he had joined organized baseball. "Burdette was involved in at least one racial incident in the minor leagues when in 1949 he hit Jim Pendleton (one of the first black players in the American Association) in the head with a fastball, sending Pendleton to the hospital."[30]

Burdette was traded by the Yankees to the Boston Braves in 1951 for $50,000 and pitcher Johnny Sain and he performed admirably there. In 1953, when the Braves moved west to Milwaukee, they took the West Virginia boy with them. Once again, however, his reputation as a racist was enhanced by a scuffle with Brooklyn Dodgers catcher Roy Campanella. Burdette knocked the catcher to the ground twice, then, according to witnesses, stood over him, yelling, "Nigger, get up and hit!" Burdette vociferously denied this, saying, "I have never cast any slurs on any man's race and never will."[31] Burdette apologists are quick to point out that Burdette was one of the first visitors to the hospital where Campanella lay recovering from the incident.

It was as a Milwaukee Brave that Burdette found the mastery that would make him one of baseball's greats, indeed, one of the top one hundred pitchers according to at least one source.³² He won fifteen or more games eight times, led the National League in 1959 with 21 games, and won 173 games for Milwaukee. Of course, he will always be remembered as one of the greatest Yankee killers of all time. His performance in the 1957 World Series is legendary. In that series, Burdette won three games, pitching one of them on two days rest, and two were shutouts. It was Milwaukee's first World Series championship since 1914. And, deservedly, he was named Most Valuable Player.

Yet it was also as a Milwaukee Brave that his eccentricities became more pronounced. He constantly fidgeted, tugging at his clothes and carrying on animated conversations with everyone, including himself and the ball. His breaking balls broke so dramatically that they evoked rumors of spitballs, an accusation that Burdette only used to his advantage by not denying. Burdette was always known as a prankster and his jokes became odder and larger as his fame grew. He faked drunken pratfalls in hotel lobbies and slipped small snakes into the pockets of the unsuspecting. And the mountain boy had developed an ego as big as any peak in the Appalachians from whence he came. When he buddied up with Warren Spahn, the two became almost unbearable. A West Virginia newspaper reported on the woes suffered by Milwaukee at the hands of its two bad boys with a former manager bemoaning division in the ranks. "Dressen ... goes on to tell of the prima donnas, Burdette and Spahn, whom he contends are now money mad and wrapped up in their own self-importance.... That Burdette possessed one of the league's most unstable temperaments has been common knowledge for a long time.... 'The guy is squirrely,' is the way a veteran player on another club puts it."³³

Pity the poor residents of Burdette's hometown of Nitro, who were about to find out what success in the show had done to their boy. During the 1957 World Series, one columnist, in a tongue-in-cheek ode to the latest wonder in space technology which was currently circling the globe, said, "Safe to say, if it had not been for a young Nitro man named Lew Burdette and a few of his business associates, the impact of Sputnik on America would be much greater."³⁴ In early November, Nitro put on the biggest extravaganza in its brief history with "Lew Burdette Day." Local politicos turned out, plus a few of the state's bigger wigs, including U.S. senators and the governor. Main Street was temporarily renamed Lew Burdette Drive. The local *Kanawha Valley Leader* newspaper made out like a bandit in advertising sales.

> Inside *The Leader's* 32-page special edition—it's biggest ever—were poems, pictures, articles, and well-wishes from everyone from the gas company to the TV repair store. Comstock Furniture and Appliance offered a "Lew Burdette Special" on washer and dryers. Appalachian Electric Power's ad stated "Like Lew.... You'll make a real hit when you live electrically." One ad announced Lew's new, lifetime membership in the Nitro Moose Lodge, Number 565.³⁵

The town was so giddy with pride that it didn't realize that its native son now regarded it with very cynical eyes until a sportswriter made note of it.

> Lew paid a flying visit to his old home town after the 1957 World Series but turned this "homecoming of the hero" into a payday for Lew Burdette. Radio and TV dealers in this area had to set up a "kitty" to make his visit home like most of his other ventures—profitable. You can't blame a guy for cashing in on his fame. In the case of a baseball player, it's get it now or not get it at all. But there are bounds of propriety.³⁶

On the mound, Burdette was still a masterful performer; in 1960, he pitched a 1–0 no-hitter, supplying his team with the only run of the game. And he could be lucky to boot. The year before, for example, Burdette was handed a victory that should have belonged to Harvey Haddix of the Pirates, who pitched a perfect game against the Braves for twelve innings but lost in the thirteenth. And still the spitball haunted him. One take on the mechanics of his perfect spitball was offered in Dan Gutman's *It Ain't Cheatin' If You Don't Get Caught:*

> Next to Gaylord Perry, Burdette was the nerviest of the spitballers. When umpires asked to see the ball, he would *roll* it to them, removing any moisture in the process. Burdette's scheme was to spit tobacco juice around the mound area and make little mudpies. When he got to a tight spot, he'd bend down to tie his shoe and wipe a little goo on the ball. Red Smith used to write that newspapers needed three columns for Lew's pitching record—won, lost, and relative humidity.[37]

No matter how he played the game, Burdette had a remarkable eighteen-year run in the majors leagues, including seasons spent pitching for the Cardinals, the Cubs, the Phillies and the Angels. When he signed with the California team, the *Sporting News* seemed tickled to take a final jab at his reputation. "Burdette has often been accused of throwing the best spitball in baseball. Ironically, his signing comes at a time when the Angels are installing 56 water fountains in Anaheim Stadium. In this case, they could clearly be the fountains of youth."[38]

Perhaps so. In his final year of play, with the Angels, he pitched 18 innings and didn't walk a man. He ended his career in organized baseball as a pitching coach for the Atlanta Braves. He spent his final days in Florida. Like his fellow West Virginian Jack Warhop, Lew Burdette left the mountains and never looked back.

Chapter 10

Almost Valhalla

In Norse mythology, warriors who die noble deaths are swept up by strong—and presumably beautiful—women and transported to a magnificent hall. There, they can replay old battles and rehash the tactics used, all while drinking and eating to their hearts' content. After a night of merrymaking, they awaken renewed and refreshed, and head right back into battle, followed by another and another and another night of revelry.

For retirees of the Negro Leagues, or men whose careers might have been shortened due to injury, Raleigh County, West Virginia, was a Valhalla of sorts, offering good paying jobs with the mining companies and the chance to play out their twilight years on fast, competitive baseball teams. In these southern coalfields, an astonishing number of aging heroes worked their daily shift, then hit the ball field to help create a microcosm of the glorious Negro Leagues.

The southern West Virginia coalfields are historically unique in Appalachia, particularly for African American residents. Those who were not born in the state as the descendents of slaves had come from further south in droves from the 1870s until the 1930s, attracted by jobs in the bituminous coalfields. "Although they formed only 6.6 percent of the population of the state in 1930, they constituted 21.8 percent of all miners."[1] As for attitudes towards African Americans in the coal camps themselves, some maintain that one of the unplanned results of contentment sociology was a certain harmony between the races which was missing in other parts of the country. Part of this might have been due to the idea of uniting against a common enemy, the company, however benevolent that enemy could be when it suited. But there seems to have been more to the generally good race relations in the camps. David Corbin posits the theory that familiarity bred the opposite of contempt. "Even when segregated, the town was too small, its population too familiar, and social interaction too great to allow racial stereotyping and social distance and, hence, a culture of discrimination to flourish."[2]

Even as Jim Crow began to spread its corruption across the country in the 1890s, the more level playing field afforded blacks in the southern West Virginia coalfields meant that they were able to avoid some of the worst aspects of it. Historian Stuart McGehee points out that the isolated West Virginia coalfields were something of a country unto themselves, free from a lot of governmental interference. As long as the production of coal was unimpeded, authorities ranging from coal company operators to political and judicial authorities from outside were content to leave the towns to their own devices. One positive result of this independence was that, while black people across the south were being denied the vote that had been guaranteed them by the Fifteenth Amendment, their counterparts in southern West Virginia were able to exercise that right. They were also being elected to political office there at a time when that was an unheard of achievement in great swathes of the country.[3]

If the sports pages of newspapers are any indication of the social clout of a segment of the citizenry, then the black population of southern West Virginia wielded quite a bit. From the newspapers of the capital at Charleston, to those of the commercial centers of the coalfields, African American baseball games were surprisingly well covered as early as the 1930s. Much of the credit for this minor miracle must be given to the passion that the entire state had for baseball and to the fact that, from Charleston southward, a team's color didn't seem to matter as much as it would elsewhere. The efforts of the black teams were rewarded with coverage that was very nearly as extensive as that of their white counterparts. And the devotion shown the sport by southern West Virginians, plus their geographical location, meant that they found themselves on barnstorming circuits that drew the greats with amazing frequency; the Homestead Grays, for instance, were well-known there because they played the greater number of their games within Pennsylvania, Ohio and West Virginia. And the local papers treated the African American visitors with due deference and a certain amount of awe: "One hundred victories a season is a commonplace thing for the Homestead Grays. As early as 10 years ago they started winning 100 and they have not dropped anywhere near that figure since."[4] In blithely-dropped bombs that could make today's Negro League fan gasp, the *Charleston Gazette* and *Charleston Daily Mail* routinely announced tilts at local parks featuring the Homestead Grays, Pittsburgh Crawfords, Baltimore Elite Giants or the Black Yankees, to name but a few. Nor were the games limited to the powerhouses playing each other. The local lads got their chance at the big guys many times during the season as well. While it is painful to consider the bloodletting involved in a game between the legends from Homestead and, say, the Valley Bell club of the Twilight League,[5] other local teams could hold their own against the barnstorming giants, especially when they packed their rosters with former professional players. In 1935, manager Abe Adkins of the Charleston Tigers signed former Gray Charles "Lefty" Williams to his team. Author James A. Riley calls Williams "one of the Homestead Grays' all-time best pitchers" and continues the glowing biography:

> The dependable left-hander pitched for the Grays for the entirety of his twenty-year career, during which he is credited with 540 wins out of 625 games pitched against all levels of competition. Included in these wins are 17 no-hitters, one of which was a perfect game. He was a mainstay on the Grays' teams of 1930–31, with the latter aggregation often considered the best black team of all time.[6]

The successes of the Charleston club and those across the coalfields were such that, at the end of 1937, the Hawkmen Athletic Association, based in the huge Logan County camp of Holden, began planning an actual league of black clubs, an act of unqualified confidence. Suddenly, not only were the local newspapers reporting on the games of African Americans, they were giving periodic rundowns on the status of the league. When the season opened, the West Virginia Negro Baseball League was composed of six camps covering several counties. It included Holden, Kyle, Scarbro, Kimberly, Omar and Glen Rogers. Although it had a short lifespan, expiring after the 1938 season, it was a bold step in the right direction.

For unknown reasons, not included in the league was the most renowned of the local coalfield teams, the Raleigh Clippers, from the large, bustling coal camp just outside of Beckley. The Raleigh Coal and Coke Company, like Consolidation Coal, was a practitioner of welfare capitalism and promoted recreation among its workers to keep them happy and occupied. A physical manifestation of this was the Raleigh Mining Institute Park, a venue that served both black and white baseball teams for decades.[7] Although there is no way of knowing just when the Raleigh Clippers were organized, the name begins to surface in Charleston papers in the late '20s. In 1928 they are mentioned as defendants in a suit filed by the Colored South Alabama Old Stars baseball club. It seems the Clippers refused to pay the Alabama team the full amount agreed upon when the Old Stars showed up for a game without the lineup they'd promised. The Clippers were ordered by the court to pay damages of one cent to the southerners.[8]

The Clippers were already well-established in 1930 when a young third baseman for the Homestead Grays broke his ankle. Forced to leave the team, he returned home to Raleigh. What he found there, and what he would nurture for another few decades, was the kernel of a living, breathing monument to professional black baseball.

Born in a coal camp outside of Birmingham, Alabama, in 1903, Grover Lewis started working as a trapper boy in the mines at age nine. By his teens, his family had moved to West Virginia for better opportunities. Lewis was discovered while he was playing for the Fairmont Giants by Cum Posey, manager of the Homestead Grays. In 1925, he took the hot corner for the Grays and played with them until that fateful day in 1930 when his ankle was broken.[9] No one can know what was in Grover Lewis' heart when he was forced by dreadful circumstance to return to a life spent underground. But return he did, to southern West Virginia and the mines of Raleigh Coal and Coke in Beckley, where he began to play for the Clippers.

Of all the places he could have landed across the country, Raleigh must have felt most comfortable to Grover Lewis simply because of the company. In 1937, at a time when the Clippers had temporarily changed their name to the Raleigh Colts, the pilots of the club were Charles Jamison and E. C. "Pops" Turner, both stars in their own right. Jamison, who would serve on the mound as well as manage, had pitched for the Homestead Grays from 1932 until 1934 and had then spent a year with the Newark Dodgers. Pops Turner had enjoyed a career spent mostly as a third baseman with the Brooklyn Royal Giants, the Homestead Grays, the Birmingham Black Barons, the Cleveland Cubs, the New York Black Yankees and Cole's American Giants. Apparently he was the ideal steward for a young, highly-charged team of miners. "At the plate he had no power and lacked speed, but he was a smart, alert base runner. He was highly intelligent and used his mind more than his body, while also helping the team as a teacher for younger players."[10] Another early fixture was shortstop and third baseman James Mickey. From the Anjean coal camp, he was fresh from seasons spent with the Birmingham Black Barons, the Chicago American Giants and the Kansas City Monarchs. Playing infield with him was his brother, Harry.

As the Raleigh Colts, the team started to receive more local press. In 1937, an announcement in the *Beckley-Post Herald* described the pedigree of the team and the promise in their line-up. "After two weeks of practice the Colts are ready to go and number several stars of the Negro baseball firmament in their lineup. These include Grover Lewis, James Mickey and several others under the managership of "Pops" Turner, a former member of the Negro teams."[11]

The second season as the Raleigh Colts arrived and local writers were still referring to them as the "old Raleigh Clippers." By this time, Grover Lewis had taken over as business manager while still working the infield. In April they put out a call to "every colored baseball player in this section who thinks he can make the grade."[12] The Colts were still boasting an imposing roster which now included Tommy Sampson as an infielder. Sampson, far from being on his way back down, hadn't yet begun his climb up. He'd grown up in Raleigh and had begun working in the mines as a teenager, losing his index finger in a mining accident while still very young. Playing with the Clippers prepared him for some future glory, particularly four consecutive years, beginning in 1940, in the East–West All-Star game of the Negro American League as a Birmingham Black Baron. He is also credited with having discovered Willie Mays.[13]

Grover Lewis immediately started bringing in local teams like the fearsome Bishop State Liners and the Huntington Quick Steps. And he began hunting for more famous prey: "He also arranged to bring in professional black teams to play each other, including the Homestead Grays, Memphis Black Sox, Kansas City Monarchs, and Birmingham Black Barons. Jim Thorpe, the Native American Olympic gold medalist, once brought a team to play at the Clippers field in Raleigh."[14]

Indeed, within the following six weeks, Lewis was promoting a visit to R.M.I. Park from the Homestead Grays.[15] And in September of that year, he coaxed Satchel Paige and the Pittsburgh Crawfords to Raleigh to meet an all-star outfit made up of men from all the local black teams.[16] While Grover Lewis was promoting black baseball, there were other voices in the wilderness, asking why black baseball and white baseball had to be two separate entities. Near the end of the 1938 season, the *Charleston Gazette* published on its editorial page Westbrook Pegler's heated denunciation of racism in the major leagues. His fury was directed at the hypocrisy of Commissioner Kenesaw Mountain Landis' suspension of a Yankees outfielder for a racial slur, while he continued to ignore the rampant racism that infected the sport. It was a bold argument for the day: "Thus no Negro ever has been permitted to play ball or even to try out for a job in the organized industry, and Babe Ruth, were he a colored man, would not have risen above the rank and pay of the leaky-roof leagues in which dark men operate as semi-pros."[17]

With the beginning of World War II, the skeleton crews of the coalfield teams were doing their part for the effort and none more so than the black Raleigh club, once again calling itself the Clippers. One advantage of the war years was that black and white teams had much more opportunity, and need, to play each other. The summer of 1942 was filled with such match-ups, including one between the Raleigh Clippers and an all-star team from the white Raleigh County League to benefit the local war chest. Apparently, at least one southern West Virginia newspaper saw in this trend a brighter future and commented upon it. On Sunday, August 30, the editor of the *Charleston Gazette* applauded an announcement from the Pittsburgh Pirates that they would give three black players—Roy Campanella, Sammy Hughes, and Dave Barnhill—a tryout.[18] Unfortunately, that turned out to be nothing more than rumor.

In Raleigh County, at the *Beckley Post-Herald*, the sports editor was outspoken in his support of black baseball in general, the Raleigh Clippers specifically. Roy Lee Harmon had been made sports editor of the paper in 1937, the same year that he was named poet laureate of the state of West Virginia, the first of three tenures under that title. He immediately began a column entitled "Speaking of Sports," which was an eclectic mix of elements. Along with straight sports reporting, there was frequently a poem—sometimes humorous, sometimes bittersweet—written by Harmon himself. He gently opined on a wide variety of topics, ranging from conservation of West Virginia's mountains and streams to forgiveness of suicide. His sports predictions took the form of a mythical two-dollar bet on his pick and he bet a lot on the Raleigh Clippers. He was a rarity in his day because of his intimate knowledge of black baseball, not only on the local semipro level, but on the professional level as well. In 1949, while visiting the statehouse in Charleston, Harmon recognized a quiet capitol messenger as none other than Clint "Hawk" Thomas, who was by then working for the Department of Mines. Thomas is ranked (along with Clipper infielder Tommy Sampson) in *The 2006 ESPN Baseball Encyclopedia* as one of the Top 100 All Time Greats of the Negro Leagues.[19] Thomas played outfield and second with several teams from 1920 to 1937, most notably the New York Black Yankees. Harmon was obviously delighted to have discovered Thomas. "Although he is not a big fellow, he was, for years, the clean-up man for the Black Yankees. And, pound for pound, he could swat a ball harder and farther than the immortal Josh Gibson, who was heftier."[20] Harmon's sports reporting is different than others of his day because, missing from his descriptions of the Clippers or other African American teams, was any patronizing reassurance for white readers that this was "real" baseball; there was never a reference to "antics" or the team's ability "to put on quite a show." When he talked about the Clippers, he described a team that could hold its own with any team in the region, white or black. His respect for them was made all the more apparent when, in September of 1942, he wrote a lengthy column—part obit, part eulogy—that paid loving tribute to Clippers first baseman Robert Toney, who had died after a sudden and brief illness. Harmon's grief was palpable and, after describing Toney's brilliance on the field, he wrote about how he'd missed his chance to say goodbye to a friend:

> Yesterday I learned that he had died in the early morning hours. And it was too late to visit him, to take him some cigarettes and tell him to hurry and get well and play against the teams which will oppose the Clippers yet this year. Maybe Johnny Vander Meer[21] and his pals will come to Beckley yet and we know other strong teams, the strongest possible, will be booked to face the Clippers.[22]

Toney's death was a blow to the team, and other wounds were amassed during the off season as the Clippers lost men to the armed services. But the spring of 1943 brought big plans for the season. Again, Grover Lewis announced a tryout for local men. At age forty, he should have been giving orders from the dugout but he was planning to cover third again. The *Raleigh Register* commented on him thusly: "He is a coal miner—and a ball player who can still knock the cover off the old apple despite the fact that he's an 'old man.'"[23] The Clippers began their year on a tear, and by the time they played the Raleigh white team in a benefit on June 20, they had already tilted with three other white teams. The teams themselves may have not been integrated but the contests for the season were certainly leaning that way.

In that summer of 1943, the Clippers were invincible, primarily because of an especially gifted and loyal player who would be a fixture on the team until its end. And he came bearing an exceptionally impressive resume. Harry "Tin Can" Kincannon was raised, and possibly born, in Raleigh County. In 1950, he would tell a reporter that he remembered the Raleigh Clippers from his childhood in the area.[24] He began his career with the Pittsburgh Crawfords in 1930 before they had achieved mega-star status. By 1932, their reputation was growing and Kincannon was one reason for it; in that year, his record was 15–8. The 1935 Pittsburgh Crawfords are considered by some to be the greatest black ball team in history. Not only did that team include Harry Kincannon and his brother Roy, but Cool Papa Bell, Sam Bankhead, Oscar Charleston, Judy Johnson, Josh Gibson and Satchel Paige as well. Kincannon's pitching career also included stints with the Black Yankees, the Homestead Grays, and the Washington Black Senators. Jimmie Crutchfield, Crawfords outfielder, shared with author James Bankes one of the most colorful stories of Kincannon, about an event that took place on the team bus:

> Everybody would put their food up on a rack while they were asleep. It was pretty common to swipe it and pass it around. One night, Harry Kincannon came on board with a nice mess of fried chicken. Tincan ate some of it and then put it up. He let everybody know he had a little pistol, a gun Charleston had picked up from a politician in Cuba. We ignored his threat and when the gun fell to the floor when he was asleep, somebody picked it up and emptied out all the shells. Then we passed the chicken around. After we finished it off, somebody tied the bones in a necklace and put it around Tincan's neck. When he woke up, everybody howled. At first, he was mad, but then he started laughing with us.[25]

For Grover Lewis and the Clippers, Kincannon supplied firepower that would soon be needed. Quietly gaining power in camps to the south and west of Raleigh were teams that would present huge challenges to the Clippers: the Gary Miners, the Bishop State Liners of Virginia, and the Glen Rogers Red Sox.

By the end of June 1943, the Clippers had been beaten only once that season by the black Gary Miners from McDowell County. "They must have something besides nice uniforms and lofty ambitions," one Beckley journalist bitterly wrote. "It takes a lot of ball playing to whip the Clippers anytime and anywhere, even when the locals do get some tough breaks."[26] It is a manifestation of the respect garnered by the Clippers that, when they hit the doldrums, local sportswriters ran the gamut of emotions endured by any loyal supporter, from proud defense to a general pique directed at the team for allowing this to occur. As usual, the Clippers rewarded their supporters by surging back to the top by the end of July and continued to give all they had—they were the winningest black team in West Virginia for three consecutive years.

After the war ended, and ballplayers began returning to the coalfields, they discovered that the Clippers had become the team to beat despite manpower shortages of the previous few years. When a brand new Beckley white team from Beckley challenged the Clippers to a tilt, Roy Lee Harmon devoted most of one column to the new club. One can almost see him rubbing his hands in glee at what he considered the fatal braggadocio of its manager.

> Two or three days ago, Patsy told me he wanted to book games with the BEST baseball aggregation in this section. When I told him the Clippers might be too tough for him, he laughed. "Listen, Pal, they don't come too tough for us," he declared. "Get us a game with Grover Lewis and his buddies." Well, he's got it. But I'll still bet the orthodox $2 on the Clippers.[27]

A more deadly threat to the Clippers, the team that would become their nemesis throughout the late '40s, was lurking in the coal camp of Glen Rogers, in the Winding Gulf field west of Raleigh. They were the Glen Rogers Red Sox and had been around since the late 1930s. Taking a page from the Grover Lewis playbook, the well-connected team manager, Babe Fullen, pulled in some high-octane players from the Negro Leagues. In 1937, the Red Sox had hooked Johnny Humes, a lefthander, from the Newark Eagles. By 1946, they had landed Charles Shields who had first surfaced as a pitcher for Bluefield State College. Even as the greenest amateur, this lefty was devastating on the mound. James A. Riley's invaluable encyclopedia lists him as having played with the Chicago American Giants, Homestead Grays, New York Cubans and Birmingham Black Barons during the first half of the 1940s.[28] With this added power, the Glen Rogers Red Sox became such a force as to earn more victories than the Clippers in 1947 and 1948. With such a reputation, they were able to lure others who were finished with the Negro Leagues or taking a breather. In 1947, Harold "Head" Hairston joined the Red Sox pitching staff after leaving the Homestead Grays, and Sonny Watts, third baseman from the Cleveland Buckeyes, signed on in 1949.

In a 1994 interview, former Clipper Angus Evans aptly described the southern West Virginia black teams when he said, "We were just a step below the Negro professional league."[29] Nothing could illustrate that point better than the moment in 1949 when the Raleigh Clippers broke ground in more ways than one. In March of that year, the team members themselves began construction on their own ball park. "Fifteen members of the Clippers, who work in or around the mines, went to the scene of the new park yesterday and worked on the fences while machines were doing the grading. The players, who are ordinarily employed at the mines, are on vacation now."[30] Grover Lewis was now part owner and booking manager of the club, having given up the reins of playing manager. As an owner, he was the force behind both the new park—which would seat one thousand spectators—and the handsome new uniforms sported by the team. Some of the names on the roster included Sonny Watts (nabbed from Glen Rogers), Harry Kincannon and his younger brother Charlie in the outfield, infielders James Mickey, Nat Smith and Robert White and a new young shortstop, Albert Hill. To complete what must have been a shining hour for Grover Lewis, the man who would become one of his most faithful allies, Garson "Lefty" Totten, was there to toe the rubber. A local lad from the Lillybrook camp, an immense raw talent, Lewis snagged Totten after the southpaw had ended his professional career with the New York Cubans. Totten would prove himself not only an indefatigable powerhouse of a pitcher but one of the pillars of the team. Clad in their new uniforms and playing on the green grass of their own park, the Clippers opened the season by defeating the powerful Bishop State liners by the uneven score of 25–3.

But this would be the Clippers' most challenging year, as other teams tried to supplant them. Some tongues were now referring to the team from Winding Gulf as "the famed Glen Rogers Red Sox"[31] and a rumor, almost too blasphemous to be repeated, suggested that the Red Sox were just as good a team as the Clippers, perhaps better because of their youthful players and the power players they were starting to pull in from the professional leagues.[32] Pounding this point home and in an ominous fashion, manager Babe Fullen and his Red Sox soon tied a series played against the New York Black Yankees. After scheduling conflicts repeatedly kept the two teams from tilting, seedy talk circulated that the Clippers were scared to play the Red Sox.[33] At the *Raleigh Register*, Bob Wills, the snide, polar-opposite of Roy Lee Harmon, was one who was, self-admittedly, manipulating the tensions.

> I am given to understand that the Lewises, Gores, Harrises, Kincannons and their predecessors have turned out some mighty fine home teams under the Clipper banner—although, like Satchel Paige's age, it's always hard to pin these fellow down to statistics and provable statements.... First let me say that whether these two teams ever meet, or the outcome of such a meeting, is immaterial to me; but the Machiavellian side of my nature—always prevalent when a good fight, between two other parties, is in prospect—leads me to add a few coals to the blazing inferno.[34]

A series was finally agreed on and the first game was scheduled by the managers. In front of a crowd of almost two thousand, the Clippers lost 3 to 1, mostly because of Head Hairston's pitching and his younger brother Fred's batting for Glen Rogers. But before the next game of the series could be played, the Raleigh Clippers would tackle the Homestead Grays.

This was the team of Sam Bankhead, Buck Leonard and Josh Gibson, Jr., and Raleigh, as usual, welcomed them with open arms. George Springer, sportswriter for the *Beckley Post-Herald*, gushed over the Grays and the upcoming game. But the Clippers, especially those who had once been Homestead Grays, must have felt a chill wind when, in giving information about the tilt, he barely mentioned the Raleigh team. "These are the Homestead Grays with whom Harold 'Head' Hairston of the Glen Rogers Red Sox and a Beckley resident played with three years ago and piled up a great record. And speaking of the Sox, they are planning to tangle with the Negro leaguers sometime later on in the season...."[35]

Apparently the crown had been passed, plucked from the collective heads of the Raleigh Clippers and placed squarely on those of the Sox. Predictably, but sadly, the Clippers lost to the Grays. In this sea of buffets, a bright moment came two days later when Harry Kincannon shut out the Red Sox, 3–0. Sportswriter and Sox booster Springer was stunned, writing, "What was amazing about the whole thing was that it was the first time in four years the Rogersmen have been shut out. They just couldn't hit Kincannon, going down in order in five of the nine innings of a game that consumed only one hour and 25 minutes of playing time."[36]

The rest of the season was a brutal three-way scramble between Raleigh, Gary, and

Glen Rogers, the Clippers finally wracking up the most wins but only through excessive blood, sweat and tears.

The first half of the 1950s witnessed the death throes of the coalfield teams, black and white, throughout Appalachia. Not only were coal camps disappearing but the entertainment demands of Americans as a whole were changing too quickly for semipro baseball to keep up. For the black teams of southern West Virginia, like the Negro Leagues from whom they drew their essence, the knell was sounded when Branch Rickey handed Jackie Robinson the pen. The 1950 season for the Raleigh Clippers began in disarray and, despite moments of brilliance over the next two years, the team never regained its footing. Grover Lewis all but disappeared for long stretches, with apparently only a background involvement with the team. He had remained an active player until the age of fifty. In a mournful editorial, Roy Lee Harmon, now writing for the *Register*, mentions stopping by Clipper Park to watch a game, only to find Grover Lewis umpiring. Speaking through the guise of a hillbilly sage, he wrote, "And he looked out of place like a calf at a shootin match. I can remember back when his job was knockin home runs fer the Clippers."[37]

Harry Kincannon, who was also getting up in years, became the manager and in midsummer persuaded his old roommate, Satchel Paige, to pitch for the Clippers against the Homestead Grays. It was a rout, the Grays taking it 11–2 as the Clippers flailed defensively behind their celebrity pitcher.

Happily, by 1951, Grover Lewis, now affectionately referred to as the "Big Old One," was back in the manager's seat, and with renewed vigor. "'We'll have the best players available in this section of the state,' Lewis declared, 'and we'll play every game to win. We'll give the local fans a classy brand of baseball when we get under full steam.'"[38] He later told the *Raleigh Register* that Harry Kincannon was ready to relieve. "Later in the year, Harry expects to be ready to start—and finish—games."[39] Garson Totten was also in uniform. And the Clippers were taking advantage of the right arm of a young Slab Fork native, Earl Francis, who three years later would be signed by the Pittsburgh Pirates. Once again with the enemy camp, Sonny Watts had replaced the colorful Babe Fullen as manager of the Glen Rogers Red Sox.

A predictable casualty of the waning enthusiasm for local baseball was that coverage of the coalfield teams began to take a back seat to that of professional ball in the local newspapers and the black teams suffered the most. Even announcements of Clipper and Red Sox games became smaller and less conspicuous; results were almost never given. Box scores for the black teams, which had been instituted just a couple of years earlier, became as rare as the dodo.

In 1952, Harry Kincannon, now the field manager (and still pitching), begged for local talent to try out for the team, as they had lost many of their men to age and the Korean War.[40] The team played their season with minimal press coverage, any quotes coming from owner Clyde Taylor. Then in September appeared a blurb, tiny but at the top of the page, announcing that a South American (and one from the Brooklyn farm system), with the unlikely name of MacDuff, had joined the Clippers. Neither detail was accurate but this man did represent the last fiery meteorite to fall into Clipper Park: Terris "Speed" McDuffie. An outfielder turned pitcher, McDuffie had played for different teams including, of course, the Homestead Grays, who he'd helped lead to the pennant in 1941. For all of his skill and accomplishments, it was probably his relationship with Effa Manley, when he played for the Newark Eagles, for which he is best remembered.

> At the ballpark she would show him off for her ladies' club friends, sometimes ordering the manager to pitch him in a particular game for this purpose. In early August 1938, after a lover's quarrel at Pennsylvania Station, where McDuffie reportedly knocked her down and kicked her, Abe Manley became aware of the relationship and traded McDuffie to the Black Yankees for two broken bats and an old pair of sliding pants.[41]

He had also been one of the two black players to try out for the Brooklyn Dodgers in an ill-fated 1945 publicity stunt. McDuffie had been playing in the Latin American leagues for some time (he was 1951 MVP for Caracas of the Venezuelan League and 1952 MVP of the Dominican Republic League) when he came to Raleigh to pitch for the Clippers at the end of the 1952 season. In October, he faced Cincinnati Reds pitcher and local boy Harry Perkowski in a benefit game between the Raleigh County League All-Stars and the County Negro All-Stars. Perkowski pitched a one-hit 4–1 win. In the newspaper coverage of that match-up, three names were conspicuously absent: Grover Lewis, Harry Kincannon, Garson Totten. It had been the Raleigh Clippers' final game.

There are only a handful of men left who can talk with any firsthand knowledge about that remarkable period in the history of African American coalfield baseball. One is Albert Hill; at ninety years old, Albert may be the sole surviving Raleigh Clipper. Sitting on his front porch in the September sunlight, he seems frail at first glance, but becomes very animated when the subject of baseball is broached. When asked what his lifetime batting average might have been, he grins and retorts, "Probably .400, 'cause I never did strike out. We never did keep up with that stuff but I know they couldn't do much with me. I might hit it and get out but as far as swinging three times? No." The box scores from the two local papers, which began to be kept for the black teams beginning in 1949, the year that Albert joined, support his assertions. He was a solid hitter in almost every game he played. "Albert was a spot-hitter; he knew where to hit for the holes," says Charles Francis, Albert's lifelong friend. Although he didn't play ball, Charles calls himself "one of the boosters" and followed the Clippers throughout their existence. (Another Francis, Charles' first cousin Earl, of the Pittsburgh Pirates, briefly pitched for the Clippers. In a pithy observation about life in the big leagues, Earl once told Charles, "Any direction you walk out there, you're going up hill. You're going up hill going back to the dugout.") Joining in to contribute their expertise on the subject of local baseball are brothers Elmer and Samuel Henry, who toiled against the Clippers as right-handed pitchers and outfielders for the Slab Fork Indians. All four of these men grew up playing with homemade balls, bats and even gloves on the slate dumps of the Slab Fork Coal Company. Now, they all live within a few blocks of each other in Beckley.

The black teams of Slab Fork have a proud history, first as the Quick Steps, then as the Aces, and finally as the Indians. Samuel Henry recalls a childhood spent plucking sodden balls out of the creek for the Indians. And he recalls watching Albert Hill play for the team. When he and Elmer reached adulthood, they joined too. The brothers, indeed all four of these men, spent their lives working in the mines.

When asked how often the Indians went up against the Raleigh Clippers, Samuel replies honestly. "Not often. They had a better team. They were in a different class than we were. The way it was, about all those little camps had their own team. Every Sunday, and sometimes on Saturday, we'd go from one camp to another to play their teams. The Raleigh Clippers played more of the bigger teams. They'd play Rocky Mountain, North Carolina, or Roanoke. See, they had a fenced-in park where we just had an open field. We couldn't sell tickets; we played and passed the hat and used that to buy our equipment." The Slab Fork Indians received no financial support from the company, nor were the players given easier jobs. "Some companies gave the men a break like that—you know, good ballplayers. It never was that way in my case. Some people, like those fellows that were in the [Negro] League, the company would give them easy jobs," says Samuel.

When it comes to remembering the genius behind the Clippers, Charles Francis laughs about one game in which Grover Lewis was struck out by a pitcher named Pee Wee. "When he was going back to the dugout, Grover pointed at Pee Wee and said, 'I'll get you next time.' The last time I saw that ball, it was going on over the fence." And they all have memories of Harry Kincannon, who played with the Slab Fork Indians before joining the Raleigh club. Their recollection of him is far different from the temperamental dandy described in Jimmie Crutchfield's anecdote. "He was a good, friendly person. After he got through playing ball [for the Crawfords], he worked in the mines down at Slab Fork and played with the Indians," says Samuel. Albert interjects, "Yeah, he broke for me for a while when I ran the motor."[42] All remember Garson Totten, the brilliant left-hander that Grover Lewis so relied upon. After the Clippers disbanded, he played for other camp teams but lost his left arm in a mining accident. "Before he lost his arm, I pitched against him when he played for Affinity and the Stonecoal Giants," remembers Elmer Henry. "I don't think he was finished playing when he lost his arm." They clearly recall the Negro League members of the nemesis Glen Rogers Red Sox, including Charles Shields, Sonny Watts and Harold Hairston. But the scorebooks and stats of all those tilts are lost to history. Samuel Henry says that, while he remembers scorebooks being kept, he has no idea where they'd be now. Albert cackles, "When the game was over they just throwed 'em down!"

When the topic of the barnstorming Negro League teams arises, all their faces light up. Samuel speaks for the group, explaining, "That was always big. At the end of their seasons, they'd tour around and play the Raleigh Clippers or the Glen Rogers Red Sox or some of those better teams. I remember going with the Raleigh Clippers down to Watt Powell Park in Charleston in the fall of the year and playing a barnstorming team with Satchel Paige. I was with the team but didn't play." Albert interjects here, making a point of saying that he, himself, played in that game. Charles talks about seeing the likes of Satchel Paige, Buck Leonard and Oscar Charleston at RMI Park in Raleigh. With this steady stream of big names coming through the area, playing in coal camps, one has to wonder if these men, as youths, completely understood what they were witnessing. "I kind of realized it. We would get articles, not too much in our newspapers, but the *Philadelphia Enquirer* was a Negro newspaper, so we knew about the Negro Leagues and all that," says Samuel. "We always had our heroes. I remember following the people in the major leagues too. My

Left to right: Elmer Henry, Albert Hill (seated), Samuel Henry, Charles Francis. The Henry brothers played for the Slab Fork Indians and Charles Francis religiously supported both the Indians and the Raleigh Clippers. Albert Hill is possibly the last surviving Raleigh Clipper (courtesy Chuck Clisso).

favorite team was the Yankees—they were the powerhouse at that time. Sometimes we could pick up a game on the radio—that was before television."

As the conversation begins to die down, Albert expresses complete mystification at the lack of interest in baseball on the part of today's kids. All agree with him, each man genuinely bewildered by today's obsession with basketball. And they all grunt in agreement when Samuel blames television for the end of the Raleigh Clippers, the Slab Fork Indians and coalfield baseball. After an hour of reliving the past, the happy chatter has given way to reflection. Albert breaks the silence by saying that the teams of their youth "all just faded away, one at a time."

A few blocks from Albert's house is a small neighborhood that was once the actual Raleigh coal camp. Today, what is most striking when visiting the neighborhood is the scarcity of visual evidence that the coal industry ever supported this area. Gone are the tipples and corollary structures; the once-uniform camp houses have been so cosmetically altered as to be unrecognizable as such. Gone is any trace of the fact that Raleigh was once a busy camp, comprising mainly African American mining families.

On a street named for a former Raleigh Coal Company superintendent is the home of George Mickey, whose brothers James and Harry were Clippers. James, in his youth, had been picked up by the Birmingham Black Barons and played for awhile in the Negro Leagues, only to return to Raleigh. Both James and Harry are now deceased but they have a loyal spokesman in George. With an absolutely Einsteinian shock of wild, white hair, George is a jolly, charismatic man. Every name mentioned elicits a chuckle from him and is followed by poetic descriptions of the past. James spent his life as a miner but Harry never was. When asked why Harry hadn't worked in the mines, George's answer sheds light on a time-honored tradition in the world of mining. "Same reason I didn't. It was dangerous. My old man wouldn't take me. You couldn't go if your dad didn't take you. Your dad had to teach you about the mine. They wouldn't let you go hardly with anybody else."

When James returned from his barnstorming career, he was immediately drafted by the Raleigh Clippers. "If you could play baseball, you could get the best job around," says George. He gives an example. "Glen Rogers scooped up Charles Shields, an awesome pitcher. They [the good players] usually didn't go underground. They usually worked outside just doing nothing. Shields, they gave him a job cleaning track." When asked how one cleaned track, George howls, saying, "That's what I mean! How do you clean track?"

George Mickey was, for years, a batboy and score keeper for the Raleigh Clippers; his memories of those days are crystalline. "Baseball was beautiful here. Every Sunday they were playing. A lot of white teams too. It was just baseball country. And it all came about because of the mines." He goes on to reminisce about the men he grew up idolizing. "A long time I knew Grover. And when he came away from the Grays, it was just something at the ball park because he would just about hit a homerun every time he got up to bat. He was an awful, awesome hitter. He was a smooth kind of guy, didn't carry on too much. Cool head. He knew what he wanted you to do and expected you to do it." Of Harry Kincannon he says, "He was a man you just wanted to be around you. He was just a big fine fellow. I don't know if he was a Christian fellow or not but you never saw him into any trouble or

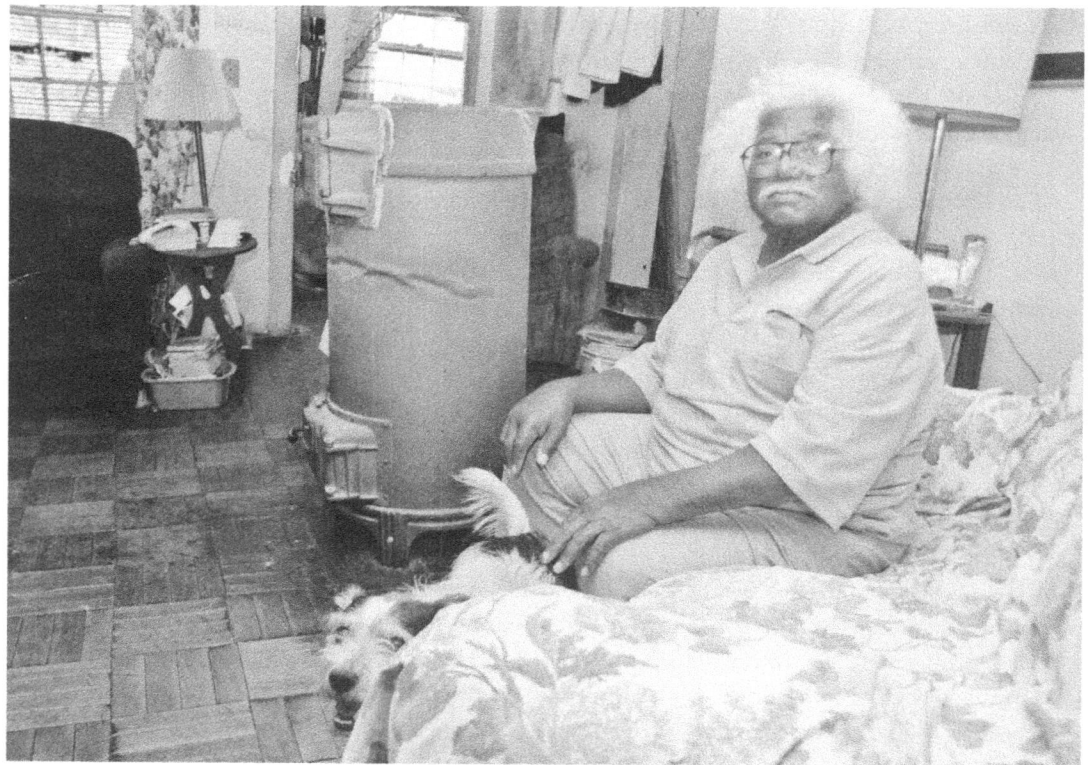

George Mickey at home in Raleigh with his dog, Patches. Two of Mickey's brothers, James and Harry, played for the Raleigh Clippers. James also played for the Birmingham Black Barons, the Chicago American Giants and the Kansas City Monarchs (courtesy Chuck Clisso).

drinking that I know of." Lewis' power to obtain the best of the local camp players was epitomized in Garson Totten, who George says "could really hum that ball."

Of course, the Glen Rogers Red Sox, under the leadership of Babe Fullen, became just as nimble at drawing the best players. George takes a special delight in discussing how the Red Sox, at the Clippers' expense, landed so much talent. "Old Babe. You're talking about one sharp dude. He was just faster, smarter, more flamboyant. You know these go-getters. They undercut, they do anything. He always had a big beautiful car and dressed, oh gosh, just wonderfully." He says that when Charles Shields went to the Red Sox, it was a mortal blow to Grover Lewis and the Raleigh club. And, it is his opinion that the Glen Rogers Red Sox were able to snag the players they did because they received financial backing from their company whereas the other black baseball teams who carried their burdens alone. He vividly recalls some of the great Red Sox players like Johnny Humes, former Newark Eagle, who was called "Crap Ear" by his fellow West Virginians. "Well, he didn't have one ear. He'd pull that hat down over so you couldn't tell if he had an ear or not." Mention Harold Hairston and George dissolves into laughter, telling that, after his baseball days had ended, Hairston worked as a night watchman in Cleveland, a position he lost when it was discovered he brought a small bed to work.

Due to the bitter rivalry between the Clippers and the Red Sox, it is natural to ask about any pervasive feelings of antagonism at their games. "'Am I gonna get out of here alive?'" is how George describes it. "It was intense but we never did hardly have fights in the park. In Glen Rogers the element outside the park was terrible. You'd see fights—I saw a woman hit a man with a coal shovel and laid him plumb out. Glen Rogers was tough. Raleigh was rough enough but Glen Rogers? Yeah, plumb."

George Mickey, in his close proximity to the team, was privileged to know some of the world's most legendary players. "I remember rubbing Satchel Paige's arm. They would holler for me and I'd get the wintergreen. He'd put his arm up on my shoulder and I'd bam, bam, bam, bam, bam—just rub it and rub it. Satchel never did remind me of a person who was very friendly until you got to know him. But after you knew him he was something. He'd come here barnstorming; he'd come by himself and play with your team. Sometimes he'd bring a team with him. Satchel was something. He was a fine fellow." George remains awestruck at the hurler's ability to take to the mound cold. "He'd get up and throw three or four balls—said he didn't want to throw his arm away." And he carries with him an indelible memory of Josh Gibson. "I saw him hit a single with one hand. He picked up the bat and swung with one hand and bang! He was a character."

George's own baseball career was limited to his teenage years. "I couldn't get out of the way of a ball. They'd hit my legs and I'd just—no. They did believe in those days in moving you back and they moved you by the head. You don't let 'em hit that head. And there wasn't such a thing as helmets. It was a lot of fun but not fun when you were getting hit." He managed the scoreboard until he tangled with a bit of lightning while hanging up a metal number plate. Honoring his father's wishes, he never went into the mines but drove a school bus for twenty-five years. One of his colleagues was Harry Perkowski, who also drove for the school system after his major league days had ended.

Perhaps one of the most engaging qualities in George Mickey is his obvious contentment in life. He loves his wife and family, he loves his dog, and he loves what is left of the town he grew up in. It shows in his face. But remembering the legendary Raleigh Clippers brings joyful sparks to his eyes. "It was beautiful," he sighs. "I wouldn't have wanted to be nowhere else."

As sad as the demise of the Clippers was, the celebration of their very existence must far outweigh any grief at their end. An odd combination of time and place and circumstance created a team that was absolutely unique, both in black baseball and coalfield baseball. Southern West Virginia's coalfields and vibrant black population lured the man who sought a good job and safe harbor. They also offered competitive black baseball. The result was the Raleigh Clippers. For the proud Negro League veteran—his bat slightly less mighty or his fastball infinitesimally slower—who needed a home, the coalfields of West Virginia offered sanctuary and a last chance at glory. Nothing less befits a warrior.

CHAPTER 11

The 1951 Hazard Bombers

The town of Hazard, in Perry County, Kentucky, is not a coal camp although it was surrounded by them. Nor did it spring into existence as a commercial center to serve the camps. Hazard existed well before powerful men from the outside world came into the Appalachians to sink their mines deep into the earth. Established by a single family at the end of the eighteenth century, it was a small settlement in the wilderness, officially named in 1854 for Commodore Oliver Hazard Perry, the hero of the Battle of Lake Erie in the War of 1812. It remained an isolated community until 1912, when, after two years of groundwork, the first train arrived on pristine and shining tracks at the newly-built Hazard station. From a pre-railroad population of roughly five hundred, by 1920 the town boasted almost five thousand people, as hundreds of coal mines opened around it. After existing for almost a century as a rural mountain settlement, Hazard began to discover what financial and social advantages coal money could bring.

This town was unusual in the coalfields. As an older, established community, it lacked the rollicking boisterousness of the camps that surrounded it. On the contrary, when the business of coal became a part of Hazard, many of the townspeople seem to have made a conscious effort to resist the rowdy culture associated with it. As bankers and attorneys and doctors came in, many of these professional people believed their town could be a beacon of civilization in the Appalachians and they set about raising their children to maintain it as such, by providing them with concerts and dance lessons and excellent educations.

Hazard is a pretty town but its maze of one-way streets can be mystifying to the uninitiated driver. Only after several circuits of the residential hillside neighborhood above the downtown area will one find the Bobby Davis Museum, but it is worth the time and gasoline expended to get there. A handsome building, built of native sandstone, it sits back from the road on four forested acres. Originally a library and park, it was the work of a local businessman who intended it as a memorial to his son who died in a train wreck at the end of World War II. It also honors the other 187 Perry County boys whose lives were lost in that conflict. Now it is a museum specializing in the history of the county. On a warm summer day, with the soothing music of fountains and the shade of its many trees, it is a cool oasis tucked away in the middle of town.

It is on such a day that Hazard natives Martha Quigley, Sydney Francis, and Bill

McGraw gather in the museum to discuss their hometown and its greatest claim to fame, the 1951 Hazard Bombers. They converse with the ease of longtime acquaintances—correcting each other, interrupting each other, always with kindness and humor. They like to talk baseball. For Bill, at least, it is about genetics: he is the great-nephew of the New York Giants' legendary pilot John McGraw. For Sydney, the only child of a widowed mother who unfailingly followed the game, being taken to home tilts is one of her most beloved childhood memories. Martha, the museum's director and Kentucky historian, interjects tidbits and disappears frequently, only to appear again with some invaluable snippet of documentation.

These three were the children of professionals, and grew up with the understanding that they would attend college, says Sydney, who, in fact, did go on to become a Latin teacher. The pervasive stereotype of the moonshining hillbilly, born of legend and bad television, is profoundly insulting to them but they seem sadly resigned to it. "People talk [badly] about eastern Kentucky but that wasn't the way we grew up. We had sort of an idyllic thing going here," insists Martha.

At the establishment of the town over three hundred years ago, Hazard was a difficult place to reach, and it still was well into the twentieth century. Sydney Francis gives an idea of the hardship involved in simply getting in and out of Hazard in the early 1950s. "You'd go up about seven mountains to get to Whitesburg and over more to get to Jenkins. It took four hours to get to Lexington. The roads were awful." And Martha Quigley points out that, there was only one road into the town at that time. The isolation of the place is evident from an aerial photograph. Hazard contorts itself along the North Fork of the Kentucky River in the only relatively flat area of a landscape that ripples like an unmade bed.

The hills that separated Hazard from the larger world also proved a barrier between it and the surrounding coal camps. As a result, while growing up, these children of the town knew almost nothing about their rowdier coal-mining neighbors. While their parents never considered the mining families inferior—and Sydney, Martha and Bill all had a friend or classmate from nearby camps—the understanding was that the camps themselves were bleak and inhospitable places to visit. "I knew very little about them—didn't even know where they were," says Sydney. Martha agrees but says she had secondhand knowledge of them. "My father went out there a lot because he was an insurance adjuster. So he told us a lot about the camps. He would take them checks or drive them over to Louisville if they had to go to the doctor; so for him, they weren't so much like a foreign country."

But Bill has a strong negative reaction to the memory of the coal camps. "It was a different world. My friend Popeye, the equipment manager for the Bombers, his father worked in a mine at Kinmont where the coal was like twenty-seven inches high. He had his back shattered in an accident. The coal camp was dark, dirty, dingy. They didn't make enough money to do anything. They could work all day and everything they could get for that day could be carried home in one grocery sack." He shakes his head, adding, "Hard way to make a living. And the coal industry still holds sway."

In a town that prided itself on edifying pursuits for its youth, it's quite natural that sports would play a vital part in local history. Baseball had come to Hazard long before the railroads—in fact, exactly 23 years before. According to local legend, in 1889, a local African

American by the name of "Tallow" Dick Combs traveled to Pittsburgh where he was introduced to baseball. He returned to Hazard with a rule book (and possibly a ball and bat) and the first game was played between Hazard and Hindman, Kentucky, in a pasture outside of town.[1] The locals got off to an auspicious beginning by winning 13–6.

Through the next several decades, most of the baseball in Hazard was played by church teams, while outside the town, it was played by the teams in the coal camps themselves. There were over three hundred camps in Perry County, from the large ones operated by the Blue Diamond Coal Company to tiny ones with descriptive names like Hell-for-Certain. Bill Gorman, the current mayor of Hazard, recalls the coal camp teams occasionally coming into Hazard to play the church teams in what must have been an interesting clash of the profane and the sacred. He also recollects some of the white teams having black players, quite a claim for pre-integration baseball ("We're very understanding here," he explains). But Hazard, as a rule, wasn't known for its baseball fanaticism. In the early days, major league towns were too distant to instill intense team loyalty. And, unlike most of the other coal towns of southern Appalachia, Hazard was too far off the map to have been on any exhibition or barnstorming circuits. No, it wasn't especially enthusiastic until a fateful day in 1948. Suddenly, a town that had enjoyed the gentility of church leagues and had avoided the raucous tilts of camp baseball, found itself with a professional team.

In 1943, Oak Ridge National Laboratory was built in the mountains outside Knoxville, Tennessee, as part of the Manhattan Project. With the birth of the Mountain States League five years later, the town organized a baseball team and named it, aptly and apparently without irony, the Bombers. In the first week of June 1948, the Oak Ridge Bombers were leading the fledgling league, but lacking an essential element: fans. For some reason, the residents were simply not turning out to support the team. In stepped Max Smith, owner of the Mary Gail mine in Kentucky, to purchase the franchise for Hazard. With local legend Hobe Brummett stepping in to the manager's shoes in July, the Hazard Bombers completed the season on an excellent note, even making it to the playoffs. It was the next season, that of 1949, that may have given the team's newly-acquired fans pause: the Bombers finished with an abysmal 35–89 record. But coal operators are businessmen and Max Smith was not about to let an investment so splendid fail so dismally. In January of 1950, it was announced that Smith had signed former major leaguer Max Macon to a two-year contract as player-manager. Macon had been a reliever for the Cardinals and the Dodgers until service in World War II and a shoulder injury ended his mound career. After that, he played first base with the Boston Braves for a couple of years. In 1949, he led the California State League in hitting with .383. He was an excellent catch for Hazard; not only was he bringing his formidable playing and managing gifts to the Bombers but, with his connections, he immediately established an affiliation with the Brooklyn Dodgers. When spring training began, he took his team, which included some of the best of the local talent (like Lonesome Pine veteran centerfielder Jack Kilgore), to the Dodgers' Vero Beach camp, where he was also able to sign a few gifted rookies.

In addition to Macon and all the bright young talents he could land, Hazard was getting a new venue in which to show them off. "Max Smith went down about a mile outside the city limits and he built what they call Bomber Field. It was state-of-the-art construction—box seats, reserve seats, all that stuff," says Mayor Gorman. "It was a very, very fine facility and he used all his own private money." Indeed, photographs at the Bobby Davis Museum show a large grandstand, with lettered, separated sections; Virgil Q. Wacks, president of the Mountain States League, was impressed enough to declare that he would use Bomber Field "as a model park for the circuit."[2]

Suddenly, a tiny town historically isolated by the mountains was flooded with new faces. From all over the country and deep in the Hispanic world came the new Bombers. Rooms were found for them in local boarding houses and the Lincoln Hotel downtown, the traditional haunt of visiting railroad men. On Main Street, Don's Restaurant became the hotspot for player watching. Sydney recalls them pouring into Don's for huge breakfasts before hitting the field for practice. When opening day rolled around, the new Hazard Bombers started the season with a bang by shellacking the Jenkins Cavaliers 22–5. Macon immediately made an impression on the two thousand spectators who turned out for the game by going 4 for 5. It didn't take long for the sportswriters at the *Hazard Herald* to understand what Macon was capable of; he was leading his own team in hitting at .467 by the middle of May. And when he wasn't giving orders from his position on the first sack, or from the dugout, he was doing it, despite his perpetually sore arm, from the pitcher's mound in relief. "The Bombers won yesterday, 7–4, as the chief Bomber strategist—Max Macon—gave his mound men a demonstration of what he means in the game yesterday at Morristown when he took the hill to relieve Snyder, and struck out four of the first five men who faced him. He allowed 3 hits in $3\frac{2}{3}$ innings."[3]

Macon quickly developed a loyal following that passionately backed him as he began a long string of ejections. His run-ins with umpires only seemed to enthrall the fans more. By the end of the season, gate receipts were reported at an all-time high, the Bombers had made it to the playoffs, and the town paid tribute to their new favorite citizen with Max Macon Night. Fifteen hundred fans turned out to shower Macon and his family with gifts and watched as the boys honored their pilot by winning a double-header over Jenkins.

Back at Vero Beach the next season, Macon was shopping for an unusually large number of players, having lost a quite a few to the Korean War. One of the best prospects was catcher Louis Isert who would serve him well that year, doubling as a coach. And, in one of the most fortuitous transactions of spring training, he obtained Costa Rican right-hander Daniel Hayling from the Class D Pony League. Hayling had been noticed and signed the previous season by a Dodger scout who assigned him to Hazard.

When he returned to Kentucky with his horde, Macon didn't exaggerate when he informed the writers at the *Hazard Herald* that he had "several boys who could throw the ball just as hard as anyone in the Dodger organization."[4] And, as if to prove his point, the Bombers opened the season with hurler Juan Ravelo pitching a no-hitter against their bitterest rival, the Harlan Smokies and their manager Battle "Bones" Sanders, a two-year veteran of the Pacific Coast League. Ravelo followed that performance with a shut-out of Big Stone Gap. Shortly thereafter, Danny Hayling took the mound for his debut appearance, clinching the first victory in what would become a 24–4 record. Then, on May 16, the *Herald*, in a tiny aside, announced the arrival of newly-acquired pitchers, one of whom was John Podres whose Hazard debut was a win in the second game of a double-header, the first game having been taken by Hayling. The Bomber pitching staff, with help from Brooklyn, was a stable of young warhorses, able to go the distance better than any others in the league. In a late May tilt against the Pennington Gap Miners, for instance, Vince Pankovits was forced to go to his bullpen four times while Hazard's Ed Bobrick lasted until the end. Behind the mound staff was assembled a more-than-capable defense, with the entire enterprise backed by the safety net of its heavy-hitting, relief-pitching, first base-guarding manager. It is little wonder that the historians at Minor League Baseball have ranked the Hazard Bombers as one of its top one hundred teams of all time.[5]

Early in the season, the team established a pattern that would carry them to the end, one in which they would win in streaks of several games each. At the beginning of June, they'd already won six games in a row for the third time. And the team wins weren't the only streaks that were being followed. Hayling and Podres both seemed to be trying to set records in organized baseball. By June 15, Hayling had pitched his tenth straight win, Podres his sixth.

Late June brought Hazard fans and their hometown newspaper their first major confrontation with Virgil Q. Wacks, who in a curious mix of micro-managing and laissez faire had temporarily cost the Bombers their main catcher and very nearly their beloved man-

The 1951 Hazard Bombers, off duty and in civilian attire, at Bomber Park. On the far left is Max Macon, their dazzling pilot. Third and fourth from the front left are pitching phenoms Johnny Podres and Danny Hayling (courtesy Bobby Davis Museum).

ager. It seemed that, weeks earlier, catcher Isert had been involved in a tiff with an umpire and Wacks suspended him for ten days but without notification or explanation to anyone but another umpire who, on game day, informed Macon that Isert was not allowed to play. The team was mystified as to the reason for this punishment. Macon attempted to reach Wacks by phone without success, so he sent Bomber business manager Robert Mansfield to Virginia in an attempt to resolve the problem. The *Herald* reported what it had learned about Isert's suspension and then some.

> But the dope on Isert was not all that resulted from Mansfield's flying visit to the Old Dominion state. No sir, it seems that Wacks had several things to say about Max Macon. One was to the effect that if Max had another run-in with an umpire, he would be suspended for a year. Further, said the wheel, he had been checking on Macon's record in organized baseball and that "it wasn't good."[6]

The newspaper was furious at this mysterious pronouncement from the league president, as were the fans undoubtedly, especially as Max Macon was the rocket fuel propelling the team while batting nearly .400 himself. The paper openly suggested that Wacks had it in for Macon and the Bombers. "You can well imagine Macon's reaction—he hit the ceiling. And you can't blame him—when you start running down a fellow's reputation in his profession you're jeopardizing his future and that's a serious matter."[7] Adding to the fray were threats of probation (due to Macon's use of the word "hell" when addressing an umpire), reneging on those threats, and eventual half-hearted apologies by Wacks and his nettled umpire.

The Bombers hit a dry spell in the middle of July, losing not only against the Mountain States League All-Stars but dropping two to Morristown in the presence of Fresco Thompson, Dodger vice president in charge of farm operations. But Danny Hayling was sitting at 18–0 at the end of July and his colleague Johnny Podres pitched an 18–0 shutout of the Big Stone Gap Rebels and tied a Mountain States League record by striking out seventeen Harlan Smokies. This gave him his fifteenth win to three losses. Only two other pitchers in the league could claim the same accomplishment, fellow Bomber Juan Ravelo and Bob Bowman, superstar submariner of the Middlesboro Athletics.

The town of Hazard was in love with its team. Mayor Gorman talks about the interaction between players and fans. "Max Macon—I remember him well—he was quite a ballplayer and just an all-around nice guy. Johnny was the same way. You'd go to the theater and see them there. They wandered all around and everybody accepted them real well. I never saw any arrogance in them." Sydney Francis' mother was one of the regulars at the games, having use of a box seat. She religiously kept scorebooks and could quote statistics on all the players. And, for Sydney and some of her friends, the athletes became heartthrobs. She describes her playtime as a child in the summer of 1951. "I was an only child and played with the neighborhood kids and I always had an imagination. We used to play on the side porch with our little play kitchen utensils. We'd get leaves and flowers and flour and water and pretend we were cooking dinner for our husbands. My husband was Johnny Podres. We would play act about our husbands playing baseball and we'd be fixing little treats." An unfortunate aspect of the game was the ingesting of the prepared meals. "That's one of the reasons I can't stand any green vegetables today," says Sydney with a grimace.

In a bit of power overkill, in early August, Bones Sanders, manager of the Harlan

Smokies, defected from that team only to join the Maconmen, neatly transferring his loyalties. "Sanders said last night that he considered the Bombers the best team in the league and was glad to be with the club. 'Now that I am with Hazard I will do everything possible to help win the pennant,' he said."[8] And apparently he meant it because in his first appearance in a Bomber uniform, he went 5 for 6.

On August 25, Johnny Podres pitched his twentieth victory of the season (against three defeats), joining his colleague Danny Hayling and a Morristown player as the only hurlers in the league to win that many. That game over Pennington Gap was also the pennant clincher. In addition to their glee at winning the pennant, Hazard was also celebrating the announcement from Max Smith that negotiations had been completed for the continued relationship between Hazard and the Brooklyn Dodgers. But there was sad news as well and there couldn't have been a dry eye in Hazard, from the diehards in the stands to little girls cooking imaginary dinners. His sterling season in Kentucky having been noted by the men in New York, Johnny Podres was ordered to report to Montreal for spring training.[9]

But before the grieving could begin, there were playoffs to win. The first series saw Hazard pitted against their archrivals, the Harlan Smokies. Keeping in mind the historic rivalry between the teams, it is no surprise that fists began to fly in the first game.

> According to authentic sources, Harlan manager John Streza was at bat and, after being driven back by two inside pitches, claimed the Hazard hurler was throwing at him. Streza got on first and there made derogatory racial statement with reference to the Hazard club. After the inning, Lou Isert, on his way to the third base coaching box, passed Streza and told him "you'd be afraid to make that statement in our ballpark." Heated words ensued between the two and Streza is said to have held Isert by his hair and kicked him with his knee several times before the fray was broken up. Both players were ejected from the game.[10]

The Bombers lost that game but won the next three in the series, ending the season for the Smokies. The last obstacle for the Bombers was the Morristown Red Sox. Podres pitched his twelfth straight win for a 2–1 victory. In the second game, Max Macon did what he always seemed to do best—he saved the day. The starting pitcher walked six batters, forcing in three runs; a reliever came in with the bases loaded and walked in another one. Macon took the mound to steal a 13–6 victory from opposing pitcher Rudy Parsons, who took the loss for Morristown. Game three had barely reached the second inning when the benches cleared for the second time in Hazard's post-season, creating a brawl that had to be broken up by the local police and delaying the game by an hour. Predictably, Max Macon was ejected from the game, but it did carry on, with Danny Hayling recording his twenty-fourth win. The brilliant play and management of Macon plus the firepower of the Brooklyn Dodgers and a dash of raw coalfield talent had paid off. The Hazard Bombers were the 1951 champions of the league.

When the official stats came out, Max Macon had dropped to third in the league in batting at .409. If there were the slightest bitter taste in his mouth at placing third, Macon could at least take comfort in the fact that he also led in runs (139), doubles (54) and RBIs (148). Johnny Podres led the league in pitching with twenty-one victories and three defeats. He struck out 228 batters and walked only 35. Danny Hayling won twenty-four and lost four; he completed the most games in the league (24) and worked the most innings (236). The Hazard Bombers had won an astonishing 93 victories to 33 losses.

Everyone knows what became of Johnny Podres after 1951; his name is still whispered with reverence in Brooklyn. His shutout in the seventh game of the 1955 World Series sealed the only championship for the New York incarnation of the Dodgers. But two years before that legendary performance, in September of 1953, 150 residents of Hazard proved their enduring loyalty to Podres by trekking to Cincinnati to see him pitch (he was removed in the first inning by an injury).[11]

Danny Hayling stayed with the Dodger organization for a few years. His winters were spent playing in warmer climes, with the Mexican and Nicaraguan leagues, and eventually he played exclusively for them.

At the end of the 1951 season, a reporter from the local newspaper asked Max Macon what his plans were for the next year. "'I want to play about a hundred games somewhere and hit around .400,' he said. We don't have anything to say in the matter but, if we did, the place would be Hazard."[12] But that was not to be. Macon was bumped up to the Miami Sun Sox of the Class B Florida International League, which he led to the championship in 1952. Like his Hazard Bombers, Macon's Sun Sox have achieved ranking in Minor League Baseball's top one hundred teams; they sit in the number forty spot.[13] Macon used the same innate skill with which he'd molded the Bombers and turned the team a defensive juggernaut, although it remained weak offensively. (Interestingly, one of his catchers was Cecil Dotson from Clintwood, Virginia, who played for that team in the Lonesome Pine League in 1948. In 1951, playing for Douglas-Bisbee, he set a minor league record by hitting for the cycle and driving in five runs in the same game.) For Macon, an uneasy relationship with the Miami owner (finding hidden microphones in the dugout was hardly helpful) compelled him to leave after one season and he spent most of his remaining career in the farm systems of the Dodgers and the Detroit Tigers.

As for the Bombers, they validated Hazard's faith in them by winning the pennant again in 1952 but were forced to fold the next spring because of debt. The equipment and uniforms were sent for storage to Brooklyn where, by now, they have long since turned to dust. Only the batboy's woolen uniform and a few photos are left in Hazard, enshrined in glass at the Bobby Davis Museum.

The wonder is that a team this significant ever existed in a place as isolated and hard to reach as Hazard. As Mayor Gorman says, "It was quite an experience. There wasn't much difference in sitting watching the Hazard Bombers and seeing the Cincinnati Reds except a whole lot more people. The Bombers were hero-type people. They were superstars in a small town."

CHAPTER 12

The Choices We Live With

God, if you had but the moon,
Stuck in Your cap for a lamp—
Even You'd tire of it soon,
Down in the dark and the damp.
Nothing but blackness above,
And nothing that moves but the cars,
God, if You wish for our love,
Fling us a handful of stars.

—Anonymous[1]

Southern Appalachia has its share of historic battlefields that are not designated as such by the government. These sites were part of the large, unofficially-declared war between union organizers and coal companies. The battles, and the men that fought them, are probably unfamiliar to people from the outside but they are the stuff of ballad to the locals. Their names ring in the collective memory. In Matewan, West Virginia, in 1920, legendary sheriff Sid Hatfield defied Baldwin-Felts agents who'd come to the camp to evict mining families from their homes for speaking of the union. A deadly shootout ensued, with men killed on both sides, followed by the eventual assassination of Hatfield by agents of the same agency. In 1921, at Blair Mountain, an army of miners, numbering as high as ten thousand in some estimates, marched into the southern West Virginia coalfields and took positions atop the two thousand-foot peak. Their enemy was a three thousand-strong militia of company-paid men and eager volunteers who smelled the menace of Bolshevism in the union. What that company army lacked in manpower, it made up for in weapons, including private planes employed to drop homemade bleach and shrapnel bombs on the miners. The arrival of federal troops brought about the surrender of the miners who refused to fire on American soldiers. In Harlan County, Kentucky, in 1931, the firings and evictions of unionizing miners resulted in the deaths of three miners and the arrest of many others, including the UMW president. And in 1941, in the town of Crummies, also in Harlan County, a company man set a machine gun on the meat counter of the commissary and killed four picketing miners when they entered to buy a soft drink. Five more were officially reported as injured.

In the long and complex history of the United Mine Workers of America, Harlan County, Kentucky, stands out. Not only did it suffer so much violence as to gain the nickname "Bloody Harlan," but it was the last coal mining county in the United States to unionize.[2] Even after the union wars had ended, tension between union and non-union miners still existed and was exemplified by two towns, sitting side by side at the foot of Kentucky's tallest mountain.

In the first twenty years of the twentieth century, two titans of industry set their sights on the rich bituminous coal deposits in isolated Harlan County, Kentucky. At the base of Black Mountain, Benham and Lynch were established by these companies. So close as to be virtually the same town, historically they have been light years apart in their philosophies of labor. Lynch was a UMWA town by the early 1940s but Benham remained the only company mine, out of 147 in Harlan County, never to join the union. For years, because of these differences, each would regard the other with, at best, suspicion and, in the worst cases, outright hostility and violence. But this is not a story of two warring towns; it is more a tale of how lives were shaped by battles and votes. The protagonists just happened to be baseball players.

Benham, whose population sits today at around six hundred, is the older town by roughly ten years and was built by International Harvester around 1910 to supply coke for its steel mills. Twenty years later the town had a population of forty-five hundred. It was as cosmopolitan a town as any in the coalfields, a mix of mountaineers, European immigrants, and African Americans newly-arrived from the sharecropping south. And, like every other Appalachian coal town, Benham reveled in the boom years and suffered through the busts until International Harvester finally sold its interests in the mid–1970s. Now, after years of decline, the town has proudly managed to secure a spot on the National Register of Historic Places. The Kentucky Coal Museum, located in the heart of Benham, is a fascinating journey into the lives of mining families. Housed in the former company store, it is packed with displays and memorabilia, yet the cavernous air of the structure keeps the visitor from feeling restricted. Benham, particularly its museum, is well worth a visit in the warmer seasons; however, like most coal towns, in winter the mountains cast a pall over the entire area.

A stone's throw down the road is Lynch, the model town begun by U. S. Steel a few years after Benham was established by International Harvester. Lynch is home to about nine hundred people, having once boasted ten thousand. It was one of the coalfields' best examples of welfare capitalism or contentment sociology at work. The houses were sturdier and more modern than those of most camps and included amenities like indoor plumbing. They were designed by architects and delivered in kit form. Several different models and varied exterior colors assured a break from monotony. A modern bathhouse was built for the miners and, in a coal town rarity, there were paved streets and sidewalks. Beautifully-wrought stone buildings show the artistry of the early Italian masons. And the mines at Lynch were models of safety in their day, ventilated and electrically illuminated throughout. One cannot visit Benham without visiting Lynch, although the same midwinter warning applies. The watery high-noon sunshine of the cold months cannot keep a pervasive gloom from settling on everything, from the sturdy buildings to the sculpture garden of rusted mining machinery that sits outside the fenced-off portals. The town plans to turn its Portal 31 into a tourist attraction, allowing visitors to experience for themselves the darkness and confines of a mile underground.

Today, little evidence remains of the ill will once felt between the towns. But Carl Shoupe, who was born in Lynch but now lives in Benham, tells a tale of Saturday night meetings at the Masonic Lodge in the not-too-distant past. The Benham Masons would sit on one side of the room, the Lynch Masons on the other, neither one addressing the other. Carl is uniquely qualified to talk about Benham and Lynch and the mine wars that separated them. His father, Buck Shoupe, who could have been the subject of a Woody Guthrie song, was an early union organizer in Harlan County. Born near Evarts in 1911, Buck Shoupe grew up in the coal camp of Highsplint where his father was a miner. Buck used to joke that he'd been thrown out of the fourth grade for having to shave so much. As tall a tale as that might have been, he did start working underground early in life. He may have spent his very early years cleaning coal (picking out the slate) but before mechanization, he also handled the mules that pulled the cars. Carl remembers his father describing those pitiful animals that were born underground and never saw daylight until they were retired (it is said that mining animals, when finally released into the sunlight for the first time, would prance and gambol the last of their days away). Later in life, Buck became a roof bolter, a position he kept until retirement. "He was one of the old miners, from the pick-and-shovel-type mining. He was reluctant to get on the big machines," says Carl. Carl is the first one to admit that there's a lot he doesn't know about his dad. He does know that at one time his father was known as "the meanest man in Harlan County." But his history is hard to pin down and with good reason. Buck Shoupe was a man who had to live life along a shadowy edge, for his own safety and that of his family and other union organizers. Carl's mother told him that, in Buck's early days of activism, he would leave his home for extended periods of time to preach the UMWA gospel throughout the coal fields, frequently under an alias. Arrested at the battle of Evarts, he was tried, convicted and served time on a charge of "banding and confederating."

There's a lot that Carl doesn't know about his father's days as a baseball player either. He does know that Buck was a catcher and played for, among others, the Highsplint camp team, whose games took place in a cow pasture. Bordering that pasture was the ubiquitous mountain creek into which flew many a ball, inevitably becoming a heavy, dripping mass to be fired back to the infield. Buck Shoupe talked a lot about ringers brought in by the company and the high stakes gambling going on in the stands. What Buck didn't talk about very often, or at any length, was the event that ended his baseball days; in the conflict at Crummies in 1941, he was one of the picketing union men who were shot in the company store. He retreated before the authorities arrived, heading toward sanctuary with a bullet in his left hand. After recovering from the wound, he went to Lynch, at about the same time that the workers there were voting out the company union that had long been in power, and saying yes to the UMWA (Carl insists that the accepted date of 1937 for the unionization of Lynch is inaccurate, that it was actually in the early '40s). Buck was immediately hired and, interestingly enough, by a company man with whom he'd tangled on many past occasions.

For a man who spent the first half of his life fighting, Lynch was a good place to land. Many companies, having seen the union voted in, reacted in anger. Howard Sparks of Van Lear, Kentucky, says, "When the unions came in, the coal camp said, 'We took care of you all these years, now you can just take care of yourselves.'" By contrast, the relationship forged between U. S. Steel and the UMWA was a healthy one that lasted until the company's final days in the area. Carl attributes this to a sensible bottom line that the company understood: when the union is in, the miners feel safe and comfortable, which leads to increased productivity.

It is often assumed that unionization of the mines spelled an end to the glory days of coalfield baseball. It is true that a man hired for his playing abilities would not gain seniority because of them, making him the first casualty in a layoff. But Carl Shoupe says, "Even when the union came, it was a lot easier to get a job if you could play ball." He mentions "sweetheart contracts," suggesting that the unions might have turned a blind eye to the hiring of men because of their playing talents.

Although Buck Shoupe was never able to play baseball again, he coached his son's team. Watching his father coach, Carl saw some of what had given Buck the reputation for meanness. "My friends and I still laugh about it. I'm not going to lie to you—it embarrassed me to death. I'm just a kid twelve or thirteen years old. My father and this other coach got into it. My dad was a pretty big man—about six foot, two inches, probably two hundred twenty pounds—and this other coach wasn't the biggest guy in the world. This little guy reached up and got Dad by the shirt collar. Dad took his left hand and he hit that guy smack in the face. That guy went down but he didn't turn loose of Dad's shirt—just ripped it as he went down."

Buck's toughness later saved his son's life. After a tour of duty in Vietnam as a Marine, Carl came home to Lynch to work in the mines as a roof bolter like his father. After less than a year of working underground, he was caught in a roof fall and pinned under a rock the size of a pool table. In addition to his massive injuries, after three months in the hospital, he contracted a deadly staph infection. When Buck questioned the quality of care Carl was receiving and requested that he be transferred to another hospital, the doctors refused to release him. "I was literally laying there dying. I believe that hospital would have let me die if not for my father and father-in-law." Buck informed U.S. Steel of his son's condition and the company immediately located a better hospital elsewhere. With an ambulance borrowed from the local funeral home, Buck Shoupe went to work. "My dad had kind of calmed down in his later years and my father-in-law was a primitive Baptist preacher, but they were both old mountain men and pretty well meant what they said. The hospital wasn't going to let me leave. This is the truth: my father had a pistol in his pocket. He didn't pull it out or nothing, he just showed it to the people and said, 'I'm getting that son of mine and I'm gonna take him out of this hospital. You get all the security guards you wanna call, but this boy is leaving.'"

Carl spent an additional year in hospitals and now his injuries are evident only in the gingerly way he carries himself or shifts his weight in a chair. He worked for the UMWA for years, a devoted employee of the union that had seen him and his father through some dark times. These days, however, there are no UMWA mines in eastern Kentucky. So now, like his father before him, Carl is engaged in a war with big coal but on a different front. He is one of the many people fighting to keep the Appalachians from being destroyed by strip mining and mountaintop removal. He speaks emphatically about his crusade: "You gotta stand for something on this earth, dadgonnit. I look back to when I was raising my family and I was too busy running that engine, trying to keep my kids in Nikes. But I could kick myself 'cause I've got grandchildren." He shakes his head as he ponders the devastated landscape that those children will inherit. "It's total destruction. It's a disaster." Despite that, this battle is one that Carl approaches with energy and superhuman optimism. "I've got a lot to be thankful for. I went through Vietnam, and made it through that mountain falling on me. God's got something else for me to do here. I love every day that I wake up."

Just as he loves the mountains, he still loves his hometown, which he refers to, along with Benham, as a "Cadillac coal camp." "The good thing about growing up in a coal camp like Lynch was that the company people, the upper echelon people, were from Pittsburgh and wanted their children to have the best, so us working class people got to take advantage of that. You can't tell by me, of course, but they had some of the finest teachers, the finest doctors, the finest food that money could buy." And for children, the mountains surrounding the camp were a paradise. "Man, we were going around here, wading in the little streams, swinging on grapevines, digging ginseng—it was such a great childhood."

As for Buck Shoupe, he stayed with U. S. Steel for the rest of his professional life. "He was blessed. Most miners retire and don't live very long but he lived for eighteen years." On a personal note, he adds, "He was one of the most intelligent men I ever knew. And he was a trooper, I'm telling you. I think that's why I joined the Marine Corps. I wanted to be mean like my dad."

As Lynch voted the UMWA in, their neighbors in Benham decided against it, remaining loyal to the company-sanctioned Progressive Mine Workers of America, a renegade of the UMWA that never effectively protected their workers. Carl Shoupe describes the tactics used by the PMWA in collaboration with the coal companies, saying that, when a raise was negotiated for the UMWA, the PMWA leaders stepped forward to loudly declare an even larger increase for their workers, but rarely made good on the promise. "You can talk a good game," he says, "and put numbers up in front of people but if it's not in writing then it don't mean nothing. The company gave them whatever the company wanted to give them."

Proving that neither side was innocent in the union wars, in May 1941, two days after Benham voted to keep the PMWA, violence erupted in Benham when pro–UMWA snipers fired at miners who were leaving their shifts. "Those were dangerous times," says Gean Austin, who worked for U.S. Steel at Lynch. While he disagreed with their judgment, he believes he understands why the Benham workers voted against the UMWA. "They were scared because International Harvester had put the fear in them that they would lose their jobs—that something might happen to them." Don Griffey, who worked at Benham, and has many reasons to regret the anti–UMWA choice there, agrees: "Some of them probably couldn't read and write. And then they'd have their families so they'd be stuck there. Whatever they [the company] would tell them to do, or how, that's what they'd do."

Griffey was hired in 1940 because he was a talented left-handed pitcher and Benham had enjoyed a reputation for its great African American ball clubs dating back to the teens. Don was born in Gatliff, Kentucky, his father died young and Don was schooled in the art

The 1948 Benham Harvester Sluggers. *Back row, left to right (staggered):* **Don Griffey, Melvin Bledsoe, Arthur Williams, R.D. Hester, Ralph Tedford, Wolford Griffey, Frank Allen, Willie Watts.** *Front row:* **Leonard Henderson, Henry Rodgers, Benny Evans, Robert Burrell. In what was apparently a little mugging for the camera, brothers Don and Wolford Griffey had agreed to stick out their tongues (courtesy Coal Mines Benham Magazine).**

of baseball by some of the men at Packard, a nearby camp—a couple of them had spent time in the Negro Leagues. "Some of the people that helped teach me how to play played with some of them. There wasn't enough black people in Gatliff or Packard to make a team so we used to walk the four miles to Packard to practice and play." The former ball players saw promise in the young left-hander and urged him to practice throwing rocks at a can placed sixty feet away. "They said, 'When you come back over here, we want you to be able to hit that can.' I would do that and that way, I got pretty good control," he explains. His control was admired enough for him to be hired at Benham and, on his recommendation, two of his brothers were hired as well. His brother Wolford was a right-handed pitcher and Robert was a shortstop. They were both fine players but Don stresses Robert's versatility. "My brother? He could play any part of the field he wanted to. If we hadn't been born too soon, we probably could have gotten in the big leagues."

As players with the Benham Harvester Sluggers, the Griffey brothers also came up against some of the best African American teams from the area, particularly those from the southern West Virginia coalfields. "When the West Virginia players would come, they'd put me in there pitching. You had to be good because some of them would knock the daylights out of that ball," Griffey remembers. "They were all good. They'd go to the coal mines around there and get the best players from each team and bring them into Kentucky. That way, we'd go up against some good players and, fortunately, we got to where we could beat 'em." Indeed, the Sluggers were fairly frequent visitors to ball fields throughout West Virginia, including Clipper Field in Raleigh. They also played barnstorming teams, including the Birmingham Black Barons, the Detroit Stars and the Kansas City Monarchs, among others. But some of their fiercest sporting encounters were with their natural rivals at Lynch.

Don's sister-in-law, his brother Wolford's widow, Lacey, remembers those days well, especially the combustible mix of the Benham Harvester Sluggers and the Lynch Grays. "When we played, we had to be protected from Lynch because, if they lost, they'd beat us up. We'd have to leave the before the game was over if we were winning." Pausing for a moment, she meaningfully adds, "They were an entirely different kind of people from us. I think we were a lot nicer." Gean Austin, who is from Lynch, agrees that the two towns tangled violently in all sports but sees things somewhat differently than Lacey Griffey does. "Benham," he explains, attempting to be tactful, "was often very rough." Whichever team was the rougher, Don Griffey says that the games had to be monitored by the company police to keep the peace. He sums up the animosity in a phrase that aptly describes both sides, saying, "If you're in the UMWA, you're in the category. If you're not, you're an enemy of the UMWA."

Don and Wolford Griffey worked for International Harvester their entire lives. Wolford, in fact, was that company's first black mine foreman, getting promoted to that position in the 1970s. Wolford, now deceased, cannot comment, but Don says that the black employee felt the disadvantages of a non-union company more profoundly than a white employee did. Since its inception in 1890, the UMWA had wisely understood that "divided" meant "conquered." The large African American presence in the mines was an essential element to the success of the organization, but anti-union companies often employed racial scare tactics. "Operators exploited the bigotry of white miners by claiming that democratic tendencies of unions threatened the racial balance of the workforce."[3] When an African American employed by U. S. Steel suffered workplace harassment or other injustices, he could go to the union for redress, but it would have been futile, and even dangerous, for Don Griffey to report his experiences in the mines to the PMWA authority at Benham. Besides the taunting that he continuously endured, one of the most costly examples of racism involved the metal tag, or "check," used by coal loaders like Griffey to identify the cars they had loaded. A strong loader, Don could fill many cars per shift, and because he was paid by the weight of the car, he should have done well. But for a few years, he was the victim of tag switching; a white employee, whose cars were meagerly filled, put his tag on Don's filled cars. "That was breaking my heart but I couldn't do nothing about it. I couldn't leave. You got a family and you had to look out for them and that had me tied down. For about four or five years they robbed me blind but I had to stay there." Despite years of this type of unfair treatment, Griffey was not bowed. "I never did believe in getting down and letting somebody pat me on the head," he says. "I always tried to stand up and be my own man. I had two boys and I didn't want them to go through what I had to go through."

The inequality shown to black miners in a non-union company could show up in the ballpark as well. "U.S. Steel reserved aboveground, 'outside' work to recruit baseball players for the white Lynch Bulldogs, later named the Lynch Steelers, and for the African American Lynch Grays."[4] Gean Austin concurs, stressing that the black ringers at Lynch always had a choice of where they wanted to work. When asked about ballplayer job options for African Americans at Benham, Don Griffey replies, "No. All the black folks' jobs was under the mountain." As they have entered old age, the Benham miners have suffered a final blow. Don Griffey retired from loading coal at age 75, when his health benefits were discontinued.

As for choices that he's made, Don Griffey looks back on one with particular wistfulness: he turned down an offer to play baseball for the Bishop State Liners. "Well, if I had it to do all over again, I think I would have gone to Bishop. They told me once, 'If you don't find a job here, you can just walk around. Just walk around the mines.' But you know, I had three sisters and my mother and my baby brother back home and I was sending my earnings to them. If I quit my job, that would have put them in hardship so I stayed."

There is no more labor strife in Benham and Lynch, just common small-town struggles. Like all little communities in America, survival in the twenty-first century is a huge endeavor. It takes a valiant effort to keep their remarkable histories alive, but they are trying. The days of bullets and ballots are in the past. Now, in the shadow of Black Mountain, all is quiet.

Chapter 13

Bob Bowman

Middlesboro, Kentucky, is a lively little city on the west side of the Cumberland Gap; its broad thoroughfares lined with buildings and structures done in the Victorian style are testimonials to what once was—or almost was. In 1886, a young Scotsman named Alexander Arthur first saw the valley in which Middlesboro now sits and had visions of a steel town along the lines of Birmingham, Alabama, only much more prosperous, and infinitely more English. With the financial backing of some of the biggest moneymen in the United States and England, he began work on his city the minute he'd snapped up thousands of acres in Kentucky, Virginia and Tennessee. The area had everything, all the resources—iron, lumber, coal—that an enterprising man could exploit. The fact that he would need to dig a tunnel through a mountain and build a 65-mile rail line from Knoxville to transport those resources was no obstacle to this intrepid young entrepreneur. Arthur was a brilliant salesman. Trips to the east and to England allowed him to work his magic on every listener, and soon hordes of people from all walks of life were beating a path to what was now called Middlesborough (the original spelling). Everyone was eager to be a part of the boom.

And what a boom it was. From every class and every part of the world people came. While laborers sunk mines and built sawmills and furnaces, physicians, lawyers and mercantilists hung up their signs. Awed mountaineers descended from the surrounding hills to find British dandies strolling the muddy streets, having arrived from across the pond in search of the great American adventure. So many people came and threw themselves with such passion into the building of the sparkling city that very few people, including Alexander Arthur himself, dedicated themselves to the economic infrastructure that was supposed to maintain them all. Instead, most of the energy went into golf courses, spas and luxury hotels.

In 1890, the first clouds began to darken the horizon. In May, a massive fire destroyed a good portion of the town. A bank failure in England combined with a depression in the United States stalled any further development in Middlesborough. Then, after closer inspection, it was determined that the iron deposits upon which Arthur had gambled everything were of only middling quality and there was not as much of it as formerly believed.[1] By 1895, the dream had died and all that was left of Middlesborough was the architectural proof that the dream had ever existed. "But the English imprint remained in the imposing walls, towers, turrets, arches, and architraves."[2]

Today, Middlesboro (the modern spelling) has a population of about ten thousand. Most of the surrounding coal camps that operated through the twentieth century are gone because, in a second irony that Arthur probably didn't expect, the quality of the local coal was also mediocre. Middlesboro's biggest claim to fame is its location at the Cumberland Gap and the massive modern tunnel that connects the states of Kentucky, Tennessee, and Virginia. It was built in the 1990s to replace a twisting 2.3-mile stretch of road, infamous as one of the nation's most dangerous drives and aptly referred to as "Massacre Mountain."

There was baseball in Middlesboro by the 1890s and the city had a team in the original 1911 to 1914 Appalachian League, along with sundry local leagues throughout the years. The Middlesboro Athletics enjoyed enough success to compete in the 1946 National Amateur World Series and to join the Mountain States League in 1949. But for the better part of the twentieth century, the dominant team in the little city was an African American one, the Blue Sox, originally organized in the 1920s.[3] They garnered a surprising amount of attention in the sports pages of the *Middlesboro Daily News,* even if it was limited to short announcements of upcoming games and the occasional scanty report on one already played (there were no box scores provided for those). Those frequent yet brief notices are valuable today because, as they list the Blue Sox' opponents (such as the Jellico Alley Cats or the Bonny Blue Tigers) they give clues to the numbers of the African American coal camp teams of the region. As early as 1932, the Blue Sox began playing exhibition games against white teams from the local camps and often hosted tilts with teams from outside the area. In addition to playing locally, at least before the Depression hit, they barnstormed fairly extensively. In an interview for the Bell County Historical Society, former player Eugene "Snooks" Sprigs was asked about the team. He says, "I don't know how the Blue Sox started. But I hear tell they used to be a big thing, went on trips for a month or two at a time, went into Alabama, West Virginia, Tennessee. They played teams, they beat teams from Birmingham and Charleston and Chattanooga. But by the time I started playing, times was hard. Couldn't make a living like that. We all had to have regular jobs and just play on the weekend." Sprigs went on to explain the distribution of gate receipts (60–40, winners-losers) and modes of transportation. "When we went out of town to play, we usually went in an open truck with benches in the back. Seems like we had some kind of heater back there for cold nights."[4] He said that the crowds drawn by the Blue Sox were large and comprised both whites and blacks. In the same article, James Hodge discussed his tenure with the Sox. "I was the youngest member of the team when I started. I was still in high school back then; they had an afternoon study hour and I would sneak out. The Blue Sox' truck would drive past the school and I'd just hop aboard." Of all the teams that the team played, Hodge's clearest and fondest memories were of the Ethiopian Clowns. "Well, when they came here, they were without one member for some reason. Anyway, I played on their team. Well, of course, we beat the Blue Sox. And they asked me to stay with them. I played with the Ethiopian Clowns for one season. We played all the small towns. We put on a show!" Hodge goes further to explain why they enjoyed a mixed-race fan base by pointing out that, during the time he played for the Blue Sox, there was not a white team in Middlesboro.[5]

The Blue Sox might have been lost to history like many of the other black coal town teams had it not been for one man who, very early on, caught the attention not only of the fans but of local sportswriters. First mentioned in the *Daily News* in 1930, Bob Bowman would rivet the locals, both black and white, for another 25 years and, in a very quiet way, would make history.

In a short article in July of 1930, it was reported that the Blue Sox had lost to Jenkins, Bob Bowman having pitched his second day in a row.[6] At that point, he was 24 years old, a big right-hander at six feet, two inches tall. He was born across the Gap in Lee County, Virginia, and his father moved the family to Middlesboro when Bowman was a small child. And, like any child, Bowman liked to skip rocks but apparently did it obsessively enough to become one of the finest submarine hurlers of his time. Along with the vicious sidearm delivery, he had an unusual grip, according to his nephew George Ferguson. Ferguson claims that Bowman held his index finger over his third. When asked about this grip, veteran pitcher Dave Hillman said he'd never heard of such but that it might well help with spin and a dramatic sinker effect, causing the ball to break down and in to a right-handed hitter or down and away to a lefty.

Bowman apparently galvanized the Blue Sox and by age thirty was player-manager. But before the 1937 season could get underway, the business manager of the team arranged a game with the Ethiopian Clowns. For the next three years, there is no mention of Bob Bowman in the *Daily News*. Future references, however, suggest that, like his teammate James Hodge, he might have been traveling with the famous barnstormers at that time. A bit in early June 1940 announced that he was at home after an unspecified amount of time with the Clowns and that he was to pitch a game for the Blue Sox. He is not mentioned again that season as being on the Blue Sox' roster.

Unfortunately, there is no memory within the Middlesboro community or Bowman's family about the period in which he might have been with the Ethiopian Clowns, or even how many years it might have lasted. But it is tempting to think that he was with the barnstorming team during a few seminal seasons. The years of the early '40s saw the Ethiopian Clowns at their peak. Alan Pollock, whose father Syd was the team owner, wrote, "The 1940 Clowns had an overwhelmingly winning record, as they did in 1941 and 1942. And they beat good teams, including a large percentage of wins against Negro Leagues opposition. The Clowns never again had a pitching staff equal to the 1940 mound corps."[7]

But fielding a team like the Clowns meant double the hardship faced by other professional managers or owners. Pollock described one of the main difficulties faced by his father: "The nature of the Clowns created a problem other clubs didn't face—entertainers. Good baseball entertainers were not quite as hard to find as practicing Druid brain surgeons or retired ace kamikaze pilots. Many players wouldn't do comedy, even for pay. Others would, but lacked the style or timing to do it successfully."[8] Bowman had the talent to pitch for the Clowns, but descriptions of him from the people who knew him best paint a picture of a man perhaps temperamentally unsuited to the job. "My dad was a very quiet man—didn't smoke, didn't drink, didn't cuss," says Patricia Bowman Edwards. Eddie Ballinger, who grew up as a Blue Sox batboy and was later coached by Bowman, says of his mentor, "He was a no-nonsense person—didn't take no foolishness from anybody." A truly gifted pitcher he was, a comic performer he was not, which may explain why his tenure with the Clowns is vague. He certainly was not a personality to compete with the comic genius of Spec Bebop or King Tut. But he did absorb a bit of Clown showmanship and at least one classic barnstorming move. Nephew George Ferguson, among others, well remembers that, when playing with the Blue Sox, in the final inning, Bowman would either send his infield and outfield to the dugout or simply order them to sit down at their positions. Left alone on the field (or virtually so) with just a catcher to assist, he would neatly dispatch an inning's worth of batters. Ferguson recalls another trick frequently performed by Bowman; he would purposefully walk three batters to load the bases, and then whiff the fourth.

In 1945, the Negro Southern League was formed and a North Carolina franchise, the Asheville Blues, was organized by C.L. Moore, a veteran of semipro play. Again, exact dates are missing but Bob Bowman played for the Blues for at least one season, probably more. His daughter, Patricia Bowman Edwards, has his contract of 1948, signing him from March 17 until September 1 at a monthly salary of $275. As might be expected, there was little attention given Negro League teams in contemporary mainstream newspapers. But in 1946, an African American newspaper in New York reported a game between its home team and the Asheville Blues in which they list the Blues pitcher as Bill Bowman, who managed to strike out twelve.[9] Back in Kentucky, a 1948 *Middlesboro Daily News* article announcing that Bowman might be back to pitch a game for the Blue Sox refers to him as having pitched for Asheville for "several years"[10] and an article in 1950 says that he played with them until that year.[11]

While the records of Bowman's career with the Blues may be sketchy, the mark he left is indelible, at least to a few who found themselves the victims of his brutal delivery. Author Brent P. Kelley found two former Negro Leaguers who had very clear memories of the submariner. When asked about great pitchers, Merle Porter (of the Kansas City Monarchs, to name but one of the many teams he played for) gave this response: "The best pitcher I faced, the guy that gave me the most trouble—his name was Bowman. I couldn't hit him for nothing. He played with the Asheville Blues in the [Negro] Southern League. They were a good team. He was a good pitcher."[12] When Kelley asked the same question of former Birmingham Black Baron Jim Zapp, the response was even more dramatic. He said, "I didn't see Satchel but a few times in 1951; he was with the American Giants then and he'd only pitch the first 3 innings each night. He was great, but I'm thinking in the Negro Leagues, Sam Jones, and we had another boy, I think he played for Asheville, and he never did play in the Negro Leagues, by the name of Bob Bowman. He came from the side with everything—hard from the side like Ewell Blackwell. I think he and Sam Jones were the hardest pitchers I ever faced."[13]

While Bowman was hurling for the Asheville Blues, back in Middlesboro, the white Athletics had been reorganized, this time to join the Class D Mountain States League in 1949. That year they finished third in the league and in 1950 finished fourth. They closed that season with an exhibition game against the Blue Sox. A small article, in length and in typeface, announced the game, obviously considered something of a dénouement to the professional season. Bob Bowman would take the mound for the Sox, it was reported, having recently returned from Asheville "where he annually hung up a brilliant record."[14] The next morning's edition, however, featured the screeching banner headline "Bowman Whiffs 15 A's But Loses One Hitter 3–1."[15] Suddenly, the hometown boy who'd been laboring away every summer for twenty years was the talk of the town. The amazement felt by Middlesboro is almost palpable in the words of the press. Julian Pitzer, the sports editor at the *News*, described the event in his column: "Several times during the game, Bowman got two strikes on a batter.... And right away Bowman would come up with his submarine delivery that had the Athletics fanning the breeze. It was very seldom that the A's even fouled off the underhand delivery of Bowman."[16]

The game had apparently given food for thought. Pitzer went on, in the same column, to suggest that entering a local team in the Negro Southern League might be the very thing to keep the park busy throughout the entire summer. And it seems that Bowman's performance might have inspired a new brand of thinking among local baseball officials as well.

It was the spring of 1951 and, as the Blue Sox optimistically planned an organizational meeting for the upcoming season, the management of the Athletics was beating the bushes for able players. Julian Pitzer bemoaned the lack of dependable pitching in an early April column and guessed that the Athletics would, once again, fall far behind the Brooklyn-backed Hazard Bombers and Max Macon. Then, on May 7, he dropped the following bomb on the reading public.

> For a number of years, Middlesboro baseball fans—white and colored alike—saw Bob Bowman pitch win after win for the Middlesboro Blue Sox. Many has been the time a fan has wondered just how Bowman would fare in white professional baseball. Now the answer may be in the making, although it must be remembered that Bob is past his prime as a pitcher. It is our belief that Bowman can win a number of games for the Athletics. He should be especially effective as a relief hurler with his submarine pitch to throw at the batter. Members of the A's can vouch for the difficulty in connecting solidly with Bowman's slants. We believe the other teams in the Mountain States will have just as much trouble with their bats when Bowman takes the mound. It may be a tough road that Bowman has to follow. But other of his fellows have been able to make the grade. It will be that he just happens to be the first in the Mountain States. Some fans may be prone to disagree with the idea that Bowman can win for the A's. Only a few pitched ballgames can definitely determine that and judgment should not be passed until a fair trial has been given the local pitcher.[17]

The next day, May 8, 1951, it was announced (with an accompanying photograph) that Bob Bowman had signed with the Middlesboro Athletics on the previous Sunday, just two hours before he took the field as an eighth-inning reliever against Big Stone Gap. The A's took the game 10–8. In the same edition of the *News*, on a different page, Mountain States president Virgil Q. Wacks gave Bowman a tepid blessing and said, "I know this is the first Negro player signed in organized baseball below the Mason-Dixon line ... as I checked this last year when Pennington planned to sign a Negro."[18] He went on to question the reaction of other clubs in the circuit. And the event was set in stone a week later when a headline from the *Sporting News* announced that the first Negro to join organized baseball in Dixie had made his debut.[19]

And how did his hometown react to this historic event? Pretty enthusiastically, if attendance is any barometer. The gate receipts for Bowman's first home game were roughly triple what they had been in the 1950 season. "Naturally it was a partisan crowd and Bowman got a nice round of applause every time he struck out a batter, and each time he strode to the plate for his turn at bat."[20] Even though the A's lost that tilt to Harlan, Bowman struck out twelve men. But a couple of weaknesses became evident to the crowd. One was an inability to hold runners at first, an issue that could be easily corrected, at least in Pitzer's belief. The second was far more threatening: he seemed to tire easily. What the world probably didn't understand was that, when the A's made history in signing the first black man to organized baseball in the South, they might have been signing the oldest rookie ever. In 1951, Bob Bowman was 45 years old.

But he was still the greatest pitcher eastern Kentucky had ever seen and the town was smitten with him. He began to be referred to affectionately as "Big Bob." His first victory on May 16 was an eight-and-two-thirds-inning shutout of the Morristown Red Sox. And at the end of his first month in organized baseball, Bob Bowman and the Athletics had people scrambling for the record books after a 27–1 victory over the Norton Braves, to the everlasting chagrin of their skipper, the other Bob Bowman. But Bowman wasn't always a superman and the A's lost to Hazard (with Max Macon on the mound for a couple of innings) at the beginning of June, putting them in fourth place. But they recovered the next week when Bowman struck out a pinch-hitting Johnny Podres in two games. A July 10 victory over Norton notched Bowman's third win in four days. More and more often, usually after another pitcher had lost a game, Bowman was featured in a reaffirming headline or sub-headline as being slated for duty the next game. At the end of that month, Middlesboro was still in fourth place in the league but the fans' honeymoon with Bob Bowman showed no signs of ending as he continued to throw consistently well; by July 28, he had struck out 111 batters in 122 innings.[21] An early August 15–0 shutout of the still-unfortunate Norton Braves led the *Daily News* to surmise that he might be leading the league in strikeouts.

In a rather interesting twist later in August, Bowman was slated to become one side of a pitching duel that was touted as making Mountain States history. Vince Pankovits, manager of the Pennington Gap Miners, scheduled a black pitcher by the name of Dick Mims (some papers reported the name as Minns) to take mound duty against Bowman. The scuttlebutt was that Mims was a former Homestead Gray[22], now with the Lynch Grays of Kentucky, and, if so, was a force to be reckoned with. Whether there was a contract involved or not, he had recently pitched the Pennington club to a couple of victories. Julian Pitzer thought it promised to be a good game, if only for one interesting Satchel Paige–like aspect, writing, "No one seems to know just how old Mims actually is. Some say that he is around 50. Others contend that 55 or 58 would be much closer to the facts. But all agree that he has seen a number of winters and springs. Anyway, the duel this evening should prove to be an outstanding one all the way."[23]

For all the fans who were expecting a dramatic contest between the two titans, it was a disappointment, for neither man fared well. Bob Bowman gave up five runs on three hits and was gone by the top of the third. Mims fell victim to the A's five runs on ten hits and was pulled in the fifth. While certainly not Bowman's first loss, it was an oddly flustered performance for him. But he soon recovered his bearings and several days later handed Mims and Pennington a 12–6 loss.

September 4 was a playoff game and Middlesboro's last of the 1951 season. It was also

Bob Bowman's final professional game. The Morristown Red Sox eliminated the Athletics in that last game of the series by a score of 3–0 in thirteen innings.

> There are few words to give an accurate description of probably the greatest game ever played in Middlesboro. At least, that was the opinion of several fans who have been watching games here for manyyears. Bob Bowman and Gordon McDonald hooked up in a sizzling pitching duel for 12 innings, and the fans were holding onto their seats all the way. Hardly ever was there a dull moment as Bowman sent 11 Red Sox down swinging and McDonald fanned 10 Athletics. The edge lay in the fact that Bowman finally walked 7 to McDonald's 3, and one of the walks led to the winning run.[24]

As everyone had expected, Max Macon steered the Hazard Bombers to the Mountain States League championship for 1951. He had pulled the very best from Johnny Podres and Danny Hayling, who ranked first and second in the league for strikeouts. Bob Bowman was third.

Nothing more was heard, in the Mountain States League at least, about Dick Mims; Pennington Gap dropped out of the league for a year after 1951. In 1952, the Norton Braves signed Billy Williams, an African American from Clinchco, and in 1953, Knoxville and Maryville-Alcoa of the Mountain States opened their doors wide to black players.

In his remarkable book *Brushing Back Jim Crow*, Bruce Adelson writes about the initial integration of the minor leagues.

> Nineteen fifty-one marked the first time minor-league color barriers in Texas (J. W. Wingate), Tennessee (Bob Bowman), and Virginia and North Carolina (Percy Miller) collapsed. The achievements of these men began the slow process of southern baseball integration. However, their organized-baseball tenures were quite brief, ranging from a handful of games to three weeks.[25]

While he was right about the year and the contribution of all the men to integration, two points must be disputed, the first a minor error of geography, made by other writers as well.[26] But it is important to note that Bob Bowman played for the Middlesboro Athletics for the entire 1951 season, his final performance a thirteen-inning scorcher that saw his team eliminated in the Mountain States playoffs.

As for the Middlesboro Blue Sox, they never recovered from the loss of Bob Bowman, but then all small town teams were beginning to lose their crowds by then. In 1963, an old-timers' game featured surviving members of the team was announced. Snooks Sprigs, James Hodge and Bob Bowman all showed up to play.[27]

After he left the Athletics, Bowman settled down into a quiet life in Middlesboro with his family. He managed a pool hall, something he'd done in the off seasons for years. He worked with local kids, who idolized their hometown hero, on the fundamentals of baseball. Eddie Ballinger was one of those kids. "A lot of us who played little league back in '52 or '53, we emulated him. Because that's the way [submarine] that some of us pitched," he says. George Ferguson says that he also wanted to copy his uncle's delivery but Bowman refused to teach him, warning that that it could damage his arm. But George had a biological reputation to uphold among the local boys. "They thought I was gonna be like Bob Bowman when I got a little older and started playing ball in the neighborhood. I was always the pitcher because I was Bob Bowman's nephew," he laughs. "One day I thought I had it—the way he was throwing it—and the next day, I couldn't raise my arm up." Both Eddie and George agree that Bob Bowman's patience in teaching kids the game was boundless. Eddie says, "You'd make boo-boos and he'd just look at you like, 'You gotta try that again.'" Bob Bowman's love of children went past coaching. He helped many of his small fans attend Blue Sox games, finding premium seats for a lucky few. "He'd always pick me out of the crew and take me to ball games and set me behind the catcher," remembers George. And Eddie Ballinger, as a frequent batboy, was granted the privilege of riding the bus with the Blue Sox to various games when he was six or seven. "With the Blue Sox, every time they played, he pitched."

Patricia Bowman Edwards was born in her father's later years; he had given up baseball by the time she came along. For many years, she didn't quite understand the basis of his celebrity. "As I child, I just thought of it as baseball. I would go places and people would say, 'Oh I know Bob Bowman—he played here or he played there,' but I didn't think of it as nothing but baseball until I got older," she says. "Then I started looking and I'm like, 'Dad had a contract!' And I'm thinking that back in '47 or '48, two hundred and seventy-some dollars—we was rich!" She doesn't recall that he ever formally coached

Bob Bowman, the first African American to play organized baseball in Dixie. This photo was taken in May of 1951, on the day that he signed with the Athletics of Middlesboro, Kentucky. Two hours later, he would take the mound in relief, clinching a victory for his new team (courtesy Patricia Bowman Edwards).

a team but that he was always a presence on the local diamonds. "I can remember him hanging around at Lincoln field where we would play ball, where we had this black girls' league. He'd be over there sometimes, hanging on the fence while we was out there playing ball. And I can remember him throwing and catching with us." When asked if baseball was just a job for her father, Patricia says firmly, "No. He loved it." And Eddie Ballinger agrees. "His passion was baseball. Most of them, at that time, it was their passion."

In the early 1970s, Bob Bowman suffered a stroke from which he never really recovered. Patricia remembers that C. L. Moore, one-time owner of the Asheville Blues, made the trek to Middlesboro to visit with his former star. Bowman died shortly thereafter on June 25, 1975.

The signing of the first African American to a contract in organized baseball in the South went virtually unnoticed in the nation's newspapers. Even the *Middlesboro Daily News* played it down, although they did run a photograph of Bowman, with pen in hand, gazing serenely into the camera.[28] And despite Middlesboro's love affair with him, his name disappeared from the sports pages after 1951, only to appear in the occasional fond remembrance by aging sportswriters.

But on August 22, 1951, Bob Bowman's name made it to the pages of the *Sporting News* when the season averages of the Mountain States League were posted.[29] His record of 16–3 was just below that of Johnny Podres' 17–3. But his name was finally there, on the pages of that venerable periodical, where it should have been all along.

Chapter 14

Vince Pankovits and the Mean Season

In the very early spring of 1953, Vince Pankovits arrived in Knoxville, Tennessee, as the playing manager of the latest addition to the Mountain States League, the Smokies. He was familiar with the area, having piloted the Pennington Gap Miners of that league in 1950 and 1951. With his knowledge of the area and the league, Pankovits seemed ideally suited to the position. He was blessed with fortitude and a strong constitution, which were distinct advantages, because what happened that summer in Knoxville would have left a lesser man weeping in a dark closet.

Vince Pankovits was a man who knew baseball. The son of a blacksmith, he grew up in Groton, New York, where he played amateur, semipro and professional ball. He'd tried out for the Cardinals and the Yankees, but his reward in those endeavors was limited to getting Babe Ruth's autograph on his Yankee tryout letter. Suspecting that his chances in the majors were limited, he opted for a career in the minor leagues and it was there that he established a solid reputation. In 1950, he was thirty-one years old, single and playing catcher and managing for the Bridgeport Bees of the Class B Colonial League. When that league folded in July, Vince answered a call issued by the desperate owners of a ball club in southwest Virginia. In the summer of that year, Pankovits accepted the position of player-manager for the ailing Pennington Gap Miners of the Mountain States League. It took months for the local paper to get his name right, referring to him through much of the first season as Vince Pankouts. By the next season, they'd gotten his last name, but, for a while, at least, changed his given name to Steve.

Hearing descriptions of Vince Pankovits, it is easy to imagine a manager who, with his straightforward Northern demeanor and intense work ethic, molded striplings into the very best ballplayers they could be. "He was a New Yorker—very cocky and brash and outspoken," says Jim Pankovits of his father. "He was a very hard worker—meticulous and organized—and a no-nonsense person at the field. I can imagine he was pretty tough to play for, probably pretty demanding if he was anything with his players like he was with me as I grew up." Having a taskmaster for a father was obviously good for Jim; it landed him with the Houston Astros where he played from 1984 to 1990 and he now pilots their Salem Avalanche club of the Carolina League. Jim was the happy outcome of the marriage of Vince to the daughter of a Pennington umpire. Jim not only inherited his father's talents but the surname that, a generation later, still seems to leave the world baffled. It is claimed that no other Astro has had his named misspelled on baseball cards more often than Jim Pankovits has.[1]

Vince Pankovits enjoyed living and working in Lee County and would undoubtedly have been delighted to continued managing Pennington's Class D team indefinitely had it not folded, never to be revived, after the 1951 season. Furthermore, the town would have been happy to keep him; his tenure there had produced far superior teams to those of the previous Mountain States entries from the county. In fielding and hitting, they always did well as a group and individually. And, in a dramatic testament to his success as a coach, he was once jailed for his own protection when defeated opposition fans slashed his tires, according to son Jim. Vince Pankovits even remained popular with the local fans despite his attempts to integrate the team. After much prodding and several failed attempts, he eventually won that battle and was able to use an African American pitcher—the only black player in Lee County's professional baseball history—at the end of the final season.

As it was, with no Lee County team in 1952, he accepted the helm of the Jackson, Tennessee, team of the Kitty League. But Appalachia had gotten into his blood. "Going to southwest Virginia and that different way of life was very relaxing for him," says Jim. "And that hard-working coal miner mentality was right down his alley." So, when the Mountain States called him with another offer in early 1953, he was happy to respond, and packed up his family for the hills of Knoxville, Tennessee.

As the crow flies, Knoxville is an hour south of Middlesboro, Kentucky, just to the west of the Cumberland Plateau of the Appalachian Mountains. Although most of the coal mines and coal camps of the area were established in next-door Anderson and Campbell counties, Knoxville was home to coal operators and speculators who carved fortunes out of the region. While not a coal powerhouse like Virginia or Kentucky, eastern Tennessee, in its day, followed an almost identical history to theirs, from company towns to union wars. The former camp of Fraterville, barely thirty miles from Knoxville, holds the unhappy number eight spot in the top ten American mining catastrophes; 216 men (only 184 of whom were identified) died in an explosion of built-up coal dust in 1902. Most of the miners who worked in the camps outside of Knoxville were immigrants from Wales. Today, their descendents number enough to merit their own Welsh society.

In early 1953, Knoxville was in the early stages of a high stakes gamble to win a coveted franchise in higher class baseball. Their ball club, the Smokies, was facing imminent ejection from the Class B Tri-State League (and from the parental arms of the New York Giants) because of a delay in the construction of a new ball park. City officials phlegmatically accepted this as a necessary sacrifice towards a bigger payoff: Knoxville was betting that their expensive new ball park would land them with the big dogs of the AA Southern Association.

The very last thing that the city movers and shakers expected was a syndicate of inexperienced local businessmen who noted the baseball void and thought they'd like to try their hand at running a team. When a spot opened in the Mountain States League, these aspiring magnates, with the collateral of a rundown park seven miles outside the city limits (and across the border in neighboring Sevier County), approached league president Virgil Q. Wacks, who happily accepted them. When word spread, it sent mightier parties, political and journalistic, racing for torches and pitchforks.

There were several reasons for the violent reaction. Primarily, the opponents believed that going from Class B to Class D was a demotion of the most embarrassing kind. Secondly, according to the rules of minor league baseball, the existence of one club froze the territory within a ten-mile radius, with no other professional clubs allowed. Opponents of the venture feared that, once it took root, the Class D club would ruin the chances for Knoxville to field a higher-ranked franchise. Were these less-than-civic-minded owners considering blocking the city from greater professional glories? Sports columnists of the *Knoxville News-Sentinel* thought so, openly accusing the new club owners of the most sinister designs on territorial rights. Furthermore, Maryville, Tennessee, also of the Mountain States and less than twenty miles away, protested the proximity of the new Knoxville Smokies' planned field to theirs.

Knoxville's mayor, George Dempster, was particularly incensed. "'It's Southern Association or nothing, for Knoxville,' declared Dempster." The quintessential politician, he righteously blasted the club owners and the Mountain States League for trying to inflict such degradation on the city, then followed up with some unctuous feather-smoothing. "I make this statement with all due respect to the fine towns in the Mountain States League. It is just that Knoxville is a metropolis along with Memphis, Chattanooga and Nashville and deserves better baseball than it has been getting—not worse."[2]

Further, Mayor Dempster insisted that, because the park the team was planning to use was not even in Knoxville, it shouldn't be allowed to use that city's name. An injunction against the use of the name was threatened by the city law director. Despite the furor, plans proceeded and in March, officials of Knox Baseball, Inc., as it was now known, announced the hiring of player-manager Vince Pankovits.

It's hard to say whether or not Pankovits was fully aware of the hornets' nest he was walking into, but he approached spring training with the same practicality he'd shown in Lee County, saying, "Our main interest is to field a winning team from the start. We have the promise of help from the Chicago Cubs and Cincinnati Reds and we're scouting around to find some good players."[3] He began the methodical business of assembling a team, borrowing players from farm systems and reaching back into Pennington Gap and St. Charles for familiar talent. He held a tryout for locals. He put every player through his paces and didn't hesitate to return, trade, or sell outright anyone who couldn't pass muster. He searched desperately for pitchers. Jim Pankovits, as a coach now himself, appreciates what he learned form his father about managing a club. "Being the son of a coach, you grow up with an awareness of all the positions—you grow an appreciation for how important each position is." Not only did he nurture each man's ability at his post, Vince Pankovits filled each position admirably himself when called upon, especially his chosen one, that of catcher. As he built his team, Knox Baseball, Inc., set to work refurbishing its antiquated ball field in faraway Sevier County. The *Knoxville News-Sentinel* begrudgingly covered the efforts but referred to Pankovits and his boys not as the Smokies but as the Chapman Highway Park team.

While turf was being laid and bleachers built in east Tennessee, in Hot Springs, Arkansas, a volcano was about to erupt and for Vince Pankovits and his Knoxville Smokies, it would mean the only bright spot in a hellish season. Jim and Leander Tugerson, two African American brothers who had built a name for themselves with the Indianapolis Clowns, were signed by the Hot Springs Bathers of the Cotton States League. The other teams were irate, as the league had always been—and they were determined it would always stay—lily white. The Tugerson brothers understood what they were walking into when they signed. "'We know our place in the South because we are from the South,' Jim told reporters. 'We know we come into the Cotton States League with two strikes against us. All we want is an opportunity to prove our ability as baseball players.'"[4] Barely had the ink dried when the Cotton States League went into a meltdown. The other seven teams called for the ouster of Hot Springs. As insults and racial epithets flew like shrapnel in the Deep South, Vince Pankovits and his Smokies sprang into action, and opened their arms to the beleaguered brothers, getting them on an option from Hot Springs. On April 21, Knoxville was introduced to its first black players by the local paper. "Receipt of a pair of Negro brother pitchers from the Hot Springs Bathers today helped Manager Vince Pankovits solve the pitching problem for his Knoxville baseball club entry in the Class D Mountain States League."[5]

Having guided the town toward integration, Pankovits was emboldened and shortly signed two more African American players. Opening day of the Mountain States League found a few of the teams well-integrated and with an international flair: Knoxville and Maryville each had three black players and Morristown boasted eleven Cuban players and a Cuban manager.

The lead-up to opening day brought more squabbling between Knoxville and Maryville over territory; each side wanted the validation of the first game of the season being played on their field. A compromise was reached when it was agreed that the game would be played at a neutral park where additional seating was arranged for the expected surge of black fans (the Maryville Twins were debuting future Giants and Indians outfielder Willie Kirkland).[6] In a gloomy portent of the year to come, Vince Pankovits, arguing against what was referred to by a sympathetic writer as a "screwy double play," was ejected from game in the second inning. The Smokies lost 9–5.[7]

But the Smokies and their manager recovered and it was immediately apparent to everyone watching that the Tugerson brothers, especially Jim, would live up to their reputation as terrific hurlers. In a double-header played against Middlesboro in early May, Jim not only won the first game but came in to relieve Leander in the second, ensuring the victory. (Sadly, Leander was sidelined with a shoulder injury shortly thereafter and wouldn't play again that season.) A week later, Jim Tugerson recorded his fifth win of the new season. When he was recalled by Hot Springs in the third week of May, the Cotton States League reacted by threatening to forfeit any game in which he played. Under that threat, Hot Springs returned Tugerson to Knoxville within forty-eight hours. National Association president George Trautman, when asked about the issue, "refused immediate comment,"[8] although he did send out a toothless memorandum in June to the effect that the actions of the Cotton States League were "at war with the concept that the national pastime offers equal opportunity of employment to all."[9] In July, Tugerson said he would give up "for this season" the fight to be played by Hot Springs.[10]

In the meantime, while still not referring to the team as "the Smokies," the newspaper was reporting the scores and allowing the team a little publicity although usually not the favorable kind. At the end of May, it was rumored that the club, its owners in debt to the tune of $21,000, was moving to Hazard, the *Knoxville News-Sentinel* felt entirely vindicated in its distaste for the upstart Chapman Highway Park team. Sportswriter Tom Siler, in an editorial entitled "MSL Smokies Fail to Excite Fans, Give City New Baseball Black Eye," wrote, "It is never pleasant to witness failure. You have to see money wasted, hopes blasted, the future blighted—all in a project that was hopeless from the start. We refer, of course, to the Knoxville Smokies." Joining the elite club of journalists who were all for riding the Mountain States president out of Appalachia on a rail, he lambasted Wacks for not investigating the investor's finances to begin with.[11]

A day later, another columnist and a gentler soul, Harold Harris, expressed sympathy for the luckless team and its manager. He also revealed how the players were suffering as a result of a now-infamous lack of financial foresight on the part Knox Baseball, Inc. In the roughly five weeks since the season opening, the team had been paid for five days. Like his colleague, he stood opposed to Class D ball in the town. "But even so, these kids deserved a kinder fate than whatever happens to baseball in Knoxville. I sincerely hope the kids who gave it all they had at CHP [Chapman Highway Park] will get their full pay. They deserve no less. They should have more for the embarrassment it has caused them."[12]

While fate and a few inept officials attempted to chart a bleak course for the Smokies, all Vince Pankovits and his young team could do was to hold up their end of the bargain by playing the very best ball they could. Sadly, local sporting goods stores and credit bureaus began to loom menacingly, with mortifying results. Add to a temporary loss of uniforms the shame of this banner headline which appeared on May 29:

KNOX GAME FORFEITED; CLUB HAS NO BASEBALLS[13]

Sports fans throughout Appalachia were greeted by this news as they downed their morning coffee. By happy hour, the story had crisscrossed the country. Vince Pankovits must have been wondering why he'd ever returned to the mountains.

> "I've been with about 15 ball clubs in my career and I've been following baseball all my life," Pankovits said, "but I've never seen anything like this. It's embarrassing to me and the players and we're willing to move anywhere at any time.... I've fought with the umpires, with opposing players and, at times, even verbally scrapped with my own players to win games. It's certainly galling to lose a game just because we don't have any new balls with which to play."[14]

To rub salt into the wound, abashed local boys began showing up at the park that very afternoon to return balls that had been fouled out of the park during previous games. Added to the salt came a dash of battery acid when Al Helfer, "Mr. Radio Baseball," during a Yankees/Athletics "Game of the Day" broadcast urged fans across the country to send balls to Knoxville. Mortified local sportswriters renewed their denunciations of the club. "It's a shame and a disgrace that Knoxville has to bear the brunt of such publicity when the city is in no way connected with the Mountain States team. The Mountain States League team, which calls itself 'Knoxville,' is located in Sevier County, more than seven miles from the Knoxville city limits."[15]

Worse was yet to come, however, because the generous spirit of the American people came through and soon the clubhouse was filling up with donated baseballs or small amounts of money with which to purchase new ones. A few of the accompanying letters still exist, tucked away by Vince Pankovits in those dark days and saved by his son Jim. One can see why Vince saved them; they are a testament to what is best in baseball fans. Shaky penmanship betrays the advanced age of a Mr. L. E. Sanders from Leachville, Arkansas, who sent a dollar in cash and wishes for "the best of luck for '53." On engraved stationery, a woman from Abilene wrote, "Our Class C team here is currently in seventh place in the West Texas–New Mexico League and they will probably be calling for help soon, if we can't improve on this standing." Saying that she wished she could send more money, she signed off with "Yours, for the grand old game, Ina Wooten James." Eleven-year-old Joe Lancaster from Utah sent one of his extra baseballs. He wrote, "I am the catcher here on the Ogden Midget League team, but I am laid up in the hospital with a broken nose because I didn't wear my mask."[16]

In a break from the relentless pounding by the *News-Sentinel,* columnist Harold Harris found some humor in the situation and recalled a few other quirky local sports stories: "Add to the list of zany players who formerly played for Knoxville, the name of Babe Benning.... Benning used to eat a hatful of electric lightbulbs at times as a pre-game attraction at Caswell Park to help lure more customers to the park."[17] Perhaps Harris was attempting, with a little gentle humor, to disassociate himself from his colleagues whose anti–Mountain States hysteria was beginning to draw unfavorable attention from other newspapers. In a late May editorial entitled "Open Letter to Virgil Q. Wacks," *Kingsport Times-News* columnist Jack Kiser wrote the following:

> Then we read in a Knoxville paper that Norton is ready to give up the ghost. A few phone calls to that Virginia city reveals that the Braves have no such thoughts in mind. It seems, Virgil, that the Knoxville papers are the Mountain States League's worst enemies. They would like to see the league fold. They are ready to print any bad news on the loop, even though it hasn't been substantiated.[18]

The storm clouds cleared a bit when a local physician, saying he was acting on behalf of Knoxville's children, took control of the Smokies. He made no bones about his desire to see the city get a higher class of ball, and winning full territorial rights was a first step in the right direction. If it meant leading a Class D team to get those rights, he would do it.

While attention was diverted by recriminations, a growing surplus of baseballs in the clubhouse, and new leadership, the Knoxville Smokies had quietly climbed into third place in the league and were pulling in growing numbers of fans. Vince Pankovits was managing from his position behind the plate, working with Jim Tugerson to build one of the most effective batteries in the league. In early June, the Smokies' winningest pitcher was honored with his own night at Chapman Highway Park. Jim Tugerson returned the favor with a one-hitter. "Tugerson pitched before about 1,100 fans—about half of them Negroes like himself, who were admitted free on Big Jim Tugerson Night. Tugerson ... was presented with a radio, fishing tackle, a dozen or so new shirts and 16 gift boxes from the fans. He increased his pitching record to 10–3 with the victory."[19]

As the first half of the season wound down, and the team managed to go for a few weeks without a new crisis, the kindly Harold Harris tried to get past the embarrassments of May, even suggesting that the Smokies, now with a full bullpen, might be a real threat in the second half.[20] Even Chapman Park hater Tom Siler begin his June 26 column with the following praise of at least one member of the team: "Who is this upstart, Robin Roberts? Jim Tugerson of the Knoxville club has won 14 in a shorter season, two more than the Phillies' star. A check of the current Sporting News failed to reveal any other pitcher who has won as many as the lanky Negro right-hander."[21] And the day after Tugerson was named to the All-Star team, he threw his seventeenth win. Siler continued the love fest and devoted his entire column to an interview with the pitcher. In it, the readership learned that Jim Tugerson had left the Indianapolis Clowns for organized ball at the urging of Roy Campanella. "'He told me it would be rough, especially playing in that section; yet, I was willing to sacrifice a better salary to see if I could climb up in the organized leagues.'" Readers also learned that he was married with five children and worked as a hotel cook in the off seasons. Siler wrote, "Tugerson's 1953 season—his first in organized baseball—portends a brilliant future."[22]

Soon, the *News-Sentinel* got a little pennant fever and began to pay real attention to the club. When Knoxville took second place in the league, after winning a double-header from Muscle Shoals' Kingsport team (the second game being Jim Tugerson's twentieth victory), they referred to the club with phrases like "red hot." Finally the team, and the town that heretofore wouldn't claim it, began to garner positive press. A United Press article commented on Tugerson's career in Tennessee: "Knoxville is all Dixie, but Tugerson has had nothing but the warmest of treatment. Knoxville manager Vince Pankovits said, 'Maybe it's a novelty, but there are a lot of Southerners on this team and they respect him as much as anybody else as long as he does his job.'"[23]

August began happily for the Smokies. They were allowed to play their first game inside the city limits on the second, a benefit for the Negro American Legion Post. Vince Pankovits was finally getting some much-deserved credit, not only for managing the team into a high position in the league but also for his hitting. It seemed that all was forgiven until August 14, when in a final, nightmarish event, Pankovits again found himself in quicksand and with another bull's eye on his head. "Anything can happen in baseball, and the Knoxville Smokies must be wondering today just how far that statement goes ... and whether there is any limit," wrote the local press by way of announcing what the rest of the world was soon to hear.[24] From the newspapers of the Appalachians all the way to the *Sporting News*, the same story was bugled: the Smokies had blown a 14-run lead. Tom Siler and the *News-Sentinel* called it "bush league baseball at its bushiest."[25] It was an overblown reaction because Vince Pankovits, with the cushion of an 18–4 lead over Big Stone Gap, was doing what any manager might have done. He was experimenting with shifting players' positions and lost control of the game. Had he tried it in any other city, with any other team, in any other year, and with any sportswriter than Tom Siler looking over his shoulder, it probably would have come off without a hitch.

Siler never forgave that loss. The day after Jim Tugerson scored his twenty-seventh victory on August 23, tying Johnny Podres' 1951 record with Hazard, and with the Smokies now in second place in the league, the writer's vitriol still could have reduced the page

Vince Pankovits early in his career. Pankovits found himself in the midst of a political, journalistic and racial maelstrom in 1953 Knoxville, Tennessee. Despite the turmoil, he managed to lead his Smokies to the league championship (courtesy Jim Pankovits).

to ash. "This meaningless Mountain States League season, using the name of Knoxville in a Chapman Highway operation, is drawing to a close. It is to be hoped, and most fervently, that never again will the baseball fans of Knoxville be humiliated with such a spectacle. Class D is just what it says and the fans of Knoxville deserve much better."[26]

The regular season ended with the Maryville Twins in first place, Knoxville in second. Playoff berths were claimed by Morristown and Kingsport as well. With the elimination of the latter two, it was Knoxville against the pennant-winning Twins, their longtime enemies from just down the road. The Knoxville Smokies won a Labor Day double-header to take the championship. The second game was Jim Tugerson's fourth playoff victory and his thirty-first for the season. Vince Pankovits played right field in both games, with four hits in the first.

The season had ended and the players headed for their respective homes the next day. But before he left, one of them sent an anonymous letter to Tom Siler in response to his biting editorial of a few days before. For the men who sweated through the unbroken desert of minor league baseball, it could be a manifesto.

> As a member of this year's Knoxville Smokies, I as well as the rest of the players on the club, deeply resent the implications set forth a few days ago. How many players in higher classifications would even set foot on some of the fields we are forced to play on this season? Then, too, how many major leaguers attained their present position without at one time working here in the lower minor leagues? All things considered, I would say we have performed pretty well. As you should know, many things go into the makeup of a winning ball club, Class D or AAA. Good fields, decent uniforms, good equipment in ample supply, and the support of the press and public. We have had little or none of the above all season. The "adverse" publicity brought upon this "fair city" was not brought about by the personnel of the club, but by the front offices of clubs in this and other leagues. Was it our fault, as players, that there were no baseballs here one night, causing a forfeit? Did we sanction the surrender of our uniforms to a credit bureau? Is it our fault that only 12 baseballs nightly were available to us? Is it our fault that our ace pitcher was shuttled back and forth between two leagues because of his color and not his abilities? I am sure you will be forced to answer "no" to all of the above questions. It put us at a distinct disadvantage to play at a park eight miles out of the city limits, and then the playing field was almost invariably in a pitiful condition. I ask you, Mr. Siler, how can ANY team help but error [sic] on diamonds such as this one? Or don't you take things such as these into account when you write your columns? I am very sorry to read how little was thought of us, this year by you and by others, but regardless, we think we've done a pretty fair job, all things considered and anything you or others thoughtlessly print will not alter our opinion.

Far from being chastened by this letter, Siler responded to it in the same column by saying, "I would hasten to agree with this ball player who thinks the players 'did a pretty good job.' The job they did was OK ... for Class D.... The newspapers try to give the sports fans what they want; most certainly this is not Class D baseball."[27]

The 1953 Knoxville Smokies left the mountain town and were blown to the four winds. Jim Tugerson led the Mountain States League in wins (29) and strikeouts (286). He was finally allowed to play in Hot Springs in October, while barnstorming with the Negro American League All-Stars. He notched a 14–1 victory in that game over the Indianapolis Clowns. Earlier, in September, a $50,000 lawsuit filed by him against the Cotton States League for civil rights violation was thrown out by a district judge in Hot Springs. He took it to a higher court in Fort Smith where, in December, it was dismissed by a federal judge. Hot Springs eventually sold him to Dallas.

Tucked away in the few papers that Vince Pankovits saved from that dreadful year was a letter written in July 1953 from an Air Force Reserve captain in North Dakota who wondered if Jim Tugerson was the same man who had once pitched for the black team at an air base in Texas where he had served.

> I have noticed the write-ups in our local paper concerning your troubles with the Cotton States League about playing ball. We have a pretty fast league up here in Minot, N. D. and several Canadian teams but I do not know what class they are in. We have a number of colored players on the teams and Minot can use a good pitcher these days so if you looking for a place to play where you would be treated as an equal, this would be the spot.

It was signed "With my best wishes to see you in the big leagues."[28] It must have been a bittersweet memento of the year for both Tugerson and Pankovits.

Near the end of 1953, the *Sporting News* ran an article written by Tom Siler, announcing the near readiness of the new municipal baseball stadium. "Knoxville excused itself from Organized Ball the past season, although a Mountain States League club known as the Knoxville Smokies operated at Chapman Park, just outside the city."[30] Knoxville returned to the Tri-State League in 1954.

At the end of what was presumably the most brutal (and yet surprisingly successful) season of his career, Vince Pankovits returned to Pennington Gap, where he had friends and family and the respect of the local press. The next baseball season found him playing and managing the local boys in the semipro Lonesome Pine League. Jim Pankovits believes that there, in the slower tempo of Lee County, his dad found what he needed. "I think that toward the end of his career, when he was playing and managing there, even though it was obviously very competitive, it was probably a great environment for him to finish his career," Jim says. "Not as much pressure and a lot more fun."

CHAPTER 15

The Old Man of the Mountains

Dynamite Rudy Parsons was giving an exhibition of Air Tight pitching to the thirty men that faced him.—Powell Valley News, 1933[1]

If coalfield baseball could be distilled to its essence, it might take the shape of a tall, right-handed pitcher named Rudy Parsons. Beginning his career in 1932, he ended it almost twenty years later, having become by that point a favored topic of most regional sports pages and a legend in several states. He played in virtually every ballpark, from the most isolated coal camps to municipal fields from Knoxville to Charleston. In southern Appalachia, he was easily the best-traveled and one of the most sought-after pitching ringers of his day. One season's play always included several different teams for him. And his dreams of glory took him from New York to California, where he was, for one golden moment, a whisper away from the majors.

Three people, experts on Rudy Parsons, sat down with me to discuss him; they are Shirley Pearson, Harriet Roberts and Connie Nunley, the only girls of his nine offspring. Shirley is the eldest, lucky enough to have seen her father in action in the sunset of his career. Harriet is the middle sister, just old enough to have enjoyed the thrill of having a baseball player for a father. Connie, whose middle name is Lou, is the youngest sister; she was named by her father for Misters Mack and Gehrig. They are an entertaining trio to be around. Each sister is bright and attractive, with a well-honed sense of humor, a family trait, apparently. The women play off each other but Shirley, the most dynamic by virtue of birth order, leads the band. Each has her own memories of their father but all agree, either from memory or hearsay, that he was a presence on the mound and in the history of coalfield baseball.

Born in 1909, Parsons was raised on a farm in Lee County, Virginia. He was the baby and the only boy. Although the daughters don't know when or how he began playing baseball, he was playing in his teens, and, by 1932, he was making a name for himself with the Dryden team of the infant Lonesome Pine League. "He had two passions, I think we would all agree," says Shirley, "our mother and baseball." Those loves intertwined like vines throughout Parson's life, one consistently affected by the other. Shirley continues: "He played baseball and was kind of a local hero when he began chasing my mother. He was a dashing man about town. Their courtship involved their friends taking her to see him play."

Marriage to Irene didn't slow his pursuit of the sport at all; by 1934, he had played with both the Charleston, West Virginia, Senators of the Middle Atlantic League and the Knoxville Smokies of the Southern Association. Shirley tells about the scores of Virginia fans who would take the train to attend his games in Knoxville. In 1935, he devoted most of the summer to pitching for the Verda, Kentucky, team of the Lonesome Pine League, considered by some local writers to be one of the best teams the region had ever witnessed. Its players—legendary locals like Cowboy Barker and Carl Doyle—were of such quality that Frank Rickey, brother of Branch, stopped by in July of that year to have a look and was disappointed that some had already signed professional contracts.[2] The *Middlesboro Daily News* reported on Rudy Parsons' signing with Harrisburg.

> Rudolph Parsons was slated as the Lonesome Pine League's twelfth player to sign a professional contract today as he made preparations to shove off to Harrisburg, Penn., for training with the Harrisburg club in the New York-Pennsylvania Class A league.[3]

Marrying a peregrinating baseball player at the height of the Depression didn't win Irene Parsons any accolades, from family or townspeople. "Her father had such a rigid mind. Of course he didn't approve of her marrying a baseball player and you can see why—they're bouncing around trying to find their break," says Shirley. "He didn't look upon Dad with great favor. He was very angry, we hear."

Connie interjects, "And the money wasn't great either so baseball players weren't considered a catch for your daughter." Harriet agrees, saying that baseball players were not held "in high esteem. When my father was born again, we used to walk to church together where he taught a Sunday school class. I can remember some kind of an uproar because some of the people in the church felt like a baseball player shouldn't be teaching a Sunday school class."

After the New York-Pennsylvania League, Parsons returned home to play with Johnson City of the Appalachian League that year as well, in addition to mound duty in the local coal camps. Even though he'd taken a step backward from the Class A league, he was not defeated and continued his dogged pursuit of a higher level of baseball. In the isolation of Appalachia, this was no mean feat. "Early on, geography and lack of communication was a hindrance," explains Shirley. "You had to be extraordinary to be found in these backwoods. I think his record from one of the surrounding teams got someone's attention."

In the late '30s, Rudy Parsons continued to pitch for several teams in the Appalachian League, teams that paid next to nothing. To support his burgeoning family, he supplemented his income by continuing to work as a ringer for the coal camp teams. The family enjoyed the extra income in the summer months but keeping food on the table in the winter months was the real challenge. Connie says, "Every time the baseball season was over, he didn't have a decent prospect here." Shirley agrees, adding, "He had to be resourceful. They both had to be resourceful. He became an electrician, he could paint, one year he did roofs, he could plumb, he worked in the mines...."

"He worked in the mines a lot," adds Connie. Laughing at the memory of those meager days and the lack of money, she says, "Tight? Things were more than tight."

"We were poor but we didn't know we were poor," adds Harriet.

"And we didn't care," says Shirley. "We weren't shunned."

Connie agrees. "No, I never felt that way at all."

"I was too little to know what was going on," says Harriet. "I just knew that my dad was a pitcher and I was so proud of him and I was taken up with the excitement of everything. All our friends wanted to come over to our house because there was so much going on." While they may not have been rich, the Parsons children were already showing signs of the accomplished adults they would turn into. All were exceptional students and excelled in sports. While their father's presence during the baseball season could be infrequent, their home was a buzzing hive of activity and frequent visitors.

When asked if, as children, they ever wished their father had what would be considered a more responsible job, Connie chuckles, "Oh ho, not when I was a little kid but when I got bigger I did!" As for their mother's feelings about her husband's chosen career, Shirley answers, "She supported him, she didn't hold him back. There must have been thousands of times that she wished that he had a regular job, when she was home alone with all of us kids for such long periods. But by the same token, she knew how important it was to him. I never knew of a time when she failed to be supportive."

Rudy Parsons was jubilant when he signed with San Francisco. The *Sporting News* reported it:

Rudy Parsons, righthanded pitcher who was with Utica of the Canadian-American League in 1942, is draft insurance for the San Francisco Pacific Coast League Seals. Thirty-three years old, Parsons is the father of five children.[4]

The press presented him as a sort of yokel comedian and christening him with nicknames like "the Virginia Bear Fighter."[5] Harriet says, "I know the newspaper reports that I used to love to read, they really razzed him because he had such a wit about him, such a good sense of humor. They would write really funny articles about him traveling all the way from the mountains to San Francisco."

"They were quite taken with him in San Francisco," says Shirley. "One of the sportswriters wrote that Rudy Parsons had finally shown up six or eight days late for spring training but considering the distance he's traveled and the family he left behind—"

Connie adds, "They always referenced the number of kids he had."

"And how he had to fight a few Indians on the way or encountered a bear," Harriet chuckles.

"All very tongue in cheek," finishes Shirley. "When he was playing for San Francisco, he would liked to have moved out there because he had lots of opportunities (one of his best friends was Lefty O'Doul). There were career options other than baseball. But by then there were several of us children and Mother was very reluctant to move."

Connie says, "And you've got to be realistic about it. They weren't paying baseball players any big money back then and you've got a family. It wasn't like you could uproot. And neither one of our families were in a position to help him, they weren't financially well-enough off to help a man and woman move."

"Not only help him, but they wouldn't have encouraged him at all," Shirley agrees.

The children dealt well with their father's absence but separation was always difficult for their parents. "They wrote letters back and forth, because there weren't plentiful telephones. Their letters were their only communication for months and months and months," Shirley says. So close to realizing his dream, Rudy Parsons saw it evaporate.

> Skipper Lefty O'Doul immediately ordered a press meeting to announce Rudy would be given ample opportunity to become a first line flinger and that he was no longer to be confused with the Parsons of 1943 whose main job was hoisting the flag before every ball game.... The father of five children, Rudy arrived in San Francisco with a 1-A card in his pocket and calculated he wouldn't be called for at least three months. But two days after Rudy arrived, so came greetings from his draft board to report for physical induction, outcome of which has not been learned.[6]

Shirley reflects on this development with obvious sadness. "Dad was drafted into the navy at the height of his career, one step from the majors. And he had at least six kids which was phenomenal. That's how bad they needed manpower in World War II. Maybe it was five kids and one on the way (there was one on the way just about every other year). The navy had him playing baseball in the upper Midwest and at Sampson Naval Base in New York."

When the war ended, along with Parson's chance at the big leagues, he returned to Lee County where he was enthusiastically welcomed by any number of area teams. But the makeup of coalfield baseball had been altered by the war. Gone were the days when every camp fielded a team. Now, baseball was limited to the larger camps and the commercial coal towns, which were looking toward a future with professional teams.

Parsons was now in middle age. He still had a powerful pitching arm, although now he relied more on strategy than velocity. After two seasons of post-war play, he took the logical next step into managing a team. Big Stone Gap had just given birth to its first professional club and offered Rudy the helm, which he accepted. The *Kingsport Times* even predicted that Big Stone Gap, "under the management of Rudy Parsons, could be the team to beat in the Mountain States League this season."[7]

Not only did he draft local talents like Jack Kilgore and Cherokee Lawson but he scoured the minors for suitable players. It was a short-lived experiment for him. After an early June losing streak, he was handed a ten-day suspension, which he apparently threw back into the faces of citizen-stockholders with the velocity of his old fast ball. Says Shirley of her father, "He didn't suffer fools gladly and he usually expressed it. It wasn't always to his advantage." His tenacity was commented on by the *Middlesboro Daily News*.

> Opposing ... will be that Old Man of the Mountains, Crafty Rudy Parsons. Parsons has been around longer than he cares to admit in these parts as a pitcher but remains one of the toughest of them all when he takes the pitcher's mound.[8]

Rudy Parsons spent the last two years of his baseball career with the Mountain States League, playing for Pennington Gap and Morristown, Tennessee. He was very well liked by his teammates, mostly very young men, who flocked to the Parsons' house after games. They'd stay late into the night, gathered around Irene's kitchen table for home-cooked meals, and, most likely, a little comfort. Shirley remembers them well. "First of all, they came from all over the country, they were young kids, and it's just a little bit hard when you're outsiders in a small town. They'd be traveling late at night, so they slept late and that just wasn't a small town's view of a proper job."

These are the days that the sisters remember most vividly now that their father was around, or at least in the area, for the entire summer. Shirley, now a teenager, walked to every home game in Pennington Gap, followed by a line of smaller siblings, like so many ducklings. "I took everybody that wanted to go that could walk," she laughs. "Sometimes I had five with me." When asked if their dad was a local hero, they all shake their heads doubtfully. When Connie answers, "They [the town] thought he was an outstanding ball player—"

Shirley finishes her sister's thought, saying, "—but a ne'er-do-well. I hate to generalize but that was the opinion of people who didn't hold baseball a suitable career path. But a lot of them didn't know. They didn't even go to games. They just had pre-conceived notions and small minds. But to the fans he was a hero, especially when he won. And he won a lot."

The *Middlesboro Daily News* had this to say about Rudy Parsons in 1951.

> Rudy is about as smart as they come in the manner of pitching nowadays. Rarely does he give the hitter anything good to hit at. Always he is hitting the outside corner or the inside corner, high or low, mostly low. Parsons didn't mind getting behind the hitter to any great extent. With three balls and one strike, down he'd come with that curve ball just as if he were ahead of the batter. On the three-two pitches it was the same thing. Even when the batter hit the ball, it was a spinning curve and the hit didn't go too far. We can remember when Parsons' stock in trade was a fast ball. All he did then was rear back and fog the ball through. It took a pretty good hitter to connect solidly with his fast one. But with the passing of the years, naturally some of the speed is gone and Parsons has turned to smart pitching to get him by.[9]

Shirley describes her father's pitching style as one of supreme confidence. "When he was on the mound, he was a very cool, collected pitcher who knew what he was doing. I never did see him show any emotion on the mound at all. Often when the inning was over, there'd be lots of players rushing up, especially if there'd been a lot of strikeouts. But he was very professional."

Even when his ball playing days had ended, Rudy Parsons' passion for the game never cooled. The Parsons household was one of the first in town to get a television so that he could keep up, especially with his beloved Cincinnati Reds. "I don't remember us ever being without shoes, but if it had been a matter of television or shoes, it would have been the TV to get the ball games. And we would have voted with him!" Shirley declares. Harriet remembers daily life with Rudy: "He'd have the newspaper spread out over the bed, maybe two of them, following all the stats and what was going on, while a game was on the radio and a different one on TV. He'd be keeping track of all of that. He was totally immersed, even after he wasn't playing." They tell of him walking down to the corner newsstand every day for the *Sporting News*. "He talked about it all the time and never quit loving the game," says Shirley.

But he was also keenly interested in his nine children and their pursuits. Connie says, "He was so proud of all of us because most of us were athletic and excelled in sports." Shirley, who grew up playing sandlot baseball and assiduously attended local ballgames throughout her teens, suffered the constraints of her gender. "I knew all the ins and outs of the game. I loved it. I always wished I had been a boy so I could play. It broke my heart."

After the death of his wife, Rudy spent time with his daughters, now grown and with

The legendary Rudy Parsons in 1951, one of his last professional seasons, playing for Morristown, Tennessee, in the Mountain States League. A steely personality on the mound, he had a career that lasted more than twenty years (courtesy of the Parsons family).

families of their own. Connie and her husband took him to Cincinnati to see the Reds play. He spent an early spring with Shirley, who lived in Florida; his demands to attend spring training games often exceeded her ability to get him there, but she did her best. "He still knew all the coaches and they treated him royally."

Rudy Parsons has been dead since 1983 but former ball players from the area still speak of him with awe; he was the greatest asset a team could have or a batter's worst nightmare. It is worth noting that in 1953, Knoxville shortstop Bobby Grose brought pitcher Jim Tugerson on something of a pilgrimage to meet Rudy. And while Harriet says that he could be quiet and conservative, his sense of humor and conviviality still drew people to him, making his home a gathering place for people from every walk of life.

The Parsons sisters are wealthy in the memories of their remarkable and colorful parents. Older people who knew them still comment on Irene's beauty and Rudy's skill on the mound. Although their father never broached the subject, it's apparent that the children sometimes wonder how his family life affected his career. Connie speaks for all of them when she says, "I guess if it hadn't been for all of us young'uns, things would have been different for him." She adds sadly, "He really wanted to see the world."

But after talking to these women, one is given to believe that Rudy Parsons' family helped to ease the pain of any wounds he suffered at not making it to the big leagues. The picture painted by his daughters is of a perpetually-lively household, full of laughter and great zeal for life. Each member of the family delighted in every other member—they obviously still do. The man who sired this brood definitely knew sacrifice, but probably was a stranger to regret.

Chapter 16

The Women in the Stands

On June 7, 1949, on the sports page of the *Middlesboro Daily News*, was a large photograph of an elderly woman, sitting in a grandstand clapping and smiling. The accompanying article described her as the most ardent fan of the Middlesboro Athletics. Aunt Bessie, as she was called, was at least the most consistent of game attendees. "'Well, I haven't missed a home game in four years,' Aunt Bessie reported. 'And I haven't missed too many of the ones away from home either.'"[1] She was also one of the most vocal team supporters, reading the riot act to umpires and players alike when they fell short of her expectations. Aunt Bessie ran the boarding house at the Premier-Jellico camp on the Tennessee-Kentucky border where her husband was a miner. The newspaper article both applauded and chuckled at this woman, whose away-game attendance was hampered only because of the unreliability of her 1929 Dodge. But if the reporter considered her an engaging oddity, he was wrong; the coalfields were chock full of Aunt Bessies. As back-breaking and mind-numbing as mine work could be for a man, the women of the camps were in equal desperate need of diversion. Their lives were filled with toil and worry and they needed baseball as much as the men did.

In the first few decades of the twentieth century, women's roles in coal mining communities was strictly defined and enforced. "Both company policy and superstition prevented women from working in the mines; therefore, other than doing laundry for the single miners or company officials or taking in boarders, the miner's wife was housewife and mother."[2] In the 1930s, First Lady Eleanor Roosevelt visited Bellaire, Ohio, and, in defiance of a long-held belief that a woman's presence in a mine would cause disaster, actually took a tour of the underground operations. A reporter informed the First Lady that in Alabama workers would leave a mine if a woman entered it, for fear of the curse. "Mrs. Roosevelt was inclined to think this superstition, like the much-sung stars, fell only on Alabama, but another member of her conference assured her it also prevailed in some sections of West Virginia."[3] Apparently the curse didn't hold true in Bellaire for there were no reports of cave-ins or explosions resulting from her visit.

In the 1970s, affirmative action legislation and a coal boom changed laws, if not all attitudes, and women were allowed to go underground as miners. But women had begun filling diverse professional positions in the coal camps since the 1930s. Many of these women

Women and children of the Dorchester camp loading coke, ca. 1918. Their very cheerful approach to the task belies the arduous nature of it (courtesy Gladys Stallard).

were not only wives and mothers, but secretaries, teachers, nurses and service workers. For all the circulated stereotypes of the Appalachian female as a pipe-smoking, bear-wrestling, man-trapping woman, the reality, of course, was far different. For all the beauty and pathos of Russell Lee's photographs, not every coal miner's wife was a bedraggled skeleton, clawed at by a passel of hungry children. These images, while accurately conveying the difficult lives in some of the early camps—usually small, individually-owned, and definitely non-unionized ones—do not speak for them all. Look at a photograph of a woman from Dante or Coalwood from 1945 and the image is no different than that of most middle-class American women. Usually fashionably attired, the coal camp woman gazes into the lens with poise and no small amount of confidence. She was leading a life similar to that of any other woman. She cared for her family and tried to make a secure and happy home. She washed her husband's clothes and chatted over the fence with her neighbors. Her children joined debate teams, flirted at soda shops, and tortured her throughout their adolescence like any other American kids did.

There were, of course, a few darker aspects that made these women's lives different from those of their sisters in Pasadena or Ithaca. First and foremost, the fear of losing an important male relative—husband, father, son—to an early death was a very real one and had to be faced everyday. In Carol Giesen's *Coal Miners' Wives,* one of the women interviewed talked about the psychological burden.

You're told that if you're going to marry a coalminer, you might be a widow. And you know that from what you see growing up. There's no mining camp where everybody don't know at least one family where someone died or got hurt bad. You're told, "Don't talk about it too much," and "Don't rock the boat," and "We'll get by if it's God's will." But you know ... that's one thing when you're a child, and another thing if it's your husband that you're thinking about.[4]

Billie Leho of Norton was raised in a coal mining family. Her father was killed by spooked mine ponies on the tipple when she was a year old. Her husband John, a brother, and all of her uncles died of black lung, which was euphemistically referred to in those days as "miners' asthma." "It was a living back then. That was all," she says resignedly. She says that John had presentiments of disaster while working in one particular mine. She and a girlfriend would drive their husbands to the company store and the men walked to the mine entrance. "Many was the time we'd get to the company store and they'd decide they didn't want to go to work. They knew the mine was gassy." John Leho's instincts served him well as he narrowly escaped death in a gas explosion at that very mine in 1957. He typically worked in the section that blew up but that night was in a different area, filling in for an absent colleague. After his narrow escape, he chose never to go back underground.

For the early pre-union coal camp woman, her world was just as likely to be surrounded by barbed wire as suburban sprawl. The anti-union coal operators, in their determination to prevent unionization, were not above erecting fortresses (often with sub-machine guns) to keep their workers in and the union agitators out. Early coal camp mothers quickly learned where to safely park their small children when bullets began to fly.

In some camps, it was the norm for officials of the company to drop in for unannounced inspections of the house and family. Tacit demands by the company for domestic stability among its workers made it incumbent on the woman to keep harmony in the coal camp home. "A marital break-up guaranteed the loss of company housing, after which the miner would be assigned to a dormitory for unmarried men. Divorced women and their children lost access to the company store, housing, and schools."[5]

Even for the inhabitants of the model communities of the 1920s and '30s, where the standard of living could be quite good, there was never any doubt that the families were lab rats in the great "contentment sociology" experiment, no matter how carefully tended by their keepers. Howard Sparks of Van Lear, Kentucky, a Consolidation Coal town, likens it to a socialist state, saying, "From the time I can remember, they did everything for you. The coal camp wanted you to be happy and contented and work. They controlled you in every way and you didn't realize it because they tried to do everything good for you too." Even though Van Lear was an incorporated community, the company chose the candidates for municipal elections, and, not surprisingly, those candidates, whether qualified or not, always won by a landslide.

For a better look into the lives of the coal camp women, one must first imagine their physical environment. Nothing about the mining of coal is aesthetically pleasing—not the sight, not the smell, not the noise, not the dust. One might be spared the sight of the underground activities and live away from the mouth of the mine but every company had aboveground operations including a latticework of railroad tracks, tipples (where the coal is dumped into waiting trains cars), and sometimes preparation plants and coke ovens. The constant thunder of trainloads or truckloads of coal going by was as unpleasant as the eye-stinging smoke from the ovens. Undoubtedly, an added psychological disadvantage was the sheer darkness of the camps due to the enclosing walls of mountains. Winter days in an Appalachian camp are some of the shortest anywhere. For those women who were new to the coalfields, the effect could be shocking. For Violet Smith, who'd grown up in the gentle meadows of Lee County, Virginia, the Crossbrook camp she came to when she married her husband left her feeling claustrophobic. "It was confining. I'd had space where I came from. It was different," she says. Wanda Osborne describes her introduction to the area. "First time I ever seen the coalfields, when I saw the coke ovens in Ramsey, I thought the whole town was on fire." Her husband had been given a job in a coal camp, but she drew the line at living in one. She says, "I guess Dante was the first one I ever saw. The roads were so narrow ... and all that old black dust and stuff...." She shudders at the memory. Indeed, the dust was the worst physical aspect of camp life, whether below ground or above. In his landmark *Night Comes to the Cumberlands*, author Harry M. Caudill gives this particulate matter a life of its own.

> Over the tipple there reared a monstrous coal dust genie which, as the ascending sun warmed the air, grew to immense proportions. Silent itself, it emanated endlessly from the rumbling machinery, and twisted and bent and soared in the changing winds. Sometimes it rose mountain high, strait up in the August sunlight. Again it reclined against the soggy earth under the pelting of a November rain. But always its gritty fingers tapped silently against the houses and crept into every nook and cranny in the town.[6]

Not only did the volume of dust require that porches be swept many times in one day and laundry on the line periodically shaken, but it also filled the inside of the house, regardless of defenses employed to keep it out. "When you got up in the morning, you had to clean your nostrils 'cause, the windows were closed, but it would seep in the house," says Betty Sabo of Dante. She marvels at the fact that more non-mining residents of her town didn't get sick. "We had a friend that we played cards with and she went to see her doctor for something or other and he told her, 'If you worked in the mines, you'd get black lung [compensation].'" Even if a house could have been hermetically sealed, there was no escaping the dust. Carol DeHaven of Coalwood remembers a coal-burning Heatrola in the living room that would periodically eruct clouds of dust which settled on furniture and floors. And the constant cloud of dust was a mobile one, escaping the boundaries of camps and settling in nearby towns. Sydney Francis of Hazard, Kentucky, a town in the midst of several camps, describes an essential ritual of spring cleaning. "There was this clay—I can smell it now—you could get in a can, like a paint can, and you rolled it up in a ball and scraped the dirt off the wallpaper. I can remember my mother coming home from work and climbing on a ladder to scrape walls."

As for architecture, a coal camp could be nothing more than a ramshackle collection of shanties, with walls of tarpaper and roofs that leaked. But wealthier camps often had substantial and attractive public structures. Larger camps could be lively and convenient places to live, with amenities that would stir the envy of any small town resident of the same era. In the Virginia camp of Keokee, in the early 1900s, for instance, there was swimming, golf, and tennis—even an opera house. Visitors to the Keokee hotel dined off of Wedgwood china that sported the company insignia.⁷

As varied as were the personalities and positions of these women, so were their opinions about living in coal camps. Some considered them an ideal place to live, work and raise a family; others were less keen on them. Gladys Stallard looks back very fondly on her years in Dorchester where her husband, Cliff, played for and managed the baseball team for years. Gladys is a diminutive woman, a widow now. She first came to Dorchester as a single woman, a teacher, in the 1930s, and lived at the clubhouse. Four years after she and her husband were married, they were able to move into a house at the camp. She sits in the living room of her Norton home, a large brick two-story, the interior dotted with piles of books. Her description of the house in Dorchester makes her current home sound small. "It was a big house, with a furnace, hardwood floors, lots of closet room. I miss that here. It was a three-bedroom house. My dining room was as big as my living room." The quality of construction and materials at Dorchester was remarkable. Gladys recalls that, when the Dorchester camp was to be demolished for strip mining, her house was sold to a local man for materials. "He said if he'd known it'd be that hard to take down, he never would have tried it."

Of course, in any camp, some houses were less grand than others. Some residents never enjoyed luxuries that might be considered essentials today. Billie Jean Flanary has a slightly different memory of Dorchester than does Gladys. The Flanarys' house was situated next to the mouth of the mine. "You get used to it," she says with a shrug. "Three little rooms, no bathroom. We left there before we ever got a bathroom." For many families, it was only after they'd purchased the house from exiting coal companies that they finally were able to install a bathroom.

For Edith Harber, her memories of life in the Pruden camp are very pleasant. "It was just a little four-room home and the happiest days of our lives, I guess," she recalls. "We did have water and I had a coal cook stove. No, I didn't have indoor plumbing but I had a big washtub. But I tell you, when you're young and in love, you don't care." She says she realizes that the common image of the coal camp is a negative one and she seems pained by that. "It would be hard for people to understand how well the camps functioned."

The companies with nicer camps always encouraged residents to keep their houses and lawns neat, often awarding prizes to the nicest ones. But for company and resident, a garden was of primary importance and not merely for decoration. Always aware that hard times could be lurking, every camp family kept a vegetable garden and some even kept small livestock. Author Duane Lockard recalls how many immigrant families used the mountains to great advantage and taught the natives a thing or two: "In the towns I knew, many families of Italian heritage would use West Virginia's steep hillsides as their Italian forbears had made vineyards on steep terrain—by terracing. With their ways of growing and preserving tomatoes they introduced their neighbors to new foods as well as new ways of agriculture."⁸ Ethel Bennett, longtime resident of the former Pocahontas camp of Bishop, which straddled the boundary between Virginia and West Virginia, describes her town as having been beautiful. "All the houses were painted white, trimmed in green. In the section where we lived, each house had a stand with a tree planted in it. And everybody had flowers." Indeed, to this day one can see shadows of Bishop's former beauty, in the spacious two-story houses and the sidewalks, an unusual amenity for a camp.

Regardless of how lovely Ethel Bennett considered the camp, like almost all of them, it was segregated. In the world of "separate but equal," Ethel, as an African American, was forced to live within certain boundaries. Born in Alabama, she moved with an aunt and uncle to the coal camp of Westland, Pennsylvania, when she was three. Westland was nothing short of utopian as there was no racial or ethnic segregation. "It was unusual but true there in Pennsylvania. We all went to school together and, when anybody had a party, we were all at the party." Her family left Pennsylvania for Virginia when she was twelve and the halcyon days of her integrated childhood came to an abrupt end. "It was different for me. But after a while I adjusted—going to segregated schools, having to pass nearby schools, because there was one right at the bottom of the hill." Sixty years after the fact, she still marvels at the complicated daily commute to school for her and the other black children. Along the serpentine route were several transfers and lengthy spells of waiting. "I'll tell you where we stayed, especially when it was cold. The man that took care of the furnace in the Bank of Berwind let us come in there, to the boiler room, so you can imagine how we looked when we got to school." The morning ride to school took about an hour and a half. And when Ethel married and had a family, her children faced the same trip when they started to school; in his junior year of high school, her youngest child was finally able to attend an integrated school. When asked what she remembered feeling, as a child, in those first weeks in Bishop, when she realized just how different her life was going to be from what it had been in Pennsylvania, she answers, "Anger, probably ... a lot of disappointment."

Lacey Griffey of Benham, Kentucky, never knew any other life but a segregated one. Benham was owned by International Harvester, which, adhering to the laws of the day, kept the town segregated. Lacey points out that the company had different standards of construction for different neighborhoods, a fact still visible today. "You'll notice that all the blacks lived on this end in small houses and all the whites lived on the other end in double houses, big houses, and that's just the way it was." With an air of resignation tinged with old anger she points out the inequality of public buildings as well. "You could compare the churches: down at the Methodist church in Benham—beautiful wood and everything—and [the church] up here, it's just something they threw together, like these houses."

However dismissive it was of black families' living quarters, International Harvester was attentive to the educational needs of the children. "Although legislation required segregated black and white schools, the corporate owners of model coal towns built and equipped quality structures for black students and recruited first-rate teachers from black colleges across the country."[9] Readily agreeing, Lacey Griffey describes her school days, saying, "As far as I know we didn't mind. I'd say a black teacher would be more interested in a black kid than a white teacher would, basically. Yes, when I was growing up the teachers were, oh, very good."

Still, most former coal camp residents, black and white, agree that while separation of the races was taken for granted, there was a consistent civility between all groups, at least above ground. This eventually led some individuals to push social boundaries; Betty Sabo's Hungarian-born father, Steve Gyetvay, was the first white person in Dante to invite black co-workers to his home. But his widow, Elizabeth Szakacs Gyetvay, says that when she was a child, there wasn't even interaction between the European immigrant population and the native-born whites. Elizabeth, who was born in Pennsylvania but came to Dante at age three, has a noticeable Hungarian accent, despite never having left these shores. She is vigorously patriotic. "I was born in Tamaqua [Pennsylvania]," she stresses. "I didn't know nothing about those other countries." She spent her entire childhood and early married life in Straight Holler, the immigrant neighborhood, which, along with family housing, had a massive boarding house for single immigrant workers of all nationalities.

At age 101, Elizabeth is a perpetual motion machine, with seemingly inexhaustible enthusiasm and humor. Every point she makes is driven home with dramatic gesticulating. She now lives in Castlewood, next door to her daughter and son-in-law. As a child, she and the other children of the Hungarian community were taught to read and write by the Hungarian preacher. Their education ended after roughly the third grade and they found work. For Elizabeth, gainful employment began at age ten, when she began to board the train every day for an hour's ride to Clinchco where she babysat.

Situated as they were in ethnic enclaves, the immigrant populations enjoyed the benefit of being able to keep their cultures intact. The Hungarian communities of every regional coal camp held a grape harvest dance in the fall, which would be widely attended by compatriots from other camps. Elizabeth wasn't able to attend too many of those because she was a bride by sixteen, and in traditional fashion, her marriage was an arranged one. There is a charming photograph of the wedding which took place in 1922. The large wedding party, with Elizabeth dressed in gossamer, stands in front of a maze of frame buildings, fences and livestock pens. A traditional Hungarian band is in the background, poised to play. She points to an outhouse in the picture and chuckles, "We didn't have bathrooms in the house so whatcha gonna do? We got those catalogues free and they was good soft papers!" As the children born to immigrant parents had children of their own, their native languages began disappear. But Betty Sabo recalls it still being in use when she was a child, especially when addressing grandparents. "You either spoke in Hungarian or you didn't speak at all," she says. As for the quality of housing for the immigrant families, Betty thinks it was about the same as in any other section of Dante. And, she's sure that her family, at least, were glad to be in this country. "America was better than what they had over there. It wasn't great, but better."

As the coalfields became less ethnically segregated, old world and new world sometimes clashed. Billie Leho's husband John was a first generation Hungarian American baseball player. Not from a Hungarian family herself, Billie found it a lifelong challenge to gain the approval of her in-laws who, according to old-world tradition, should have chosen their son's wife for him. "They was funny people. I don't think she ever did like me. We got along but I could tell she didn't approve of me a lot 'cause I was American. You'd go over there and her and him would start talking Hungarian so you didn't know whether they were talking about you or not." It is often suggested that immigrant parents saw baseball as the best way for their sons to become Americanized, but the Lehos were not of that opinion. Although their son showed considerable talent for the sport early on, they (particularly his mother) were opposed to him playing. Billie says that her husband always told her that he could have had a chance at the majors if not for his hovering mother who hated the sport with a passion. At a young age, he stole away to Bristol, Virginia, to try out for the professional club there and was signed. His distraught mother eventually located her runaway when his name was pointed out in the game highlights of an area paper. He was promptly retrieved.

As in the rest of the country, one of the largest immigrant populations in the coalfields were the Italians. Rosemary Fara Walker who was raised in MacArthur, West Virginia, just outside of Beckley, is heir to a rich family history, as all her grandparents came from the old country in search of a better life. Her maternal grandfather, Giovanni Tallerico, was a sheep herder and farmer when his cousins, who had become coal miners in southern West Virginia, wrote him of a guaranteed job and house if he'd join them. He did and when he had established himself, he sent for his young wife, Maria. Because she spoke no English, when she boarded the ship for America, officials pinned a freight tag to her coat. After arriving at Ellis Island, she was put on a train for West Virginia, where she eventually ended up in the coal camp of Stickney. In her first years in Appalachia, Maria (now called Mary), still having trouble with the language, would peel the labels off of jars or crates and take them to the company store to identify what she needed.

Giovanni, now known as John, was partially paralyzed in a mining accident when he was in his thirties and the company put him to work as a janitor at the camp school. He determined that his sons would never go into the mines. "He said he'd beg for food first," remembers Rosemary. "He said he wanted them to be educated." And Mary concurred. As a child in Italy, she'd been allowed to attend school for one day. When her father denied her further schooling, she angrily told him that when she had children of her own they would all attend school, girls as well as boys. Rosemary recalls that although her nana never learned to read, she made certain, from the time her first child was born, that the house was filled with newspapers and magazines, which she'd peruse thoroughly every day. All of the Tallerico children finished high school and several went to college. Although their parents' inability to read meant they could never take the tests necessary for citizenship, John and Mary were fiercely patriotic. All of the sons served in the military and each child was ordered to register to vote when they reached the age. While she was still a child, Rosemary's school offered Italian classes and she quickly enrolled, hoping to impress her beloved grandmother. "I came home and was saying numbers and colors in Italian and she said, 'Speak English—you're an American!'"

On her father's side, Rosemary's grandparents, the Lancianeses and the Faras, were also immigrants from Italy, but were eventually able to escape the mines and establish themselves as merchants. Although her father, Dante, spent the first several years of his adult life in the mines, it was work that he disliked intensely. "He was almost glad when the war came along and got him out of the mines," she says. "He hated being underground. He liked the people he worked with but he was claustrophobic." Indeed, being underground inspired such fear in him that, he gave away his burial plot at a local cemetery and bought mausoleum space instead.

When he returned from World War II, Dante (his name now Americanized to Danny) bought a market outside of Beckley which he and his family ran until 1978. It catered mostly to miners on their way to work. Because she began working in the store at age seven, Rosemary recalls many years of waiting on miners while standing on a milk crate behind the counter. The men would stop there to pick up necessities for their dinner pails, which she says consisted of sandwiches, cakes, fruit and endless rolls of antacid tablets. Because of the dust in the mines, the men chewed tobacco to keep their mouths and throats moist. The combination of tobacco juice and having to work most of their shift bending over to pick at coal resulted in constant discomfort. The store also sold mining supplies such as belts, carbide for lamps and kneepads for working in low coal. The miners would bring cakes of Ivory soap that the company supplied at the bathhouse to trade for Ivory dishwashing liquid, which was easier to keep and better to wash off the coal dust.

Though each side of her family was determined to become as American as they could, thankfully, they remained loyal to the foods of their birthplace. Rosemary's childhood was one of homemade breads, pastas, and wine, complemented by the occasional imported Italian cheese. In the early days, all their vegetables were raised in steep, terraced gardens which climbed up the hillsides behind their houses. "I don't remember either side of the family ever having soup beans and cornbread," says Rosemary. "They'd have pasta fasul, the beans with pasta, like a soup. But you didn't have cornbread—you had bread." As a result of growing up with exclusively Italian food, Rosemary and her sister came to regard soup beans and cornbread as a delicacy. But greens cooked the Appalachian way came as a shock to her after a life spent enjoying her father's greens which had been lovingly sautéed in olive oil and garlic and then gently simmered.

Rosemary says that after her grandparents arrived in this country, their need to be Americanized was so strong that they were reluctant even to speak of Italy. They rarely mentioned relatives and never expressed a desire to return. It was only after their deaths that the family discovered bank books belonging to each grandmother and grandfather, written entirely in Italian, which showed that they'd been sending money back home for decades, even in the darkest years of the Depression.

While the lives of many coal camp women were devoted to work in the homes, some were professionals. Carol DeHaven was a secretary for 35 years in the offices of Olga Coal Company, in Coalwood, West Virginia. Working outside the home wasn't a novel idea in her family; her mother had managed the company movie theaters in Coalwood and the nearby camp of Caretta for years. Being at the command center of the mines put Carol at the heart of the action. "Of course, we were owned by a big steel company up in Ohio and they had all these directives that we had to follow in case anything made the news. We had to go through protocol and their people got involved in what was released to the news." Unfortunately, she was also in the position of usually being the first woman in the camp to know the identities of men who'd been killed or injured in the mines.

Ethel Bennett, who was a nurse in Bishop for fifteen years, also learned about mining disasters before most people but, because she had a husband in the mines, didn't accompany the doctor to the scene. Ethel is a woman of surpassing elegance, but spend fifteen minutes with her and the steel underneath the surface becomes apparent. The doctor and his wife/nurse, who hired her, certainly must have seen it. They convinced her to attend classes at a nearby school; what training she couldn't get there, they'd give her on the job.

She found the work both exhilarating and harrowing, given the rough conditions of the area. She tells of helping to deliver a baby in a snowstorm. "The water had frozen so there was no running water. She was on the couch with a kerosene heater because the power was off. We delivered that baby and the doctor was so concerned," she relates. But, returning a few hours later, they were surprised to find the new mother back at her chores. "She was up with what they called a 'kneebaby,' about two years old, carrying him around on her hip. That woman had delivered a baby that morning and she was up. But the baby did fine." Nodding, she adds, "She was a miner's wife." Because the doctor didn't drive, Ethel provided all the transportation for their many house calls. "He knew all the miners. We went up into hollows I didn't know existed." With a gleam in her eye, she talks about the car she used. "I had a Corvair—*that's not a Corvette, now*. That Ralph Nader made me get rid of my car and I loved it. I was just sick when I had to get rid of mine." When asked what she'd say to Nader should she ever have the chance to meet him, she adamantly replies, "I'd say to him to mind his own business."

When Gladys Stallard first arrived in Dorchester, the ink was barely dry on her teaching certificate. Having grown up in East Stone Gap, in Wise County, Virginia, she applied to that school board for placement within the district. A personal connection with the Dorchester principal helped land her in the camp school. She was needed to replace the first-grade teacher who'd created a scandal by marrying in secret two years before and continuing to teach, a flagrant violation of school board rules. "The awful thing was that the other teacher could do anything—she played the piano like mad, put on plays—she could do anything. I went in and I'd never even taught in the first grade. I had to learn my ABCs along with them, the poor kids," she says. Gladys was given a room, along with the other Dorchester teachers, in the clubhouse. This building also housed office workers and visiting mining officials. Dinnertime around the crowded table was a lively affair and there was often dancing to records afterwards. She remembers life at the clubhouse, and in the camp at large, as fun. "There was always something going on according to season." And any entertainment options lacking in the camp were available in nearby Norton, accessible by bus, taxi or foot—it was just a mile away. "We just had a good time," she says. "They kept a barn full of horses—Uncle Jack Fawbush was in charge of them. They always had him lead a parade on the Fourth of July over here in town. He would sit up so straight and tall on his horse. I rode up to High Knob on one before the road was paved. I rode Brown Betty—she was a kind of feisty horse." After eight years of teaching and a seven-year courtship, she married Cliff Stallard, a catcher for the Dorchester Cardinals. She was forced to retire from teaching because of the Wise County rules regarding married women, but stayed busy, their first child arriving within fourteen months of the wedding.

On the border of Kentucky and Tennessee, at the Pruden camp, Edith Harber was the principal of the elementary school and she was hired and paid by Claiburne County, Tennessee. Her husband Tye was the principal of the high school, hired and paid by Bell County, Kentucky. They had to keep duplicate records on each student. For Edith, teaching in the camps was immensely gratifying. "They were the finest children I have ever taught," she says. "That's when the mining camps were booming. The schools were nice buildings, well kept. You got all the help from the company." And the parents were her greatest supporters. At the camp in Fonde, Kentucky, where she taught before she married, the school year was only seven months long. The miners voluntarily relinquished enough of their pay to keep her teaching for an additional month. In Pruden, the school was located just across a swinging bridge from her house. "We would come in from school, have our evening meal, and go right back. I might go in and get work ready for the next day and Tye had baseball games going outside for the camp kids."

Surely some of the most interesting stories of coal camp women at work come from Dante where a surprisingly large number of the young ones went into the defense industry during World War II. As the country emptied of most of its young men, the girls discovered a unique opportunity to try their wings.

Lela Fox sits on a sofa in her nicely-appointed living room in St. Paul, Virginia. She is the picture of old-style femininity, demure and gracious, so it's a bit startling when she daintily declares, "I built bombs." Or, more accurately, she helped brew a volatile concoction called Composition B which was used for detonation. Holston Ordnance Works in Kingsport, Tennessee, was, by 1944, one of the largest makers of high explosives in the world. Lela was part of a group of girls from Dante who went over the border into Tennessee, looking for employment that wasn't available to them at home. Innate patriotism and a desperate need for income drove some of them to bend the law just a bit. "I was only seventeen and a girl from Dante worked on my birth certificate a little bit and made me eighteen," Lela says. Each prospective employee had to undergo a physical and the doctor who saw her was suspicious of her age. She laughs, "He said, 'Little girl, why don't you go back home?' But they hired me."

Another Dante girl who left home to work was Lillie Mabry. She and her sister, plus several classmates, moved in a group to Akron, Ohio, to build Corsairs in the aircraft division of Goodyear. At the peak of the war, roughly forty thousand people were employed. Lillie was a riveter. "That's the reason all those planes was fallin' out of the sky," jokes James, her husband of sixty years. The Dante girls found lodging with a single mother of four who gave them two rooms in which to sleep. She says they bought their own food and cooked for themselves. Far from the wild ride one might expect from mountain girls on their own in the big city, the girls stuck pretty close together and pretty close to the boarding houses. Entertainment was limited; they played parlor games like pokeno ("You know, for pennies"). Lillie is a quiet person and shy. She downplays her part in the war effort. Of her experience as a working woman away from home she says, "It was okay. It was nice."

For Betty Sabo, her adventure into the defense industry began with schooling not too far from home, and in the company of a large number of other girls from Dante. "They had a school in Bristol and they'd bus us there. They were teaching blueprint reading, riveting—aircraft jobs—and there were several of us from Dante who went. They wanted me to go to [Glen L.] Martin in Baltimore but I didn't want to go to Baltimore. I had an aunt up in Michigan and she wanted me to come there. So after I learned what I wanted to learn in Bristol, I went there." Like Lela Fox, Betty Sabo wasn't above fudging her date of birth: "My Aunt Rose lied for me to get on down there at the school. I was eighteen when I went up to Michigan." Once there, she was hired at the Willow Run Plant built by Ford outside of Ypsilanti. Willow Run built B-24s and Betty went to work riveting gun turrets. At its peak, its workers could produce one aircraft an hour. On her first day at work, she managed a problem rivet that had been plaguing the other workers, including some men. She laughs when she recalls that the boss reacted by shouting, "We've got a riveter here!"

Along with several other Hungarian girls from Dante, she roomed with a German couple. Her husband Ponnie interjects at this point. "I'll bet that was a sight to see, a bunch of those hillbilly women going up there to the city!" But she insists that there was little to enjoy about her life there. "There wasn't much fun. The men were gone, the cars were gone—you didn't get to do too much." When the war ended, Betty went to Kelsey Hayes in Plymouth, Michigan, where she did detail work on machine guns. She harbors no sentimental feelings about her contribution to the war effort. "It was a matter of survival. There was no work in Dante for a young woman."

For mothers whose husbands were overseas, wartime life in the camps was difficult. "Oh lord, the loneliness," Ethel Bennett sighs as she remembers the three long years without her husband Frank. "I wrote to him every day and he wrote to me every day and the letters would pass." Any men who'd been deferred were working in the mines so there was no one available to help around the house. "We had to do everything that the husbands had been doing. But I learned how to chop wood—and I liked it."

In the 1930s, as roads and highways began to open up the mountains, and cars became more readily available, the gates began to swing open and the people of the camps flowed out to enjoy all the advantages of larger towns within a couple of hours drive. There was shopping in the larger cities like Bristol or Lexington or Bluefield, as well as fine restaurants and nightclubs. Lacey Griffey's first date with her soon-to-be-husband found them driving from Benham, Kentucky, over Black Mountain and the state border into Appalachia, Virginia, to a nightclub. The drive today, even with the road widened, is as hair-raising a prospect as one could ever imagine. Considering the same drive, on a narrower road and at night, is absolutely terrifying.

A first date story to make any urban socialite green with envy is that of Frank and Ethel Bennett. She was in high school when they met, he a man of the world eight years her senior and a friend of her brother's. They'd been flirting for some time. "He'd come to the house to visit my brother and we just sorta..." she says, her voice trailing off coyly. They weren't allowed to go out on a date, just sit on the porch. But they eventually broke the rules and in an unforgettable fashion. "The big bands came to Bluefield—Count Basie, Duke Ellington, Benny Carter, Woody Herman. I guess I was fifteen or sixteen and my brother was taking his girlfriend to a dance and he asked my mother could I go. He said, 'I'll take care of her, I'll watch her,' and my mother said yes. Then, when we got in the car, I got in the back seat and Frank was sitting there! That was the night that Jimmy Lunsford and his band were there with Ella Fitzgerald. She was singing 'A-Tiskit, A-Taskit.'"

Lest anyone assume that entertainment on a grand scale was only available outside the camps, Howard Sparks' memory of dances in Van Lear sets the record straight. Formal affairs, featuring glittering pre-disco disco balls and rented bands, were frequent events. Attire was strictly formal. He recalls one band in particular. "I looked at that band and it was thirteen redheaded women, all in evening gowns. I was very naïve then and I asked myself, 'How in the world did they find thirteen redheaded women?'"

But beyond their roles as wife and mother, homemaker or professional, the women of the Appalachian coal camps were some of the most devoted fans of America's pastime. Not a single woman interviewed said she didn't like the sport although some, like Wanda Osborne, stress the practical beginnings of their affection for it: "It was either learn it or sit at home." After she'd mastered the fundamentals, it took no time at all for her to begin keeping a scorecard at every game she attended. And she attended every game. Wanda and most of the players' wives were loyal fans, even bringing their small children to see dad play. "Our son, I forget how many games he saw before he was six months old."

Before cars were common in the camps, the wives were at the mercy of anyone who had transportation to get them to the away games. Gladys Stallard remembers fans piling into every spare inch of a truck to get to games away from the Dorchester camp. After she had children, she didn't attend games away from home so much but did enjoy the luxury of having a house situated on a hill above the diamond at Dorchester. From the front porch, she and her small children could watch the games. Women frequently made up the majority of fans in the stands. Billie Leho says of baseball, "I couldn't wait 'til Saturday to get to the games." And having a husband on the team only enhanced her commitment to the game. "I lived it, I heared it, I ate it, I slept with it," she says fervently. Dave Hillman says he always saw more women than men in the stands and advances an interesting theory as to why: "I think it's because they stayed at home and couldn't get out. It let them holler and get things off their chests."

Sydney Francis' mother frequently took her to games in Hazard after work. "She was a widow so she didn't have to cook dinner. She'd just pile the neighborhood kids in the car and we ate hotdogs and drank lemonade." Her mother could quote the stats on any player and kept a scorebook each season. And Bill McGraw's mother, having moved to a large urban area for schooling, became accustomed to attending major league ball games for most of her adult life ("She said she saw Babe Ruth punch one one night out of the park and on top of a streetcar," he says). When she moved back to Hazard in 1929, her first act upon arrival was to head right to the ballpark.

The female fan base ran the social gamut, from the Aunt Bessies of the ball parks to the svelte wives of the coal town brass. Shirley Pearson still recalls with amazement that Perle Stewart's wife would attend the Pennington games in nothing less than haute couture. "Augusta Stewart would come into the stands and stop traffic," she says. Shirley and her sister Connie Nunley say that for certain segments of the community, the Sunday afternoon ballgame held a see-and-be-seen significance. "It was a social event. You might even see some hats," they laugh.

Ty Harber has a scrapbook, dog-eared and falling apart, that was put together by his grandmother Glessie Harber. While it holds an eclectic variety of baseball-related tidbits, it is mostly devoted to her son, Ty's father, Tye Harber. A wealth of yellowed clippings recount his career path through the years, but the scrapbook is not simply the result of a doting mother's pride. The entire family, according to Ty and his mother Edith, was baseball crazy ("I tell you, it was in their blood," says Edith). After all, Glessie and her husband had named their four sons after famous players.

Glessie and her two sisters, Chloe and Leola, were, as Ty tells it, "the reason why you have the word 'fan' from fanatic," never missing a ballgame in Pennington Gap. "They would absolutely *show themselves*," says Edith. "I think that Aunt Chloe was the worst one, next would have been Leola. I never heard about Tye's mother carrying on but she might have. Seems like they talked about Aunt Chloe being just awful." Of course Ty's favorite memory of his grandmother Glessie is of an instance in which she exacted revenge on an insensitive spectator sitting near her. "My dad was playing first base and, at that time, there were poles around and there was this guy wire that went up the poles. He was chasing a foul ball and straddled it—of course, very painful. There was this guy who started laughing and my grandmother hit him with a Coke bottle." Shirley Pearson says of the sisters, "My dad [Rudy Parsons] said you could hear them in the outfield if something didn't suit them. They were respected members of society but they took their baseball seriously." Larry Fish remembers the sisters well: "Glessie was the tartar of the group. Honey, nobody wanted to mess with Glessie. Leola I always considered the lady of the three but you didn't want to mess with her around baseball." He concurs with Shirley by saying, "We took it seriously. This wasn't something you joked about or played around with. This was serious." He recalls seeing the wife of the school superintendent escorted from the ballpark one Sunday. "She didn't like the umpire—he wasn't one of her favorite people. Here you've got this very motherly-looking lady sitting there, a Norman Rockwell mama, and she's yelling, 'Beat him to death!' and 'Hit him with the bat!' Eventually the umpire called a strike on her son when she just knew it wasn't a strike and she ended up hitting him three or four times with the humongous pocketbook she carried. So they led her off the field—this sweet, dignified lady."

Lee County's female fans weren't the only ones to react with a certain amount of vigor to events on the field. Around Tacoma in Wise County, a favorite local tale is of a woman wresting the dipper from a water boy and beating him with it out of fury at a call. Salty Smith's mother suffered self-inflicted bruises up and down her thighs as a result of unbridled enthusiasm watching him play a tense game. But most of the fury was confined to yelling. Ethel Bennett says that the State Liners' games drew many vocal female fans, some with a bit of artificially-induced enthusiasm: "We yelled out at 'em. Not only Bishop women came but from all the surrounding communities over into McDowell County. Some of them drank beer so that made a difference." And every resident, past and present, of Dante remembers one woman in particular who had served as the team's batboy for most of her childhood. "She would drown the rest of us out," recalls Betty Sabo. Jim Childress remembers a Grundy-Vansant fan he'd rather forget. "Certain people, their voice carries. You could always hear them, especially if you missed the ball. You'd hear, 'Get you a stick and kill it!' or 'Pull your apron down!'" Or, a female fan might distract a player in other ways, perhaps unintentionally. A blushing Jim reluctantly shares the tale of one unfortunate shortstop. "There was this one lady that, well, didn't cover up too well and it caught his eye. Just about that time, someone threw the ball to him and it hit him in the face."

It's conceivable that some female fans attended the games to enjoy the sight of so many able-bodied young men. Salty Smith politely declares, "I wouldn't say they throwed themselves at the players but they did flirt." Billie Jean Flanary will attest to the fact that her husband Roy had half a dozen young women interested in him and James Mabry jokes that he had an entourage of pretty fans who attended games only to flirt with him. Sydney Francis suspects that Johnny Podres might have had a rough time of it in Hazard. "I would guess that there were a lot of single girls in town that were gaga over that guy 'cause he was really handsome," she laughs. "And Max Macon was tall and had the bluest eyes this side of Texas." Shirley Pearson says that after Pennington Gap joined the Mountain States League, although it was considered bad form for the local girls to date the players who'd been brought in from outside the area, it was still done. But most of the women who found romance at the ballpark were there to begin with simply because they loved the game. For Lacey Griffey, the first sight of her future husband was a reward for being a fan. "Well, I went to the ballgame with my best friend. I asked her when he came out, 'Who's that? I'm going to marry him.'"

For many of the women in the stands, then and now, the love of baseball is bittersweet. Despite the passion they may feel for the game and the fervor with which they follow it, they are not encouraged to play. Like a lot of women around the country, many of the women of Appalachia did their best to claim a piece of the pie, if only in leisurely Sunday afternoon pick-up games. Salty Smith tells of his early years in the Crossbrook camp where all the families would get together to play "roundtown," which seems to have evolved from either "rounders" or "townball" or a combination of the two. Men and women into their fifties and sixties played alongside the younger ones. Near Dungannon, Virginia, for many decades, a cow pasture was the site of Sunday afternoon version of roundtown so brutal it would have left Ty Cobb agog.

Tressa Robbins is an artist who grew up down the road from the ever-smoking coke ovens of Ramsey, Virginia. Sundays always involved a harrowing drive through the mountains to a family farm where for generations her family has played roundtown. After the noon meal, the players, men and women (mostly the latter), would walk to a remote hollow where rocks and cow pies served as bases. "Sometimes you had to mark a spot in the dirt. But it was always the same place so if you played every week you knew where your bases were," says Tressa. They usually played with a hard sponge ball and an axe handle and she says that positioning was vague because of the small number of players.

The rules for roundtown were not that far removed from regular baseball but, according to the mood of the players, could be more flexible. One of the deviations from strict baseball rules was that the batter and the base runner, if there were one, were a team unto themselves, with no lustily cheering teammates in the dugout to boost morale. The batter was allowed three strikes but no balls and getting beaned was the only way to walk. "My aunts were great fastball throwers, with those old-fashioned sponge balls that weren't so squishy. You didn't want to get hit with one of those. I'd rather get hit by a baseball." Appalachian roundtown offered very little mercy to the old or infirm, or was compassionately inclusive of them, depending on one's point of view; they were consistently drafted as catchers.

The rules of batting show what a complex and difficult game it was. "In order to advance the batter, you had to hit the ball in front of them," says Tressa. "Like, if I got a hit and got to first, in order for me to get to second, someone would have to hit in front of me [i.e., the area between first and third base], which was easy to do. But if I was on second, trying to get to third, someone has to hit a ball between second and third to get me to third." If the players were in a strict mood, the rules could be tightened: to advance a runner from first to second, the ball might have to be hit precisely between those two bases. "The most exciting thing was to get up to bat with someone on base. If they were on second and I got a hit, if it went between first and second, they couldn't go anywhere. So I didn't really succeed, even though I got myself on first. It wasn't your job to hit a home run—it was your job to make that runner round the bases."

Outfielders had to roam far and wide but they were not completely without help. "The dogs were fillers for the outfield," Tressa recalls. "They were good at retrieving, especially sponge balls, but by the end of the game, the balls had pieces chewed out of them." Her athletic aunts spent most of the game poling the ball to the outfield. "You spent the day running after the ball. Those sponge balls were hard. You could knock them miles and miles and miles. So you were always trying to retrieve them out of briar patches and creeks, from across barbed wire, fighting the dogs to get the ball if they got it first. Being small, I always had to go under fencing and I just remember the briars they had to pull out of me. So it was a great deal of effort." And while the world may swoon over a beautiful outfield play by Beltran or Soriano, force either one of them to field around a few huge, cud-chewing obstacles and see if they can maintain their composure, let alone their fielding average. "Sometimes there were cows in the outfield that you had to maneuver around. One time a cow stood on the ball. I had to get the dog barking at the cow to get her to move, then the dog got the ball and ran into the creek. I had to pull it away from his teeth and left half of it in them." She grins and adds, "I think the game ended early that day."

But base running was where the game grew dangerous. Tressa recalls a particularly vicious second baseman: her five-foot-tall mother. "She'd pinch or kick you or trip you. There was a lot of physical stuff that went on to keep the runner from advancing. They could grab your shirt so you couldn't run. Because you didn't have a lot of players to get the ball in the outfield, you had to slow the runner down as much as possible. They were a tough bunch. They'd make you pay for running their bases; you had to be real conscious of being able to knock them out of the way before they knocked you off base." And age, or the lack of it, made no difference in the style of play. "When you're small and you're playing with adults, well, there were no boundaries on how much force could be exerted, so you always hurt pretty bad afterwards." And while mean taunting of the batter was the name of the game, there could be praise lavished on the base runner who made a scorching slide or took a brutal hit or pinch and didn't cry.

Playing began early in life. "If we had little ones in the family, we'd take them to the outfield to run after balls. Sometimes we'd try to let them bat. Even now, if there's a little one around, the first thing my aunts do is to buy them a bat, a little plastic one. Seems to be like coming of age, like walking and talking. They're all rabid baseball fans."

Tressa's memories of roundtown become more precious to her as she watches those women she played with grow old. Some have died. Perhaps it is her artistic sense that gives the images in her mind the clarity of diamonds. "There's a kind of euphoria, a nostalgia associated with it. I can remember how the light looked; it would be kind of yellow-gold over those hills and over that field 'cause there'd be hay or grass or corn around us. I can remember the smell of the hay or the blackberry and raspberry bushes lining the creek. Sunflowers. There were always sunflowers leaning over the fence. And butterflies coming off the field. It all kind of mixed together in some sort of thing that still sits in my brain when I drive by a summer meadow. We had to walk pretty far up into that holler to play. It was really like you were in your own little world. Time out from everything."

Time out from everything. In the end, what more can we ask of baseball?

Epilogue

The juxtaposition of hard labor in the darkness of a coal mine to baseball played in the bright light of a summer afternoon could probably cause even the most practical soul to immediately run amuck with the symbolism of it all. After all, coal mines rarely induce anything but negative reactions in people; indeed, they evoke the most primal of fears, ranging from being buried alive to spending one's afterlife in a warm and unhappy place. And then there's baseball, to which fans traditionally love to attach all manner of archetypal significance or, at the very least, metaphors for life. But the great paleontologist and baseball fan Stephen Jay Gould condemned this type of thinking as a lot of hooey. He maintained that baseball, in and of itself, was perfect. To embellish it, particularly with any metaphysical sentimentality, was not just silly but criminal. And I believe that he was right. It is exquisite with just eighteen players, a ball and a bat—it needs nothing else.

That doesn't mean that, at the start of this project, I didn't find the idea of baseball-playing coal miners fraught with symbolism; it was easy for me to make my own horror at underground mining the very antithesis of the beauty I find in baseball. I waded into the first interviews expecting the same sort of weighty philosophizing from the players. The first surprise came when I discovered that most of the ballplayers, the white ones, at least, managed to avoid going under ground at all, although any mine work, even on the surface, is dangerous. But none of these men—those who worked below or above ground—had any judgments to make on mining itself. It had simply been a job, a means to feed their families. Most of them had witnessed death and injury but didn't allow themselves to dwell on it; they simply couldn't afford to waste that much time in fear. As far as baseball itself was concerned, for players and the mining families alike, it wasn't some transcending visit with the divine, nor were there life lessons to be taken from the diamond. It was just a game that they adored and that for few hours a week relieved them of their worries. As I met more and more of these remarkable people, thankfully my need to gussy up coalfield baseball with symbolic contrasts of dark and light fell by the wayside.

That said, I do firmly believe that there was an essential difference between these players and their fans, and their contemporaries elsewhere. The ballplayer of the coalfields played with a fire in his belly that burned like a supernova, as though each game might be his last. The majority of the players didn't care whether they went up or not; they just wanted to

Reunion, July 2007. *Back row, left to right:* **Bill Osborne, Dave Hillman, Salty Smith, Bill Patton, Bo Scott.** *Front row:* **Roy Flanary, Paul Kilgore, Jim Childress, James Mabry** (courtesy Chuck Clisso).

play. As far as passion goes, their fans may have ranked a notch above even a card-carrying member of the Red Sox Nation; every account attests to their unruly devotion to the sport. Perhaps the specter of death, always walking a few steps behind every resident of the camp, made player and fan more capable—than anyone, anywhere—of unfettered joy in this most joyful affirmation of life.

These days, there is little evidence of the ball fields, just as there are only ruins left of literally hundreds of coal camps that used to exist in southern Appalachia. With the amount of strip mining and mountaintop removal occurring today, the very mountains that cradled those camps are rapidly disappearing. This ancient range is swiftly being turned into a desolate moonscape of treeless, flat-topped knolls.

The good news is that even though coalfield baseball is a part of the past, the people of the region still treasure it. The older ones can remember watching the games and they still revere the players, both living and dead. The children of the players, now with wrinkles of their own, couldn't be prouder of their fathers if Cooperstown had just called. Young kids are discovering that their grandfathers and great-grandfathers had wicked fastballs and that some even signed professional contracts with teams whose names the children actually know. The wives of former players prod their husbands for memories, then roll their eyes as the stories emerge, attempting unsuccessfully to disguise the pride they felt then and still do.

As for the players themselves, it takes very little prompting to rekindle the fire they felt long ago. It starts behind their eyes, and, as the memories return, the wrinkles of their eighty- or ninety-odd years fall away. They are young again, with lightning-fast reflexes, muscles of steel, and knees that can once again be trusted.

The world at large has taken a lot away from Appalachia. Its people have been stereotyped, ridiculed, and robbed. Only now are outsiders beginning to look past what can be exploited in the area to what is there is to be honored. To the crafts, the music and the folklore that make this area special, let us add this singular brand of baseball, one of the dearest gifts the mountains could give.

Chapter Notes

Chapter 1

1. Rudy Abramson and Jean Haskells, eds., *The Encyclopedia of Appalachia* (Knoxville: University of Tennessee Press, 2006) p. 457.
2. Thomas J. Morris, "The Coal Camp: a Pattern of Limited Community Life," Master's thesis, West Virginia University, 1950, p.66.
3. Thomas E. Wagner and Phillip J. Obermiller, *African American Miners and Migrants* (Urbana: University of Illinois Press, 2004), p. 72.
4. Rhonda Janney Coleman, "Coalminers and Their Communities in Southern Appalachia, 1925–1941," *West Virginia Historical Quarterly* Vol. XV, no.2, part 2 of 2, April 2001.
5. www.msha.gov/stats/centurystats/coalstats.asp.
6. www.msha.gov/stats/charts/coalbystate.asp.

Chapter 2

1. Duane Lockard, *Coal: A Memoir and Critique* (Charlottesville: University Press of Virginia, 1998), p. 7.
2. *The Coalfield Progress*, May 13, 1948, p. 1.
3. Doug Gibson, "Remembering the Coal Leagues," *University Mine Workers Journal*, no. 3, May–June 1999, p. 5.
4. Martha Hall Quigley, *Railroading Around Hazard and Perry County* (Mount Pleasant, SC: Arcadia, 2006), p.104.
5. *The Post*, May 12, 1949, p. 1.
6. Ibid., June 13, 1901, p. 2.
7. Keokee Extension Homemakers, "The Village of Keokee," (1976) p. 50.
8. *The Coalfield Progress*, May 13, 1948, p. 1.
9. Extra Innings.
10. *Middlesboro Daily News*, October 16, 1945, p. 4.
11. *The Washington Post*, October 17, 1933, p. 18.
12. *Powell Valley News*, July 26, 1934, p. 1.
13. *Wise County News*, March 15, 1911, p. 4.
14. *Powell Valley News*, April 19, 1934, p 1.
15. William E. Akin, *West Virginia Baseball* (Jefferson, NC: McFarland, 2006), p. 116.
16. *Powell Valley News*, September 28, 1933, p. 1.
17. www.northbysouth.kenyon.edu/2000/baseball/Industrial.
18. Jim Gilley papers.
19. *The Charleston Gazette*, June 17, 1952, p. 10.

Chapter 3

1. *Powell Valley News*, May 26, 1922, p. 2.
2. *The Post*, May 18, 1949, p. 1.
3. *Powell Valley News*, July 13, 1933, p. 1.
4. *Middlesboro Daily News*, September 11, 1946, p. 4.
5. *Powell Valley News*, September 14, 1928, p. 3.
6. Ibid., January 26, 1933, p. 1.
7. Ibid., August 9, 1934, p. 3.
8. *Kingsport Times-News*, February 26, 2006, p. 5B.
9. *Powell Valley News*, April 21, 1922, p. 1.
10. Ibid., April 28, 1922, p. 4.
11. Ibid., March 1, 1932, p. 1.
12. Ibid., April 7, 1932, p. 1.
13. Ibid., May 19, 1932, p. 1.
14. Ibid., June 30, 1932, p. 1.
15. Ibid., April 6, 1933, p. 2.
16. Ibid., April 20, 1933, p. 1.
17. Ibid., July 20, 1933, p. 1.
18. Ibid., August 31, 1933, p. 2.
19. Ibid., August 3, 1933, p. 1.
20. Ibid., April 19, 1934, p. 4.
21. Ibid., June 14, 1934, p. 1.
22. Ibid., June 28, 1934, p. 1.
23. *The Post*, May 14, 1935, p. 1.
24. *Powell Valley News*, June 7, 1934, p. 1.
25. *Middlesboro Daily News*, April 1, 1936, p. 6.
26. Ibid., September 5, 1936, p. 5.
27. *The Coalfield Progress*, May 12, 1938, p. 1.
28. *Middlesboro Daily News*, August 26, 1938, p. 6.
29. *The Kingsport Times*, August 31, 1938, p. 2.
30. Ibid., December 5, 1938, p. 2.
31. *Middlesboro Daily News*, July 8, 1940, p. 4.
32. *The Kingsport Times*, December 3, 1940, p. 2.
33. Ibid., January 6, 1941, p. 2.
34. *Powell Valley News*, June 18, 1942, p. 8.
35. Ibid., May 7, 1942, p. 1.
36. *The Kingsport Times*, June 15, 1949, p. 12.
37. *Middlesboro Daily News*, August 9, 1950, p. 6.
38. *The Sporting News*, May 14, 1952, p. 37.
39. *The Kingsport Times*, June 15, 1949, p. 12.

40. *The Knoxville News-Sentinel*, August 7, 1953, p. 12.
41. *Middlesboro Daily News*, August 7, 1953, p. 1.
42. Ibid., August 8, 1953, p. 1.
43. Ibid., September 23, 1953, p. 6.
44. Ibid., April 29, 1953, p. 8.
45. *The Kingsport Times-News*, May 31, 1953, p. D1.
46. *Middlesboro Daily News,* January 13, 1954, p. 1.
47. *The Kingsport Times-News*, July 4, 1954, p. 6A.
48. *The Kingsport Times*, July 20, 1954, p. 7.
49. *Middlesboro Daily News*, December 2, 1952, p. 5.

Chapter 4

1. *The Raleigh Register,* August 23, 1942, p. 4.
2. Robert H. Zieger, *John L. Lewis, Labor Leader* (Boston: Twayne, 1988), p. 136.
3. *Powell Valley News*, June 18, 1942, p. 6.
4. Ibid., July 2, 1942, p. 1.
5. Ibid.
6. Ibid., July 9, 1942, p. 1.
7. Ibid., September 3, 1942, p. 1.

Chapter 5

1. *Middlesboro Daily News*, July 31, 1941, p. 4.
2. *Powell Valley News*, August 3, 1933, p. 1.
3. *The Post*, May 18, 1949, p. 1.
4. *The Sporting News*, August 20, 1931, p. 1.
5. A "chili bun" is an Appalachian specialty consisting of chili (no beans) on a hot dog bun with mayonnaise and onions.
6. *The Knoxville News-Sentinel*, June 27, 1953, p. 5.
7. Katharine C. Shearer, ed., *Memories from Dante* (Abingdon: People Incorporated of Southwest Virginia, 2001), pp 273–274.
8. *Grundy Mountaineer*, June 5, 1980, p. 12.

Chapter 6

1. Robert Smith, *The Illustrated History of Baseball* (New York: Grosset and Dunlap, Madison Square Press, 1973), p. 183.
2. *The Charleston Gazette*, August 5, 1938, p. 10.
3. Geoffrey L. Buckley, *Extracting Appalachia* (Athens: Ohio University Press, 2004), p. 68.
4. Lee County Historical and Genealogical Society, *Bicentennial History of Lee County Virginia, 1792–1992*, p. 50.
5. Katharine C. Shearer, ed., *Memories from Dante* (Abingdon: People Incorporated of Southwest Virginia, 2001), p. 55.
6. Peter Crow, *Do, Die, or Get Along* (Athens: University of Georgia Press, 2007), p. 2.
7. *The Kingsport Times-News*, May 20, 1951, p. 10-A.
8. Ibid., June 17, 1951, p. 11-A.

Chapter 7

1. *Middlesboro Daily News*, April 1, 1936, p. 6.
2. *Crawford's Weekly*, September 8, 1923, p. 1.
3. Ibid., April 1, 1936, p. 6.
4. *The Kingsport Times*, February 16, 1951, p. 8.
5. *The Coalfield Progress*, April 19, 1951, p. 3B.
6. Ralph Berger, "Larry MacPhail," in *The Baseball Biography Project*, Society for American Baseball Research.
7. *Middlesboro Daily News*, June 14, 1951, p. 10.
8. *The Sporting News*, July 25, 1951, p. 37.
9. *The Coalfield Progress*, May 22, 1952, p. 1.
10. Ibid.
11. *The Sporting News*, May 28, 1952, p. 15.
12. *The Coalfield Progress*, March 5, 1953, p. 4.
13. *The Kingsport Times-News*, April 12, 1953, p. 2-D.
14. *The Coalfield Progress*, April 30, 1953, p. 2.
15. *The Knoxville News-Sentinel*, June 28, 1953, p. B-6.
16. *The Coalfield Progress*, February 11, 1954, p. 6.
17. *The Kingsport Times*, February 11, 1954, p. 27.

Chapter 8

1. Jim Gilley papers.
2. *Bluefield Daily Telegraph*, May 4, 1979, p. 9.
3. *The Charleston Gazette*, September 25, 1925, p. 27.
4. *Charleston Daily Mail*, November 19, 1925, p. 9.
5. *Bluefield Daily Telegraph*, May 4, 1979, p. 9.
6. David L. Porter, ed., *Biographical Dictionary of American Sports* (Westport, CT: Greenwood Press, 2000), p. 377.
7. *Welch Daily News*, October 5, 1931.
8. *Middlesboro Daily News*, June 26, 1936, p. 6.
9. *The Kingsport Times*, September 28, 1934, p. 2.
10. Iris Webb Glebe, *The Earl of Dublin* (Ann Arbor: McNaughton & Gunn, 1988), p. 62.
11. www.legis.state.wv.us/Bi l.

Chapter 9

1. Robert Armstead, *Black Days, Black Dust* (Knoxville: University of Tennessee Press, 2002), p. 56.
2. *The Sporting News*, October 21, 1959, p. 1.
3. Ibid., January 1, 1947, p. 8.
4. Ibid., April 1, 1920, p. 7.
5. www.minorleaguebaseball.com/milb/history/top100.jsp?idx=21.
6. *The Charleston Gazette*, July 17, 1928, p. 11.
7. *The Sporting News*, March 24, 1927, p. 3.
8. *The Sporting News*, August 5, 1920, p. 6.
9. *The Charleston Gazette*, July 17, 1928, p. 11.
10. *The Sporting News*, March 24, 1927, p. 3.
11. *The Bridgeport Telegram*, September 8, 1927, p. 16.
12. Ibid., October 21, 1927, p. 20.
13. *The Charleston Gazette*, July 17, 1928, p. 11.
14. Ibid., August 26, 1951, p. 23.
15. Ibid., February 26, 1937, p. 2.
16. *The Charleston Daily Mail*, August 15, 1948, p. 12.
17. *The Charleston Gazette*, February 21, 1946, p. 13.
18. *The Charleston Daily Mail*, August 15, 1948, p. 12.
19. Paul J. Nyden, "Coal Town Baseball," *Goldenseal*, October–December 1979, p. 39.
20. *The Charleston Gazette*, May 20, 1932, p. F1.
21. *The Sporting News*, January 21, 1937, p. 7.
22. Ibid., March 12, 1936, p. 8.
23. Ibid., March 18, 1937, p. 1.

24. Ibid., September 7, 1939, p. 3.
25. Ibid., April 4, 1940, p. 11.
26. Rudy Abramson and Jean Haskells, eds., *The Encyclopedia of Appalachia* (Knoxville: University of Tennessee Press, 2006), p. 469.
27. David Driver, "Lew Burdette: The Pride of Nitro," *Goldenseal*, Fall 1998, p. 58.
28. *The Charleston Gazette*, June 15, 1944, p. 15.
29. Driver, "Lew Burdette: The Pride of Nitro," p. 59.
30. www.baseball-reference.com/bullpen/Lew_Burdete
31. Driver, "Lew Burdette: The Pride of Nitro," p. 59.
32. Brent P. Kelley, *100 Greatest Pitchers* (Greenwich, CT: Bison Books, 1988), p. 14.
33. *Gazette-Mail*, January 7, 1962, p. 54
34. Ibid., October 13, 1957, p. 37.
35. Connie Karickhoff, "Lew Burdette Day in Nitro," *Goldenseal*, Fall 1998, p. 63.
36. *Gazette-Mail*, January 7, 1962, p. 54
37. Dan Gutman, *It Ain't Cheatin' If You Don't Get Caught* (New York: Viking Penguin, 1990), p. 28.
38. *The Sporting News*, December 11, 1965, p. 25.

Chapter 10

1. James T. Laing, "The Negro Miner in West Virginia," in *Blacks in Appalachia*, William H. Turner and Edward J. Cabbell, eds. (Lexington: University of Kentucky Press, 1985), p. 71.
2. David Alan Corbin, *Life, Work, and Rebellion in the Coalfields* (Urbana: University of Illinois Press, 1981), p. 66.
3. Extra Innings.
4. *The Charleston Gazette*, May 5, 1935, p. 16.
5. Ibid., May 5, 1935, p. 16.
6. James A. Riley, *The Biographical Encyclopedia of the Negro Baseball Leagues* (New York: Carroll & Graf, 1994), p. 846.
7. William E. Akin, *West Virginia Baseball* (Jefferson, NC: McFarland, 2006), p. 109.
8. *The Charleston Gazette*, July 14, 1928, p. 7.
9. Paul J. Nyden, "Coal Town Baseball," *Goldenseal*, October–December 1980, p. 40.
10. Riley, *The Biographical Encyclopedia of the Negro Baseball Leagues*, p. 794.
11. *Beckley Post-Herald*, May 9, 1936, p. 8.
12. Ibid., April 24, 1937, p. 6.
13. Riley, *The Biographical Encyclopedia of the Negro Baseball Leagues*, pp. 692–693.
14. Nyden, "Coal Town Baseball," p. 40.
15. *The Charleston Gazette*, June 18, 1937, p. 15.
16. *Beckley Post-Herald*, September 11, 1937, p. 8.
17. *The Charleston Gazette*, August 5, 1938, p. 10.
18. Ibid., August 30, 1942, p. 6.
19. Gillette and Palmer, *The 2006 ESPN Baseball Encyclopedia* (New York: Sterling, 2006), p. 1641.
20. *The Charleston Gazette*, December 15, 1949, p. 37.
21. This must have been a private joke between Harmon and Toney. Johnny Vander Meer of the Cincinnati Reds is legendary as the only major league pitcher to have thrown back-to-back no-hitters. When Toney died, Vander Meer had just finished an 18-victory season and was leading the league in strikeouts.
22. *Beckley Post-Herald*, September 2, 1942, p. 8.
23. *The Raleigh Register*, February 12, 1943, p. 9.
24. *Beckley Post-Herald*, August 24, 1950, p. 10.
25. James Bankes, *The Pittsburgh Crawfords* (Jefferson, NC: McFarland, 2001), p. 91.
26. *The Raleigh Register*, June 27, 1943, p. 8.
27. *Beckley Post-Herald*, July 27, 1945, p. 7.
28. Riley, *The Biographical Encyclopedia of the Negro Baseball Leagues*, p. 712.
29. Extra Innings.
30. *Beckley Post-Herald*, March 22, 1949, p. 7.
31. Ibid., June 24, 1949, p. Sports-1.
32. Ibid., May 10, 1949, p. 7.
33. *The Raleigh Register*, June 14, 1949, p. 6.
34. Ibid.
35. *Beckley Post-Herald*, June 25, 1949, p. 6.
36. Ibid., June 29, 1949, p. 6.
37. *The Raleigh Register*, May 14, 1950, p. 7.
38. *Beckley Post-Herald*, June 1, 1951, p. 10.
39. *The Raleigh Register*, June 10, 1951, p. 10.
40. *Beckley Post-Herald*, April 12, 1952, p. 6.
41. Riley, *The Biographical Encyclopedia of the Negro Baseball Leagues*, p. 536.
42. Albert is referring to the electric "engine" that pulled the coupled coal cars in and out of the mine along a narrow track. The brakeman was his assistant, stopping the motor when needed to connect and disconnect the cars.

Chapter 11

1. Martha Hall Quigley, *Railroading Around Hazard and Perry County* (Mount Pleasant, SC: Arcadia, 2006), p. 104.
2. *The Hazard Herald*, April 28, 1950, p. 7.
3. Ibid., May 29, 1950, p. 5.
4. Ibid., April 29, 1951, p. 2.
5. www.minorleaguebaseball.com/milb/history/top100.jsp?idx=81.
6. *The Hazard Herald*, June 24, 1951, p. 5.
7. Ibid.
8. Ibid., August 9, 1951, p. 7.
9. *Middlesboro Daily News*, August 29, 1951, p. 4.
10. *The Hazard Herald*, September 2, 1951, p. 7.
11. *The Knoxville News-Sentinel*, September 10, 1953, p. 33.
12. *The Hazard Herald*, August 26, 1951, p. 8.
13. www.minorleaguebaseball.com/milb/history/top100.jsp?idx=40.

Chapter 12

1. From a poem published in the *Powell Valley News*, October 27, 1932, p. 4.
2. Thomas E. Wagner and Phillip J. Obermiller, *African American Miners and Migrants*, (Urbana: University of Illinois Press, 2004), p. 56.
3. Ibid., pp. 35–36.
4. Ibid., p. 88.

Chapter 13

1. Lowell H. Harrison and James Clotter, *A New History of Kentucky* (Lexington: University of Kentucky Press, 1997), pp. 301–302.
2. Harry M. Caudill, *Theirs Be the Power* (Urbana: University of Illinois Press, 1983), p. 33.
3. Ann Matheny, "Batter Up!" *Gateway: Journal of the Bell County Historical Society*, Vol. XIII, no. 3, Fall 2002, pp. 5–6.
4. Ibid.
5. Ibid.
6. *Middlesboro Daily News*, July 7, 1930, p. 3.
7. Alan J. Pollock, *Barnstorming to Heaven* (Tuscaloosa: University of Alabama Press, 2006), p. 97.
8. Ibid., p. 64.
9. *The Kingston Daily Freeman*, June 24, 1946, p. 7.
10. *Middlesboro Daily News*, July 17, 1948, p. 4.
11. Ibid., September 12, 1950, p. 4.
12. Brent P. Kelley, *The Negro Leagues Revisited* (Jefferson, NC: McFarland, 2000), p. 266.
13. Ibid., p. 203.
14. *Middlesboro Daily News*, September 12, 1950, p. 4.
15. Ibid., September 13, 1950, p. 6.
16. Ibid.
17. Ibid., May 7, 1951, p. 4.
18. Ibid., May 8, 1951, p. 8.
19. *The Sporting News*, May 16, 1951, p. 32.
20. *Middlesboro Daily News*, May 10, 1951, p. 8.
21. Ibid., July 28, 1951, p. 4.
22. *Powell Valley News*, August 16, 1951, p. 1.
23. *Middlesboro Daily News*, August 20, 1951, p. 4.
24. Ibid., September 5, 1951, p. 4.
25. Bruce Adelson, *Brushing Back Jim Crow* (Charlottesville: University Press of Virginia, 1999), p. 35.
26. Jules Tygiel, *Baseball's Great Experiment* (New York: Oxford University Press, 1983), p. 270.
27. *Middlesboro Daily News*, August 20, 1963, p. 8.
28. Ibid., May 8, 1951, p. 4.
29. *The Sporting News*, August 22, 1951, p. 35.

Chapter 14

1. www.astroland.net/pankovis.
2. *The Knoxville News-Sentinel*, March 10, 1953, p. 14.
3. Ibid., March 20, 1953, p. 12.
4. Ibid., April 1, 1953, p. 20.
5. Ibid., April 21, 1953, p. 13.
6. Ibid., April 24, 1953, p 14.
7. Ibid., April 26, 1953, p. B-2.
8. *Middlesboro Daily News*, May 21, 1953, p. 8.
9. Vince Pankovits papers.
10. *The Knoxville News-Sentinel*, July 17, 1953, p. 12.
11. Ibid, May 29, 1953, p. 12.
12. Ibid., May 31, 1953, p. B-4.
13. Ibid., May 29, 1953, p. 14.
14. Ibid.
15. Ibid., May 30, 1953, p. 5.
16. Vince Pankovits papers.
17. *The Knoxville News-Sentinel*, May 31, 1953, p. B-3.
18. *The Kingsport Times-News*, May 31, 1953, p. 1-D.
19. Ibid., June 7, 1953, p. 29.
20. *The Knoxville News-Sentinel*, July 5, 1953, p. B-4.
21. Ibid., June 26, 1953, p. 13.
22. Ibid., July 8, 1953, p. 16.
23. *The Kingsport Times-News*, July 26, 1953, p. 4-D.
24. *The Knoxville News-Sentinel*, August 15, 1953, p. 5.
25. Ibid., August 16, 1953, p. B-4.
26. Ibid., August 24, 1953, p. 12.
27. Ibid., September 6, 1953, p. B-2.
28. Vince Pankovits papers.
29. *The Sporting News*, November 4, 1953, p. 18.

Chapter 15

1. *Powell Valley News*, June 15, 1933, p. 1.
2. *The Post*, July 11, 1935, p. 1.
3. *Middlesboro Daily News*, March 20, 1936, p. 6.
4. *The Sporting News*, April 15, 1943, p. 11.
5. *The Kingsport Times*, April 16, 1944, p. 6.
6. Ibid.
7. Ibid., April 28, 1949, p. 13.
8. *Middlesboro Daily News*, May 16, 1951, p. 4.
9. Ibid., May 17, 1951, p. 8.

Chapter 16

1. *Middlesboro Daily News*, June 7, 1949, p. 6.
2. David Alan Corbin, *Life, Work, and Rebellion in the Coalfields* (Urbana: University of Illinois Press, 1981), p. 65.
3. *The Post*, June 13, 1935, p. 2.
4. Carol A.B. Giesen, *Coal Miners' Wives* (Lexington: University of Kentucky Press, 1995), p. 46.
5. Thomas E. Wagner and Phillip J. Obermiller, *African American Miners and Migrants* (Urbana: University of Illinois Press, 2004), p. 32.
6. Harry M. Caudill, *Night Comes to the Cumberlands* (Boston: Little, Brown, 1962), p. 145.
7. Keokee Extension Homemakers, "The Village of Keokee," pp. 18 and 29.
8. Duane Lockard, *Coal: A Memoir and Critique* (Charlottesville: University Press of Virginia, 1988), p. 93.
9. Wagner and Obermiller, *African American Miners and Migrants*, p. 30.

Bibliography

Books and Articles

Abramson, Rudy, and Jean Haskells, eds. *The Encyclopedia of Appalachia*. Knoxville: University of Tennessee Press, 2006.

Addington, Luther F. *The Story of Wise County, Virginia*. Wise, VA: Wise CountyCentennial Committee, 1956.

Adelson, Bruce. *Brushing Back Jim Crow: The Integration of Minor-League Baseball in the American South*. Charlottesville: University Press of Virginia, 1999.

Akin, William E. *West Virginia Baseball: A History, 1865–2000*. Jefferson, NC: McFarland, 2006.

Armstead, Robert. *Black Days, Black Dust: The Memories of an African American Coal Miner*. Knoxville: University of Tennessee Press, 2002.

Bankes, James. *The Pittsburgh Crawfords*. Jefferson, NC: McFarland, 2001.

Berger, Ralph. "Larry MacPhail." *The Baseball Biography Project*, Society for American Baseball Research. http://bioproj.sabr.org/bioproj.cfm?a=v&v=1&bid=1070&=8621.

Buckley, Geoffrey L. *Extracting Appalachia: Images of the Consolidation Coal Company, 1910–1945*. Athens: Ohio University Press, 2004.

Caudill, Harry M. *Night Comes to the Cumberlands: A Biography of a Depressed Area*. Boston: Little, Brown, 1962.

_____. *Theirs Be the Power: The Moguls of Eastern Kentucky*. Urbana: University of Illinois Press, 1983.

Coleman, Rhonda Janney. "Coal Miners and Their Communities in Southern Appa-lachia, 1925–1941." *West Virginia Historical Quarterly*, Vol. XV, No. 2, Part Two of Two, April 2001. http://wvculture.org/HiStoryvhs1503.html.

Corbin, David Alan. *Life, Work, and Rebellion in the Coalfields: The Southern WestVirginia Miners, 1880–1922*. Urbana: University of Illinois Press, 1981.

Crow, Peter. *Do, Die, or Get Along: A Tale of Two Appalachian Towns*. Athens and London: University of Georgia Press, 2007.

Driver, David. "Lew Burdette: The Pride of Nitro." *Goldenseal*, vol. 24, no. 3, Fall 1998, 56–62.

Eller, Ronald D. *Miners, Millhands, and Mountaineers: Industrialization of the Appalachian South, 1880–1930*. Knoxville: University of Tennessee Press, 1982.

Gibson, Doug. "Remembering the Coal Leagues." *United Mine Workers Journal*, no. 3, May–June 1999, 4–7.

Giesen, Carol A. B. *Coal Miners' Wives: Portraits of Endurance*. Lexington: University of Kentucky Press, 1995.

Gillette, Gary, and Pete Palmer, eds. *The 2006 ESPN Baseball Encyclopedia*. New York: Sterling, 2006.

Glebe, Iris Webb. *The Earl of Dublin: Baseball Career of Earl Webb, Major League Record Holder*. Ann Arbor: McNaughton & Gunn, 1988.

Gutman, Dan. *It Ain't Cheatin' If You Don't Get Caught*. New York: Viking Penguin, 1990.

Harrison, Lowell H., and James Clotter. *A New History of Kentucky*. Lexington: University of Kentucky Press, 1997.

Karickhoff, Connie. "Lew Burdette Day in Nitro." *Goldenseal*, vol. 24, no. 3, Fall 1998, 63.

Kelley, Brent P. *100 Greatest Pitchers*. Greenwich, CT: Bison Books, 1988.

_____. *The Negro Leagues Revisited: Conversations with 66 More Baseball Heroes*. Jefferson, NC: McFarland, 2000.

Keokee Extension Homemakers. "The Village of Keokee: A Bicentennial Project." 1976 (available at Mountain Empire Community College Library, Big Stone Gap, VA).

Laing, James T. "The Negro Miner in West Virginia." In *Blacks in Appalachia*, William H. Turner and Edward J. Cabbell, eds. Lexington: University of Kentucky Press, 1985.

Lee County Historical and Genealogical Society. *Bicentennial History of Lee County Virginia, 1792–1992*. 1992 (available at Mountain Empire Community College Library, Big Stone Gap, VA).

Lockard, Duane. *Coal: A Memoir and Critique*. Charlottesville: University Press of Virginia, 1998.

Matheny, Ann. "Batter Up!" *Gateway: Journal of the Bell County Historical Society,* Vol. XIII, no. 3, Fall 2002, 5–6.

Morris, Thomas J. "The Coal Camp: a Pattern of Limited Community Life." Master's thesis, West Virginia University, 1950.

Nyden, Paul J. "Clint Thomas and the Negro Baseball League." *Goldenseal,* October–December 1979, 17–26.

———. "Coal Town Baseball." *Goldenseal,* October–December 1980, 31–42.

Pollock, Alan J. *Barnstorming to Heaven: Syd Pollock and His Great Black Teams.* Tuscaloosa: University of Alabama Press, 2006.

Porter, David L., ed. *Biographical Dictionary of American Sports.* Westport, CT: Greenwood Press, 2000.

Quigley, Martha Hall. *Railroading Around Hazard and Perry County.* Mount Pleasant, SC: Arcadia, 2006.

Riley, James A. *The Biographical Encyclopedia of the Negro Baseball Leagues.* New York: Carroll & Graf Publishers, 1994.

Rottenberg, Dan. *In the Kingdom of Coal: An American Family and the Rock that Changed the World.* New York: Routledge, 2003.

Shearer, Katharine C., ed. *Memories from Dante: The Life of a Coal Town.* Abingdon: People Incorporated of Southwest Virginia, 2001.

Shifflett, Crandall A. *Coal Towns: Life, Work, and Culture in Company Towns of Southern Appalachia, 1880–1960.* Knoxville: University of Tennessee Press, 1991.

Smith, Robert. *The Illustrated History of Baseball.* New York: Grosset and Dunlap, Madison Square Press, 1973.

Tygiel, Jules. *Baseball's Great Experiment: Jackie Robinson and His Legacy.* New York: Oxford University Press, 1983.

Wagner, Thomas E., and Phillip J. Obermiller. *African American Miners and Migrants: The Eastern Kentucky Social Club.* Urbana: University of Illinois Press, 2004.

Weiss, Bill, and Marshall Wright. "Team #45 1918 Toronto Mapleleafs." Minor League Baseball. http://web.minorleaguebaseball.com/milb/history/top100.jsp?idx=45.

Wise County Historical Society. *The Heritage of Wise County and the City of Norton, 1856–1993.* Waynesville, NC: Professional Press, 1993.

Zieger, Robert H. *John L. Lewis, Labor Leader.* Boston: Twayne, 1988.

Newspapers and Magazines

Beckley (WV) Post-Herald
The Bridgeport (CT) Telegram
Bluefield (WV) Daily Telegraph
Charleston (WV) Daily Mail
Charleston (WV) Gazette
Coal Mines Benham, International Harvester Monthly Magazine
The Coalfield Progress (Norton, VA)
Crawford's Weekly (Norton, VA)
Gazette-Mail (Charleston, WV)
The Grundy (VA) Mountaineer
The Hazard (KY) Herald
The Kingsport (TN) Times
The Kingsport (TN) Times-News
The Kingston (NY) Daily Freeman
The Knoxville (TN) News-Sentinel
Middlesboro (KY) Daily News
The Post (Big Stone Gap, Virginia)
Powell Valley News (Pennington Gap, VA)
The Sporting News
The Washington Post
Welch (WV) Daily News
Wise County (VA) News

Collections

Bobby Davis Museum, Hazard, Kentucky
Eastern Regional Coal Archives, Craft Memorial Library, Bluefield, West Virginia
Jim Gilley papers, courtesy of R. Tim Gilley
Kentucky Coal Mining Museum, Benham, Kentucky
Vince Pankovits papers, courtesy of Jim Pankovits
Wise County Historical Society, Wise, Virginia

Video Production

Griffith, Suzanne. *Extra Innings: Coalfield Baseball.* Beckley, WV: WSWP (PBS) Presentation, 1994.

Websites

www.astroland.net
www.baseball-reference.com
www.coalcampusa.com
www.legis.state.wv
www.minorleaguebaseball.com
www.msha.gov
www.northbysouth.kenyon.edu

Interviews

Gean Austin (January 25, 2007, and February 1, 2007)
Edward Ballinger (May 10, 2007)
Ethel Bennett (March 30, 2007)
Frank Bennett (March 30, 2007)
Jim Childress (May 26, 2007)
Jim Daniels (December 1, 2006)
Carol DeHaven (April 26, 2007)
Patricia Edwards (May 10, 2007)
George Ferguson (July 21, 2007)
Larry Fish (August 3, 2007)
Billie Jean Flanary (December 18, 2006)
Roy Flanary (December 18, 2006)
Lela Fox (December 5, 2006)

Myers Fox (December 5, 2006)
Charles Francis (September 22, 2007)
Sydney Francis (April 20, 2007)
R. Tim Gilley (letters and e-mails 2006–2007)
William D. Gorman (May 4, 2007)
Donald Griffey (February 1, 2007)
Lacey Griffey (January 27, 2007)
Elizabeth Gyetvay (February 11, 2007)
Edith Harber (June 9, 2007)
Ty Harber, Jr. (May 19, 2007)
Elmer Henry (September 22, 2007)
Samuel Henry (September 22, 2007)
Albert Hill (September 22, 2007)
Dave Hillman (March 8, 2007, and May 8, 2007)
Paul Kilgore (August 21, 2007)
Billie Leho (August 2, 2007)
James Mabry (November 6, 2006)
Lillie Mabry (November 6, 2006, and February 14, 2007)
James Marsh (May 16, 2007)
William McGraw (April 20, 2007)
Larry McReynolds (November 11, 2006)
George Mickey (September 22, 2007)
Bud Miller (December 12, 2006)
Connie Nunley (May 19, 2007, and October 15, 2007)
Bill Osborne (February 24, 2007)
Wanda Osborne (February 24, 2007)
Jim Pankovits (July 11, 2007)
Bill Patton (February 7, 2007)
Shirley Pearson (May 19, 2007, and October 15, 2007)
Brownie Polly, Jr. (February 7, 2007, and March 4, 2007)
Martha Quigley (April 20, 2007)
Tressa Robbins (June 25, 2007)
Harriet Roberts (October 15, 2007)
Alex Sabo (November 14, 2006, and February 11, 2007)
Betty Sabo (November 14, 2006, and February 11, 2007)
Elizabeth Scott (November 18, 2006)
Herb Scott (November 18, 2006)
Melton Scott (November 18, 2006)
Carl Shoupe (June 20, 2007)
Terry Smith (March 11, 2007, and March 27, 2007)
Violet Smith (March 11, 2007)
Howard Sparks (August 25, 2007)
Gladys Stallard (March 29, 2007)
Tracy Stallard (March 23, 2007)
Rosemary Walker (October 2, 2007)
Woodrow Williams (November 3, 2006, and November 29, 2006)
Willie Winkles (October 23, 2006)

Index

Numbers in ***bold italics*** refer to pages with photographs.

Aaron, Hank 27, 83
Adams, Rush 62, 68, 69
Adams, William 82
Adelson, Bruce 150
Adkins, Abe 114
Affinity, West Virginia 123
Alexander, Dale 102
Alexander, Grover Cleveland 108
American Association of Independent Professional Baseball 101
American Fork and Hoe 110
American Legion 29, 53, 88, 110
American Viscose Rayon Spinners 110
Anaheim Angels 112
Anderson, Charlie 40
Anderson County, Tennessee 154
Andover, Virginia 20, 52–53, 78
Anjean, West Virginia 115
Anti-Atlas Mountains of Morocco
Anti-Broadcast Commission of Major League Games into Minor League Territory 41
Appalachia, Virginia 33, 50, 53, 181
Appalachia Railroaders 53–54, 56
Appalachian League 24, 28, 34, 36–38, 47, 50, 53, 56, 64, 66, 68, 109, 145, 164
Arthur, Alexander 144–145
Asheville, North Carolina 51
Asheville Blues 147, 151
Atlanta Braves 112
Aunt Bessie 170
Aunt Jane 53
Austin, Gean 26, 142, 143

Baldwin-Felts Agency 136
Ballinger, Eddie 146, 150–152
Baltimore Elite Giants 115
Baltimore Orioles 24, 106, 108
Bankes, James 118
Bankhead, Sam 118 120
Barker, Clay "Cowboy" 30, 164
Barnhill, Dave 117
Barron, Eugene 81
Bartley, West Virginia 100

Baseball Hall of Fame, Cooperstown 25, 39
Basie, Count 181
Bearsville, West Virginia 104
Bebop, Spec 146
Beckley Bengals 105
Beckley, West Virginia 105, 107
Beckley Black Knights 108
Bell, Cool Papa 118
Bell County, Kentucky 179
Bell County Historical Society 145
Bellaire, Ohio 170
Bender, Charles Albert ("Chief") 55
Benham, Kentucky 137–138, 140–143, 175, 181
Benham Harvester Sluggers 25, 141–143, ***141***
Bennett, Ethel 174–175, 178–179, 181, 183
Bennett, Frank 27, 181
Bennett, George Eli 87
Benning, Babe 158
Berwind, West Virginia 175
Big Stone Gap, Virginia 20, 89
Big Stone Gap Rebels 133, 166, 159
Birmingham, Alabama 115, 144
Birmingham Black Barons 26, 83, 115, 116, 119, 142, 147
Bishop, Virginia 94, 174–175
Bishop Miners 71
Bishop State Liners ***26, 27***, 116, 118, 119, 143, 183
Black, Joe 80
Black Mountain, Kentucky (coal camp) 46
Black Mountain, Kentucky (land formation) 137, 181
Blackwell, Ewell 147
Blair Mountain, West Virginia 136
Blake, Fred "Sheriff" 105, 107–108
Bloomer Girls 26
Blue Diamond Coal Company 130
Bluefield, West Virginia 24, 105, 181

Bluefield Blue Grays 105
Bluefield State College 119
Bobby Davis Museum 128, 131, 135
Bobrick, Ed 132
Bon Air, Tennessee 100
Bonny Blue Tigers 145
Boone, Daniel 10
Boston Braves 55, 87, 110
Boston Red Sox 59, 60, 101, 102
Bowman, Bob (Middlesboro Athletics) 88–89, 133, 146–152, ***151***
Bowman, Bob (Norton Braves) 87–89, 105–106, 149
Bramwell, West Virginia 98
Brewer, Chet 76
Bridgeport, Connecticut, Bears 107
Bridgeport, Connecticut, Bees 153
Bristol Twins 25
Bristol, Virginia 24, 68, 177
Brooklyn Dodgers 87, 98, 108, 121, 122, 130, 134
Brooklyn Dodgers (NFL) 50
Brooklyn Royal Giants 115
Brouton, Billy 60
Brown, Mace 61
Brown, Mordecai 19
Brummett, Hobe 130
Buchanan County, Virginia 70, 75
Burdette, Selva Lewis (Lew) 110–112
Bureau of Mines, Department of the Interior 97
Burkett, Jesse 104
Burley Belt League 55, 62, 82
Butcher, Max 108–110

California State League 130
Calloway, Frank 33
Campanella, Roy 110, 117, 159
Campbell County, Tennessee 154
Canadian-American League 165
Caples, West Virginia 78
Carbide 110
Caretta, West Virginia 94, 178
Carnegie, Pennsylvania 19

Carnegie Steel 110
Carolina, Clinchfield and Ohio Railway 65, 79, 95
Carolina League 109, 153
Carter, Arnold 105
Carter, Benny 181
Carter, George Lafayette 95
Carter Family 5
Castellano, Ed 40
Castlewood, Virginia 80, 176
Caudill, Harry M. 173
CCC (Civilian Conservation Corps) 36
Chapman Highway Park team 155, 157
Charleston, West Virginia 27, 104, 114, 123
Charleston, Oscar 118, 123
Charleston Senators 164
Charleston Tigers 114
Charlotte Black Hornets 80, 83
Chattanooga, Tennessee 145
Cherokee Indians 9
Chesapeake and Ohio Railroad 10, 106
Chester, West Virginia 104
Chicago American Giants 116, 119
Chicago Bears 50
Chicago Cubs 56, 59, 98, 99, 104, 107, 112, 155
Chicago White Sox 56, 98, 101, 104, 106
Childress, Barbara 71, 75
Childress, Jim 70–71, *74*, 75, 183, **188**
Cicotte, Eddie 98
Cincinnati, Ohio 10, 51
Cincinnati Reds 26, 59, 98, 99, 104, 107, 122, 155, 167, 193*n*
Claiburne County, Tennessee 179
Cleveland Buckeyes 104, 119
Cleveland Cubs 115
Cleveland Indians 69, 85, 92, 104
Clinch Valley League 24
Clinchco, Virginia 65, 67–69, 71, 150, 176
Clinchfield Coal Company 62, 65, 66, 78, 80, 102
Clintwood, Virginia 5, 71
Coalfield League of Wise County 33, 86
Coalwood, West Virginia **16**, 94, 95, 178
Coalwood Robins 95, 96, **97**, 98, 99, 100
Cobb, Ty 106
Coeburn, Virginia 58, 59–64
Coeburn Blues 59, 62, 64, 66
Cole's American Giants 115
Colonial Coal and Coke 54
Colonial League 153
Colored South Alabama Old Stars 115
Columbia, South Carolina 106
Combs, "Tallow" Dick 130
Connelly, C.F. 37
Consolidation Coal Company 76, 95, 100, 102, 172

Conyer, Frank 78
Cooper, Wilbur 104
Corbin, Kentucky 25
Corbin, David 113
Cotton States League 156, 161, 162
Covington, Kentucky 51
Coxville, Indiana 19
Craddock, Walt 105
Crooked Road 5
Crossbrook, Virginia 52, 184
Crummies, Kentucky 136, 138
Crutchfield, Jimmie 118, 123
Cucumber, West Virginia 94
Cullop, Nick 71
Cumberland Gap 10, 145
Cumberland Mountains 9
Cumberland Plateau 154
Currence, Stubby 98–99

Dandy, Dr. Walter 87
Daniels, Jim 57–59, **73**
Dante Bearcats 22, 67, 78–85
Dante, Virginia 15, **17**, 62, 69, 78–85, 180
Dante Miners 62, 65–67, 81
Danville, Illinois 99
Davis, Piper 76
Dean, Dizzy 109
Dean, Wayland 105
DeHaven, Carol 173, 178
Dempster, George 155
Derby, Virginia 11, **12**, 33, 49–54
Derby Daredevils 50–51
Derringer, Paul 99, 104
Detroit Stars 26, 142
Detroit Tigers 101, 105, 135
Dickenson County, Virginia 69, 70
Dixiana, Virginia 54, 88
Dixon, Walt 92–93
Dodd, Bobby 50
Dominican Republic League 122
Donora, Pennsylvania 105
Dorchester Cardinals 55, 57–58, 179
Dorchester, Virginia 20, **21**, **22**, **24**, 33, 54–59, **171**, 174, 179, 182
Dotson, Cecil 135
Douglas, "Shufflin'" Phil 98–99, 104
Dowd, Ike 81, **82**
Dowd, Pete 81
Doyle, Carl 164
Dryden, Virginia 33, 78, 163
Dunbar, Virginia 46
Dungannon, Virginia 33, 59, 184
Dunn, Jack 106
DuPont 110
Durocher, Leo 87, 97

E. E. White Coal Company 107
East Stone Gap, Virginia 50, 179
Edwards, Doc 106
Edwards, Patricia Bowman 146, 151
Egan, Jack 107
Elias Bureau 76

Elizabethton, Tennessee 24, 56
Ellington, Duke 181
Ethiopian Clowns 145, 146
Evans, Angus 119
Evarts, Kentucky 138

Fair Labor Standards Act 15
Fairmont Giants 115
Fara, Dante 177
Fawbush, Jack 179
Feathers, Beattie 35, 50
Feller, Bob 76
Ferguson, George 146, 150
Fish, Larry 31–33, 183
Fitzgerald, Ella 181
Flanary, Billie Jean 56, 174, 183
Flanary, Roy 56–57, **57**, 62, **72**, **188**
Florida International League 135
Fonde, Kentucky 180
Ford, Henry 10
Ford, Hobart 87, 90
Fox, John, Jr. 49
Fox, Lela 66, 180
Fox, Myers 66–67, **74**
Francis, Charles 122, 123, **124**
Francis, Earl 105, 121, 122
Francis, Sydney 128, 129, 131, 133, 173, 182, 184
Fraterville, Tennessee 154
Freeport, Illinois 106, 107
Frisch, Frankie 109
Fullen, Babe 119, 120, 121, 126

Galveston, Texas 108
Gardner, Ed 90
Gardner, Mrs. Ed 90, 91
Gary, West Virginia 99, 103
Gary Miners 118, 120
Gas House Gang 55
Gatliff, Kentucky 140
Georgia Tech 50
Gerkin, Steve 104
Gibson, Josh 27, 76, 117, 118, 127
Gibson, Josh, Jr. 120
Giesen, Carol 171
Gilley, Doris 103
Gilley, Frances Bragg 100
Gilley, Jim Langley 95–103, **97**, **101**
Gilley, R. Tim 96–103
Glamorgan, Virginia **28**, 88
Glasscock, Jack 104
Glen Rogers, West Virginia 115, 119, 127
Glen Rogers Red Sox 118, 119, 120, 121, 123, 125, 126, 127
Glen White, West Virginia 107
Gomez, Lefty 91
Gooch, Johnny 35
Goodyear Aircraft, Akron, Ohio 180
Gorman, William 130–131, 133, 135
Gorsica, John 105
Gould, Stephen Jay 187
Grant Town, West Virginia 104
Green Bay Packers 50

Index

Griffey, Don 25, 140–143, *141*
Griffey, Lacey 142, 175, 181, 184
Griffey, Robert 141
Griffey, Wolford 141, *141*, 142
Grimes, Burleigh 109
Grose, Bobby 169
Groton, New York 153
Grundy-Vansant team 70
Grundy, Virginia 70, 183
Gutman, Dan 112
Gyetvay, Elizabeth Szakacs 176
Gyetvay, Steve 175–176

Haddix, Harvey 112
Hairston, Fred 120
Hairston, Harold "Head" 119, 120, 123, 126
Halstead, Bill 46
Hanna, William B. 106
Harber, Edith 44, 174, 179–180, 182–183
Harber, Glessie 46, 182–183
Harber, Ty, Jr. 46, 182–183
Harber, Tye *35*, 44, *45*, 46–48, 78, 182
Harber, Walt *35*, 46
Hardy, Elijah 81
Harlan, Kentucky 46
Harlan County, Kentucky 136
Harlan Smokies 41, 131, 133–134
Harman Coal Company 70
Harmon, Roy Lee 117, 119, 121, 193n
Harris, Harold 157, 158, 159
Harrisburg, Pennsylvania 164
Harrison County, West Virginia 104
Hatfield, Sid 136
Hawkmen Athletic Association 114
Hayling, Danny 131–135, *132*, 150
Haysi, Virginia 70
Hazard, Kentucky 55, 128–135, 182
Hazard Bombers 89, 128–135, 148, 150
Helfer, Al 157
Hell-for-Certain, Kentucky 130
Henry, Elmer 122, *124*
Henry, Samuel 122, 123, *124*, 125
Herman, Woody 181
Hershey, General Lewis 43
Hickam, Homer 94, 96
Hickam, Homer, Sr. 100
Highcoal, West Virginia 110
Highsplint, Kentucky 138
Hill, Albert 119, 122, 123, *124*, 125, 193n
Hillman, Dave 59–60, 62, 64, *73*, 146, 182, *188*
Hillman, Ima Jean 60
Hindman, Kentucky 130
Hinton, West Virginia 106
Hodge, James 145, 146, 150
Holden, West Virginia 108, 114
Hollingsworth (pitcher) 34, 51, 54
Holston Ordnance, Kingsport, Tennessee 180
Homestead Grays 27, 114, 115, 116, 118, 119, 120, 121, 149

Hot Springs, Arkansas 155, 161
Hot Springs Bathers 156
House of David 26, 88, 108
Houston Astros 153
Hughes, Sammy 117
Humes, Johnny 119, 126
Hungarian immigrants 65–66, 175–177
Huntington, West Virginia 108
Huntington Booster Bees 105
Huntington Quick Steps 116

Ickes, Harold 44
Indianapolis Clowns 27, 83, 156, 159, 161
International Harvester 137, 140, 175
Isaac, Abie 53
Isert, Louis 131, 133, 134
Italian immigrants 174, 177–178

Jackson, Tennessee 154
Jamison, Charles 115
Jeanette Jays 100
Jellico Alley Cats 145
Jenkins, Kentucky 71, 88, 99, 129
Jenkins Cavaliers 131
Jenkins Cubs 68, 69, 100, *101*, 102
Jennings, Dick 92
Jennings, Hughey 19
Johnson, James 89
Johnson, Judy 118
Johnson, Walter 76
Johnson City, Tennessee 24, 164
Johnson City Cardinals 68
Johnson City Soldiers 62
Jones, "Sad" Sam or "Toothpick" 104, 147
Jonesville, Virginia 31
Jonnard, Claude 34
Joseph, J.K. "Daddy Joe" 83, 85

Kansas City Monarchs 26, 27, 76, 116, 142, 147
Kaufmann, Guy A. 37
Kelley, Brent P. 147
Kelsey Hayes, Plymouth, Michigan 181
Kentucky Coal Mining Museum 137
Keokee, Virginia 20, 56, 173–174
Kerr, Dickie 105
Keystone, West Virginia 87
Kilgore, Jack 53, 130
Kilgore, Paul 54, 56, 166, *188*
Kimberly, West Virginia 115
Kincannon, Charlie 119
Kincannon, Harry 118, 120, 121, 122, 123, 125
Kincannon, Roy 118
King Tut 146
Kingsport, Tennessee 24, 83, 95
Kingsport Braves 83, 85
Kingsport Cherokees 53, 92, 161
Kinmont, Kentucky 129
Kirkland, Willie 93, 156
Kiser, Jack 40, 158
Kitty League 154

Kiwanis 36, 69
Knox Baseball, Inc. 155, 157
Knoxville, Tennessee 153–162
Knoxville Smokies (Mountains States League) 150, 153–162
Knoxville Smokies (Sally League) 99, 100–102
Knoxville Smokies (Southern Association) 36, 164
Knoxville Smokies (Tri-State League) 154
Korean War 121, 131
Kyle, West Virginia 115

Landis, Kenesaw Mountain 38, 98–99, 116
Lane, Earl 78
Lawson, Cherokee 53, 54, 166
Lee, Russell 171
Lee Bears 36–37
Lee County, Virginia 30–42, 47, 78, 146, 154, 162, 163
Lee Miners 37
Lee Smokies 34, *35*, 46, 102
Leeman Field 34, 47
Leho, Billie 172, 176–177, 182
Leho, John 172, 176–177
Leonard, Buck 120, 123
Letcher County, Kentucky 100
Lewis, Grover 115–127
Lewis, John L. 44
Lexington, Kentucky 51, 129
Lillybrook, West Virginia 119
Lockard, Duane 174
Logan, West Virginia 108
Logan County, West Virginia 109
Logan Indians 105
Lombardi, Ernie 97
Lonesome Pine League 24, 28, 31, 33–36, 46, 38–39, 49–75, 86, 100, 102, 162, 164
Long, Lee 65, 102
Louisville, Kentucky 129
Louisville and Nashville Railroad 10, 86
Ludlow Massacre 67
Lunsford, Jimmy 181
Lynch, Kentucky 26, 137–140, 142–143
Lynch Bulldogs 143
Lynch Grays 26, 142, 149
Lynch Steelers 143
Lynchburg, Virginia 68

Mabry, James 79–82, *84*, 85, 183–184, *188*
Mabry, Lillie 79, 80, 180
MacArthur, West Virginia 177
Mack, Connie 108, 109
Macon, Max 89, 130–135, *132*, 148, 150, 184
MacPhail, Larry 87
Madisonville, Kentucky 56
Man, West Virginia 109
Manley, Abe 122
Manley, Effa 122
Mann, Les 98
Mansfield, Robert 133

Maris, Roger 60
Marsh, Jim 78
Martin Brothers Hardware 47
Maryville, Tennessee 155, 156
Maryville-Alcoa team 93
Maryville Twins 150, 161
Matewan, West Virginia 136
Mays, Willie 116
Mazeroski, Bill 104
McCoy, John 87
McDonald, Gordon 150
McDowell County, West Virginia 26, 94, 98, 103, 118
McDuffie, Terris "Speed" 121
McEver, Gene 50
McGehee, Stuart 20, 113
McGraw, Bill 128–129, 182
McGraw, John 98, 104, 129
McReynolds, Larry 66, 67
McRoberts, Kentucky 46
Medwick, Joe 87
Memphis, Tennessee 101
Memphis Black Sox 116
Menke, Frank 106, 107
Mercer, Win 104
Mexican League 61, 135
Miami Sun Sox 135
Mickey, George 125–127, **126**
Mickey, Harry 116, 125
Mickey, James 115, 116, 119, 125
Middle Atlantic League 108, 164
Middlesboro, Kentucky 22, 46, 144–152, 154
Middlesboro Athletics 88, 89, 145, 147–152
Middlesboro Blue Sox 145–147, 150
Miller, Bud 81–85, **84**
Miller, Percy 150
Milligan College 59
Milwaukee Braves 94, 110
Milwaukee Brewers (American Association) 101
Mims, Dick 149, 150
Mine Safety and Health Administration 18
Minoso, Minnie 69
Monsanto 110
Mooney, Jim 33, 55
Moore, C.L. 147, 151
Mooresburg, Tennessee 55
Moosic, Pennsylvania 19
Morgan, J.P. 10
Morrison, Walt 105
Morristown Red Sox 88, 134, 149, 150, 156, 161, 166
Motto, George 89, 90
Mountain State League (West Virginia) 24, 28, 105, 108
Mountain States League (Virginia, Tennessee, Kentucky) 31, 39–42, 55, 71, 75, 87–93, 102, 130–135, 147–152, 153–162, 166
Mungo, Van 109
Murchison, Tim 59–60
Musial, Stan 105, 108

National Association of Professional Baseball Leagues 39, 40, 41, 87, 91, 92, 102
National Industrial Recovery Act 15
National Register of Historic Places 49, 137
The Natural 94
Neale, Greasy 104, 107
Necciai, Ron 25
Negro American League 116
Negro Leagues 26, 76, 77, 80, 113, 114, 116, 117, 120, 121, 123, 125, 127, 141, 147, 161
Negro Southern League 147
New York Black Yankees 115, 117, 118, 120
New York Cubans 119
New York Giants 68, 93, 98, 101, 104, 107, 154
New York Highlanders 106
New York Mets 59, 61
New York–Pennsylvania League 164
New York Yankees 106, 110, 111, 116, 123, 153
Newark Bears 107
Newark Dodgers 115
Newark Eagles 119, 122
Newport, Tennessee 87, 90
Newport Canners 47
Nicaraguan League 135
Nicola Construction Company 52
Nitro, West Virginia 94, 110, 111
Norfolk, Virginia 106
Norfolk and Western railroad 10, 86
Northern League 69
Norton, Eckstein 86
Norton, Virginia 33, 86–93
Norton Braves 55, 69, 87–93, 149, 150, 158
Nunley, Connie 163–169, 182

Oak Ridge, Tennessee 69, 130
Oak Ridge Bombers 130
Oak Ridge National Laboratory 130
October Skies 94
O'Doul, Lefty 165, 166
Office of Price Administration 44
Olga Coal Company 178
Omar, West Virginia 115
O'Neil, Buck 27
Osborne, Bill 62, **63**, 64, **73**, **188**
Osborne, Wanda 64, 173, 182
Ott, Mel 97

Pacific Coast League 131, 165
Packard, Kentucky 141
Paige, Satchel 76, 116, 118, 121, 123, 127, 147
Panama City, Florida 46
Pankovits, Jim 153–154, 162
Pankovits, Vince 132, 149, 153–162, **160**
Parkersburg, West Virginia 104
Parsons, Gene 46

Parsons, Irene 163, 164, 169
Parsons, Rudy 134, 163–169, **168**, 183
Patton, Bill 67–69, **74**, **188**
Pearson, Shirley 163–169, 182, 183, 184
Pegler, Westbrook 76, 116
Pendleton, Jim 110
Pennington Gap, Virginia 30–38, 40, 46, 78, 93, 102, 150, 155, 162, 166, 167, 183
Pennington Gap Miners 132, 149, 153
Perkowski, Harry 122
Perry, Gaylord 112
Perry, Commodore Oliver Hazard 128
Perry County, Kentucky 20, 128
Philadelphia Athletics 104, 107, 108
Philadelphia Phillies 100, 104, 109, 112, 159
Piedmont League 100
Pikeville, Kentucky 75
Pineville, Kentucky 25
Pittsburgh Crawfords 27, 114, 116, 118
Pittsburgh Pirates 104, 107, 109, 112, 121
Pittston strike 68
Pitzer, Julian 39, 40, 148, 149
Podres, Johnny 55, 131–135, **132**, 150, 152, 159, 184
Pollock, Alan 146
Pollock, Syd 146
Polly, Brownie 50–52, 54
Polly, Brownie, Jr. 50
Pony League 131
Pope, Dave 76
Porter, Merle 147
Porterfield, Frank 71
Portland, Oregon 107
Posey, Cum 115
Premier-Jellico coal camp 170
Progressive Mine Workers of America 140
Pruden, Kentucky 48, 179–180
Purser, B.H. 100, 102

Quigley, Martha 128, 129

Raleigh, West Virginia 125
Raleigh Capitols 109
Raleigh Clipper Park 119, 121, 142
Raleigh Clippers 115–127
Raleigh Coal and Coke 115, 125
Raleigh Colts 115–116
Raleigh County, West Virginia 108, 113
Raleigh County League 117, 122
Raleigh Mining Institute Park 115, 116, 123
Ramsey, Virginia 61, 184
Ravelo, Juan 131, 133
Reider, Jack 87, 89
Richlands, Virginia 95
Richmond, Virginia 10
Rickey, Branch 98, 105, 121

Rickey, Frank 36, 164
Riley, James A. 114
Roanoke, Virginia 10
Robbins, Tressa 184–186
Roberts, Harriet 163–169
Roberts, Robin 159
Robinson, Jackie 121
Rochester, New York 99, 107
Rochester Red Wings 99
Rockefeller, John D. 10
Rocket Boys 94
Rogan, Bullet Joe 76
Rogers, H.H. 10
Roosevelt, Eleanor 170
Roosevelt, Franklin D. 44
Roush, Edd 26
Ruth, Babe 76, 101, 106, 116, 153, 182
Ryan, Jack 99

Sabo, Alex "Ponnie" 65–66, *73*, 181
Sabo, Betty 65, 173, 175, 176, 180–181, 183
Sain, Johnny 110
St. Charles, Virginia 21, 30–35, 155
St. Charles Miners 30, 44, 46–47, 54
St. Louis Browns 37, 108
St. Louis Cardinals 61, 68, 87, 99, 100, 104, 105, 108, 112, 153
St. Paul, Virginia 59, 180
St. Paul Saints 82
Salem Avalanche 153
Sally League 55, 106
Saltville, Virginia 64
Sampson, Tommy 116, 117
Sampson Naval Base, New York 166
San Francisco Seals 165
Sanders, Battle "Bones" 131, 133
Saunders, Papa Charlie 79, 81
Scarbro, West Virginia 115
Scots-Irish immigrants 10
Scott, Elizabeth 80, 81
Scott, Herb 22, 80–85, *84*
Scott, Melton "Bo" 80–85, *82*, *84*, *188*
Scott, Robert 80, *82*
Seattle, Washington 107
Selective Training and Service Act 43
Seminick, Andy 104
Sevier County, Tennessee 154, 157
Shawnee Indians 9
Shearer, Katharine C. 65, 81
Shields, Charles 119, 123, 125, 126
Shoals, Leo "Muscle" 64, 69, 91, 92–93, 159
Shoupe, Buck 138–140
Shoupe, Carl 138–140
Siftt, George 89
Siler, Tom 157, 159, 161, 162
Sioux City Explorers 69
Slab Fork, West Virginia 121, 122, 123
Slab Fork Aces 122

Slab Fork Indians 122, 123, 125
Slab Fork Quick Steps 122
Slemp, Bill 88
Smith, Howard 52
Smith, Max 130
Smith, Nat 119
Smith, Ozzie 81
Smith, Red 112
Smith, Terry "Salty" 52–54, *72*, 75, 78, 183, 184, *188*
Smith, Violet 173
Solid Fuels Administration 444
Solomon, Mose 86
Sorrell, Vic 105
Southern Association 36, 154
Southern Railroad 10
Spahn, Warren 111
Sparks, Howard 138–139, 172, 181
Spartanburg, South Carolina 79, 107
Spink, J.G.T. 105
Sprigs, Eugene "Snooks" 145, 150
Springer, George 120
Sputnik 94, 111
Stallard, Cliff 174, 179
Stallard, Gladys 174, 179, 182
Stallard, Tracy 60–62, 64, 69
Stanley, Ralph 5
Stapleton, Roy "King Tut" 30
Stephens, Captain Fitzhugh 22
Stewart, Augusta 182
Stewart, Perle 31, 33, 35, *35*, 36, 37, 38, 78
Stickney, West Virginia 177
Stone Mountain League 24
Stonecoal Giants 123
Stonega, Virginia *14*, *23*, 49, 78
Stonega Coal and Coke 49–50
Stotesbury, West Virginia 107
Streza, John 134
Suttles, Mule 76

Tacoma, Virginia 183
Tallerico, Giovanni 177
Tallerico, Maria 177
Tamaqua, Pennsylvania 176
Tate, Carroll 90
Taylor, Clyde 121
Texas League 108
Thomas, Clint "Hawk" 117
Thompson, Fresco 133
Thorpe, Jim 116
Tom's Creek, Virginia 61
Toney, Robert 117, 193*n*
Toronto Maple Leafs 106
Totten, Garson 119, 121, 122, 123, 125
Trautman, George 89, 156
Tri-County League (Virginia) 24
Troy, Alabama 46
Tugerson, Jim 156, 158–159, 161, 169
Tugerson, Leander 156
Turkey Foot, Virginia 15
Turner, E.C. "Pops" 115, 116
Tuscarora Indians 9

Unexpected, West Virginia 110
United Mine Workers of America 15, 23, 35, 37, 65, 68, 136–140, 142
U.S. Rubber 110
U.S. Steel 103, 137, 139, 140, 143
University of Tennessee 35, 50
Utica 165

Van Lear, Kentucky 138, 181
Vanderbilt, Alfred Gynne 87
Vander Meer, Johnny 117, 193*n*
Vansant, Virginia 70, 71, 183
Venezuela League 122
Verda, Kentucky 164
Vero Beach, Florida 130, 131
Vietnam War 139
Virginia Coal and Iron 49–50
Virginia League 106
Virginia Tech 99

Wacks, Virgil Q. *32*; and the Appalachian League 36–38; and Bob Bowman 148; early years in journalism 31–33; and the Hazard Bombers 131, 132–133; and the Knoxville Smokies 155; and the Lonesome Pine League 33–36; and the Mountain States League 39–42; and the Norton Braves 86, 88, 90–91, 93
Wad, West Virginia 12
Wagner, Honus 19
Walker, Ernie 100
Walker, Ewart 100
Walker, Fred "Dixie" 100
Walker, Harry 100
Walker, Rosemary Fara 177–178
Walker, Thomas 9
War, West Virginia 94
War Industrial League, West Virginia 110
Ward, West Virginia 107
Warhop, Jack 106–107, 112
Washington Black Senators 118
Washington Senators 109
Watt Powell Park, Charleston, West Virginia 123
Watts, Sonny 119, 121, 123
Webb, Earl 100, **101**, 104
Welch, West Virginia 25, 27, 99, 102, 109
Welch Senators 100
West Virginia Negro Baseball League 115
West Virginia University 105
West Virginia Wesleyan 107
Westland, Pennsylvania 175
Wheeling, West Virginia 104
Wheelwright, Kentucky 55, 56, 64
White, Robert 119
Whitesburg, Kentucky 129
Williams, Billy (Willie) 69, 91–93, 150
Williams, Charles "Lefty" 114
Williams, Ed 80

Williams, Woodrow 51–52, 54, *72*
Williamson, West Virginia 75, 105, 108
Williamson Colts 105
Willow Run Plant, Ypsilanti, Michigan 180
Wills, Bob 120

Winding Gulf Field 107, 119
Wingate, J.W. 150
Winkles, Willie 55–56, *72*, 88
Winston-Salem Twins 100
Wise County, Virginia 22, 33, 183
Works Progress Administration (WPA) 36
World War I 13, 110

World War II 24, 28, 43–47, 53, 56, 62, 67, 70, 80, 116, 128, 166; women 180–181

Zapp, Jim 147
Zulu Cannibal Giants 26

www.ingramcontent.com/pod-product-compliance
Ingram Content Group UK Ltd.
Pitfield, Milton Keynes, MK11 3LW, UK
UKHW050526150426
5217IPUK00026B/1819